Upgrading China's
Information and Communication
Technology Industry

State-Firm Strategic Coordination
and the Geography of Technological Innovation

Cassandra C. Wang

Zhejiang University, China

World Scientific

ZHEJIANG UNIVERSITY PRESS
浙江大学出版社

Published by

World Scientific Publishing Co. Pte. Ltd.

5 Toh Tuck Link, Singapore 596224

USA office: 27 Warren Street, Suite 401-402, Hackensack, NJ 07601

UK office: 57 Shelton Street, Covent Garden, London WC2H 9HE

and

Zhejiang University Press
No. 148, Tianmushan Road
Xixi Campus of Zhejiang University
Hangzhou 310028, China

British Library Cataloguing-in-Publication Data
A catalogue record for this book is available from the British Library.

This edition is jointly published by World Scientific Publishing Co. Pte. Ltd. and Zhejiang University Press. This edition is distributed worldwide by World Scientific Publishing Co. Pte. Ltd., except Mainland China.

UPGRADING CHINA'S INFORMATION AND COMMUNICATION
TECHNOLOGY INDUSTRY
State-Firm Strategic Coordination and the Geography of Technological Innovation

ISBN 978-981-4407-68-7

In-house Editor: Zheng Danjun

Typeset by Stallion Press
Email: enquiries@stallionpress.com

Printed in Singapore.

FOREWORD

The rapid growth and transformation of the Chinese economy over the last two decades has made China the research focus of the world. As a major recipient of foreign direct investment and being labeled the world's factory, China has played a significant role in global production and consumption. While "Made in China" labels are now featuring in our daily lives, "creativity in China" has become of vital importance if China wishes to reach a higher level of economic growth. How could China successfully complete the transformation from "Made in China" to "creativity in China"? How could Chinese indigenous firms establish their capability for self-dependent innovation and get rid of the technological reliance on foreign investment? What are the influential factors that affect the innovation-related motivation of the indigenous firms? How could we make sense of the uneven geography of technological innovation in China? These are some of the essential questions that intrigue not only the experts and China watchers but also any intellectuals interested in the globalized world in which China has played such an important part.

As one of the pillar industries that have received much support from the Chinese government, the information and communication technology (ICT) industry has experienced such a substantial growth that it has made a significant contribution to not only the national economy but also the global ICT industry. What does the role of China's ICT industry play in the world? What are its structural characteristics? How is China's ICT industry spatially distributed? How has the innovation-related investment and performance of this industry varied over time and space? Does the spatial clustering of the ICT industry facilitate the innovative activities and improve its economic performance? What are the driving forces of innovation behind the ICT firms?

It is no easy task to answer the questions raised above, not only because of the complexity and many facets of innovation, but also because of the difficulties in obtaining consistent and comparable data of China's ICT industry. In particular, recent theoretical attempts to understand the dynamics of technological innovation have been based predominantly on the theory of regionally concentrated clusters which sees technological innovation as the result of inter-firm interactions based on not only production but also knowledge in the process of industrial clustering. Without taking account into the innovation-related motivation of firms, the concept of industrial clustering cannot provide a satisfactory explanation for why certain firms are more innovative than others within a cluster.

Dissatisfaction with the existing literature is only a part of the motivation to engage in this book project. In recent years, Chinese authorities have started to pay much attention to the collection of industrial data that are relatively accurate, consistent and reliable. In particular, the first national economic census conducted in 2005 was to gather county-level data about the real situation regarding the scale, structure and efficiency of its secondary industry and tertiary industry which has laid a statistical foundation to create better management and better decisions for China's high-tech industry. Given the enormous size of the territory and its huge variation in economic structure, the survey was an extremely time consuming, labor-intensive and costly exercise unprecedented in the history of the People's Republic of China. The result of the 2004 Economic Census provided a valuable database to examine the structural characteristics, spatial distribution and innovation performance of China's ICT industry and to explore the innovation dynamics of high-tech firms in China.

This book documents and explains the innovation dynamics of Chinese indigenous firms taking the ICT industry as an example. It is hoped that this volume can serve as a useful source of reference to facilitate a better understanding of the mysterious nature and innovation dynamics of China's high-tech industry and, perhaps, a more effective management to stimulate the innovation-related motivation of indigenous high-tech firms and to improve the regional economic and innovation performance.

CONTENTS

ACKNOWLEDGMENTS

Many people have provided assistance for this book. I am especially grateful to Prof. George C.S. Lin for his insightful comments and constant support. His meticulous reading of several early drafts and the critical questions he raised helped me to clarify many ideas introduced in the book.

I owe special debts to Prof. Harald Bathelt in the University of Toronto, Dr. Simmon Zhao and Dr. James Wang in the University of Hong Kong and Prof. Stefan Becker in Lehman College for their critical comments and valuable suggestions which have enabled me to improve the early version of the manuscript.

During the long course of writing and research, I enjoyed and benefited from scholarly exchange with the research fellows in the Department of Geography of the University of Hong Kong, including Professor David Zhang, Dr. Yang Fan, Dr. Hu Zhiyong, Dr. Shan Xizhang, Dr. Lai Kun and Dr. Chen Yan.

I would like to express my deep gratitude to those people who provided kind help during my field work in Shanghai and Shenzhen. My special thanks go to Prof. Gang Zeng and Prof. Du Debin in the Eastern China Normal University, Prof. Yu Zhou in Vassar College, Prof. Yifei Sun in California State University Northridge, Prof. Dennis Y. H. Wei in the University of Utah, Prof. Wang Jici and Dr. Tong Xin in Peking University, Dr. Fan Hongwei, Ms. Chen Yang and Mr. Xiong Zhefei, who provided me with generous help during my fieldtrip in Shanghai and Shenzhen. My sincere appreciation goes to all of corporate respondents who took their time to accept my interviews and shared their most valuable experience and opinions with me. I especially would like to thank Mr. Liu Hongchao, Mr. Sun Zhenshou, Mr. Liang Chunlin, Ms. Liang Chunyan, Mr. You Junsheng, Mr. Liu Yongsheng and Ms. Liu Yani. They acted more like my friends than friendly informants. My snow-balling interviews would not have been possible without their warm-hearted help and unconditional support.

My appreciation also goes to many supportive colleagues at Zhejiang University, especially to Professor Chen Hanlin, Professor Wen Jiwei,

Professor Ouyang Anjiao, Professor Wang Bo, Professor Jin Pingbin and Professor Fang Youjun.

The research and writing of this book was funded by the National Natural Science Foundation of China (Grant No. 41101112) and by the "Fundamental Research Funds for the Central Universities" (Program No. 2011QNA3042). Their generous financial support is gratefully acknowledged.

Completion of this book would not have been possible without the incredibly strong support of my family. I would like to express my heartfelt gratitude to my parents and my husband for their selfless love, unreserved support and understanding. To the people who love me and whom I love so much, I dedicate this book.

LIST OF FIGURES

LIST OF TABLES

LIST OF ABBREVIATIONS

CAS	Chinese Academy of Sciences
CSSB	China State Statistical Bureau
ECNU	Eastern China Normal University
FDI	Foreign Direct Investment
FYP	Five-Year Plan
GDP	Gross Domestic Product
IC	Integrated Circuit
ICT	Information and Communication Technology
IDH	Independent Design House
LQ	Location Quotient
MII	Ministry of Information Industry
MNCs	Multi-National Corporations
OECD	Organisation for Economic Cooperation and Development
R&D	Research and Development
S&T	Science and Technology
SEZ	Special Economic Zones
SICA	Shanghai Integrated Circuit Industry Association
SMEs	Small- and Medium-Sized Enterprises
SMIC	Shanghai Municipal Informatization Commission
SOE	State-Owned Enterprises
SSB	Shanghai Statistical Bureau
SSIPEX	Shanghai Silicon Intellectual Property Exchange
SZSB	Shenzhen Statistical Bureau
TD-SCDMA	Time Division Synchronous Code Division Multiple Access
VC	Venture Capital

Chapter One

INTRODUCTION

1.1. Research Background

China's economic reforms and subsequent rapid growth have made China the "World's Factory Floor" (Hennock, 2002). The timely insertion into the restructured global economy has brought about an influx of foreign and domestic capital as well as technologies and advanced management skills to China. As part of the remarkable economic growth of the whole country, the dramatic expansion of China's information and communication technology (ICT) industry in recent years appears to be of special importance, not only because the ICT industry has been a driving force for innovation and growth in other industries but also because it involves national security as a core industry of informatization for the whole economy and society (Breidne, 2005). It is pointed out that the ICT industry has been "a Chinese pillar of success and is now the largest industry in China with a growth of nearly 20 percent annually, and there is no end in sight" (Pecht, 2006, p. xiii). China's First National Economic Census conducted in 2004 singled out the ICT industry as one of the major contributors with growing significance to the Chinese national economy.[1] With less than 6 percent of employment and less than 9 percent of the total assets of the whole manufacturing sector, the ICT manufacturing sector generated 12 percent of sales revenue to China's manufacturing industry in 2004 (CSSB, 2005a). The rapid growth of the ICT industry is a recent phenomenon as the ICT manufacturing sector started to dramatically expand only after 1994 and the software sector enlarged only after 2000. Before 1994, the ICT manufacturing sector generated less than 4 percent of output value to the whole of manufacturing industry. This ratio has remained stable at over 8 percent since 1999. Meanwhile, ICT exports have made an even more significant contribution to the whole manufacturing industry. Over one-third of total exports in

---

[1]Data generated by the 2004 economic census are arguably one of the most comprehensive, comparable and consistent sets of economic data in the history of China (see more in Chapter 4 and Appendix I).

China was produced by ICT manufacturing during the period 2003–2008 (CSSB, 2004, 2005b, 2006, 2007, 2008, 2009; MII, 2004, 2005, 2006, 2007, 2008, 2009). ICT exports increased from 142.1 in 2003 to 521.8.5 billion USD in 2008.

China's ICT industry also occupied an important role in the world economy. The industrial output generated by China increased from $14.7 billion to $20.1 billion from 2003 to 2005, accounting for 13.1 and 15.1 percent, respectively, of the world's total (Ning, 2009a, p. 74). China has not only become the world's number one producer of most electronic products such as TVs, recorders, VCD players, telephones, calculators, refrigerators, air conditioners and personal computers, but has also been identified as the number one cellular phone and integrated circuit (IC) market (Pecht, 2006). It is reported that China has been the leading exporter of ICT goods to the world, ahead of Japan and the European Union since 2003, and overtaking the U.S. in 2004 (OECD, 2005).

Given the significant role that China's ICT industry has played in the national economy and the global production chain, it is not surprising that China's ICT industry has attracted much attention from scholars and policy-makers (Breidne, 2005; DeWoskin, 2001; Fan, 2003; Harwit, 2005; Katsuno, 2005; Khalil and Hamid, 2005; Lin and Wang, 2009; Lin *et al.*, 2011; Meng and Li, 2002; Naughton, 1997; Ning, 2009a; Pecht, 2006; Wang *et al.*, 2010; Zhang, 2008; Zhou *et al.*, 2010). However, the detailed mechanism of technological innovation and its regional variation remain poorly understood, mainly because of the lack of consistent and comparable data. The rapid growth and the unknown innovative capability of China's ICT industry have raised some interesting and important theoretical and empirical questions about the innovation dynamics of Chinese transitional economies. What is the technological level of China's ICT industry and what position has China taken in the global ICT value chain? What is the spatial pattern in the economic and innovative performance of China's ICT industry? Is there any relationship between spatial agglomeration and economic performance as well as between industrial clusters and innovative performance? While a plethora of literature is available to explain the innovative performance of a region with reference to a relational framework that places much emphasis on inter-firm linkages and network embeddedness as well as learning processes and untraded assets, can the same dynamics derived from Western-based experiences be directly applicable to the ICT firms in a socialist economy under transformation such as China? If not, how can we explain the dynamics of technological innovation of China's ICT firms? These questions are fundamental to our understanding of not only the dynamics of technological innovation of China's ICT industry but also the diverse process of technological innovation in different world regions under globalization.

1.2. The Case of China's ICT Industry

This study documents the dynamics of growth and innovation of China's ICT industry. The significant growth of China's ICT industry in recent years has been the results of the efforts made by the Chinese government and the restructuring of the global ICT industry. Before the 1978 economic reform, there were very few ICT firms in China. Without any autonomy, these firms produced and sold according to the administrative commands and did not undertake any research and development activities. Although this planned economic system had been criticized for its separation of R&D and production from market demands, it produced significant technological breakthroughs through mobilizing the nation-wide resources into several important research projects, which laid a fundamental foundation for the later growth and technological progress of China's ICT industry.

The 1978 economic reform allowed foreign and private capital to participate in the construction of China's ICT industry and, since the 1990s, this industry has embarked upon a path of rapid growth. However, as a latecomer to the ICT industry in the world, China has still been stuck at the low end of the global value chain with the focus on the processing and assembly of electronic products, even though it started to produce much more sophisticated products like electronic computers rather than household video and audio equipment that used to dominate China's ICT industry in the 1980s. At the end of 2007, the sub-sector of electronic computer manufacture had accounted for 33 percent of output value, 26 percent of total profits and 41 percent of exports, much higher than those of other ICT manufacturing sub-sectors, namely telecom equipment, radar and related equipment, broadcasting and television equipment, household audio and video equipment, electronic devices, electronic components and other electronic equipment (MII, 2008).

While the strategy of a "market for technology" that China adopted at the beginning of the reform and opening-up has indeed attracted a great deal of foreign investment, a problem appeared to be related to the ICT industry's heavy reliance upon foreign capital and technology. China's ICT manufacturing industry has been dominated by foreign-invested firms that had produced 60 percent of output value, 72 percent of exports, 55 percent of total profits and 50 percent of output value of new products at the end of 2004. Although China has been the number one exporter of ICT goods in the world since 2004, the lion's share of ICT exports have been completed by processing imported materials. For example, China had become the leading exporter of TV sets and DVD players, but the most valuable chips in these products are still heavily dependent on imports.

With the core technology controlled by others, China's ICT manufacturers have a weak negotiating power in the world market and survive only on a very thin profit margin. A bitter lesson from the severe dependence on foreign technologies is the patent dispute over the export of DVD players in 2002, when Chinese-made DVD players were impounded at European ports because the manufacturers did not pay the high patent fees. As a result of this dispute, most of the Chinese DVD makers went bankrupt (Suttmeier and Yao, 2004). A Chinese DVD manufacturer complained that "the more we sell, the more we lose" because over one-third of the revenues for selling DVD players in the USA went toward royalties to the DVD patent holders (Suttmeier and Yao, 2004, p. 11). The incapability of the indigenous firms to grasp the core technology is not particularly confined to the manufacture of DVD players. This case reflects the awkward situation that Chinese ICT manufacturers found themselves in. Unable to compete with foreign firms in the core technology, most indigenous firms only engaged in low-end production, taking advantage of a cheap labor force and use of land at the expense of product quality.

In recognition of the fact that China's ICT industry is vulnerable without its own IP rights, the Chinese government tried to help its firms get out of the "patent trap" set by the industry leaders and to ensure national security through establishing homegrown standards in certain ICT fields. This action and many other efforts made by the Chinese government have exerted a positive influence on the innovation-related strategies of the firms. There are studies to make the case that China has stood on her own feet in certain technology and has managed to develop some of its core technology through indigenous and domestic R&D activities (Lu, 2000; Sun, 2002b; Zhou, 2008). This book also identified that a few regions and firms tend to be much more innovative than others. China's ICT industry has a strong tendency to concentrate in the eastern coastal area, including Beijing, Shanghai, Guangdong, Jiangsu and Fujian. However, the industrial clustering of China's ICT industry did not bring about correspondingly better economic and innovative performance, as the prevailing theoretical models have suggested.

As the most clustered area of ICT manufacturing in China, Guangdong Province has alone accounted for over one-third of the employment and produced over of the output value to China. However, its labor productivity and capital profitability are rather poor and its innovative performance, measured by both granted invention patents and output value of new products, is also disappointing. In comparison, Shanghai, with a lower employment location quotient, achieved a much better innovative performance than Shenzhen, a leading city-region in the ICT industry of Guangdong Province.

This study reveals that the innovation dynamics of China's ICT firms is not embedded in industrial clusters or in inter-firm linkages, connections and relationships, but instead lies in the process whereby the innovation-related strategies of the firms are coordinated with the strategic selectivity of the state, so-called "state-firm strategic coordination". Therefore, the different degrees of state-firm strategic coordination entailed a different extent of innovative performance of firms within a city-region and in different regions. Under an innovation-supportive regional environment that is characterized by an active strategic selectivity by both the central and local governments toward innovation-related activities, Shanghai's firms are more innovation oriented. Shanghai achieved a higher degree of state-firm strategic coordination and hence a better regional innovative performance. In sharp contrast, under an innovation-averse regional environment that indicates no interest by both the central and local governments in innovation-related activities, firms in Shenzhen suffered from a much lower degree of state-firm strategic coordination and hence a worse regional innovative performance. Why is there a mismatch between existing theories and the Chinese reality? How do the prevailing theoretical frameworks explain the dynamics of technological innovation?

1.3. Theory and Reality

In recent decades, the importance of technological innovation to sustained regional economic growth in the context of intensified global competition has received considerable scholarly attention. Ever since Schumpeter (1934) brought up technological innovation as one of the basic factors for economic development, the dynamism of innovation has never ceased to intrigue economists, geographers, planners and development specialists (Dodgson and Rothwell, 1994; Fagerberg *et al.*, 2005; Fagerberg and Verspagen, 2009). Since the 1990s, a great deal of theoretical and empirical work has been carried out to investigate industrial clusters and the geography of innovation (Audretsch and Feldman, 1996; Bottazzi and Peri, 2003; Breschi and Lissoni, 2001a, 2001b; Cooke, 2001; Döring and Schnellenbach, 2006; Howells, 2002; Kesidou and Romijn, 2008; Porter, 1990, 2000a). Among many other things, it is widely recognized that co-location of related firms could facilitate cooperation and competition, produce mutual trust and an innovative milieu, stimulate collective learning and bring about localized knowledge spillover, all of which will contribute to the growth of a regional knowledge-based economy (Fan and Scott, 2003; Florida, 1995; Porter, 1990, 2000a). A brief review of the existing literature can identify at least three prevalent explanatory frameworks that build their interpretations upon such analytical concepts as localized production networks, innovative milieu and knowledge spillover, etc. (Audretsch and Feldman, 1996; Camagni, 1991c; Florida, 1995; Porter, 1990, 2000a). Each of these interpretations tends to approach the same issue from different standpoints and is characterized by different emphasis.

The model of a localized production network stresses the importance of the production linkages based on the division of labor and vertical disintegration in an industrial cluster. A localized production network is believed to have the effect of increasing external economies of scale and scope, producing collective efficiency and reducing transaction costs (Grabher, 1993a; Marshall, 1920; Schmitz, 1995). Geographical proximity is considered to be important because it allows firms in the same region to share collective resources, facilitates the interaction between suppliers and customers, cultivates a relationship of mutual trust and stimulates competition (Bröcker *et al.*, 2003; Fan and Scott, 2003; Gertler, 1995; Gordon and McCann, 2000; Saxenian, 1994).

In the last two decades, the study of economic geography has experienced a shift of emphasis from an economic and reductionist explanation to a more contextual and discursive approach, sensitive to social, cultural and institutional environments in the understanding of industrial location and regional development (Amin, 1999; Barnes, 1999; Martin, 2000; Yeung, 2005a; Yeung and Lin, 2003). Regional unevenness in technological innovation has to be understood in relation to the variation in social, cultural and institutional conditions. The key to technological innovation, it is argued, lies in some "innovative milieu", such as the presence of a well-developed enterprise culture, supportive regulatory and promotional agencies, research-orientated universities, and locally committed financial structures, and the resulting process of mutual learning in such an innovative milieu (Martin, 2000, p. 82).

In recognition of the importance of collective learning, scholars started to pay much attention to localized knowledge spillover in the process of technological innovation (Cooke, 2001; Döring and Schnellenbach, 2006; Howells, 2002; Paci and Usai, 1999; Porter, 1990, 2000a). In the framework of knowledge spillover, knowledge is seen as a localized asset which is difficult to access for firms outside the region (Simmie, 2004, p. 1098). Because of the localized nature of technological knowledge, geographical proximity is believed to be instrumental in speeding up knowledge spillover and stimulating various forms of learning-by-doing, learning-by-using and learning-by-interacting (Malmberg, 1996; Maskell and Malmberg, 1999; Porter, 1990, 2000a). In this view, localized knowledge spillover could cut down the cost of knowledge search and scientific discovery and hence, to a large extent, reduce the risk resulting from the uncertainty of innovation (Audretsch and Feldman, 2003). The localized knowledge spillover resulting from the clustering of firms is therefore identified as a major driving force for technological innovation and regional growth (Kesidou and Romijn, 2008).

While the theories of industrial cluster have shed significant light on the dynamics of technological innovation, a close scrutiny and critical evaluation leads to a number of conceptual issues that require further clarification and interrogation. First, these theoretical frameworks stressed the importance of interactions or inter-relationships among the firms within a region, while paying little attention to the nature, attributes and characteristics of the firms themselves as active agents and actors in the process of technological innovation. Recent studies have shown that the nature and attributes of firms (e.g. size, ownership, market orientation, etc.) have implications for technological innovation no less significant than the regional environment that surrounds the firms (Beugelsdijk, 2007; Jefferson *et al.*, 2006; Lin *et al.*, 2011). It has also been observed that the success or failure of the technological innovation of a firm is, to a great extent, dependent upon the firm's capability to find a coupling between its production and a niche in the market where the firm has its competitive advantages (Brown and Fai, 2006). Meanwhile, these frameworks neglect to explore the internal resources held by the firms for technological innovation and hence fail to understand their diverse innovation-related strategies and behavior. Most of China's ICT firms are relatively small, without adequate capability to mobilize the necessary capital for innovation-related investment and without a highly-qualified workforce to potentially lead important research projects. These observations lead to questions like "what are the constraints to innovation confronting ICT firms in China? What are the options for ICT firms to overcome these barriers and conduct innovative activities? Why are some firms more innovation-oriented than others even though both of them share the same location?" These questions require further investigation.

Second, the frameworks have tended to assume that all firms in a cluster are tempted by the benefits of innovation and would therefore like to engage in research and development activities without taking into account other influential factors that may depress the innovation-related activities. Explanations as to why some firms are more innovative than others have been made in terms of the different capability of the firms to gain access to knowledge, without paying adequate attention to the motivations of firms and the opportunity costs that may be involved if a firm decides to engage in innovation. The reality has clearly been more complicated that what has been perceived in these theories. Firms are not necessarily motivated to engage in innovation-related activities because of the risks anticipated and the opportunity costs involved. It has been noticed that many firms would not be willing to commit themselves to innovation-related activities because of the risk-averse nature of private capital (Arrow, 1962; Lu, 2000, p. 15). In addition to financial constraints, there are many strategic considerations which may mean that firms are reluctant to enter the innovation cycle (Meeus and Oerlemans, 2005). It is not unusual to see that the return from imitation becomes higher and certainly safer than direct investment in innovation because the latter is plagued with risks and uncertainty and could easily end up with market failure (Christensen, 1997). Furthermore, many R&D investors have suffered a loss because of an immature market and an unfavorable institutional environment, such as in the Chinese context, whereas the imitators or competitors could still enjoy a stable economic return and a satisfactory profit margin (Teece, 1986). The extant studies fail to appreciate the significant influence of the external institutional and market environment on the innovation-related strategies of firms and hence underestimate the role of the state in the building-up of the regional institutional and market environment. These observations lead to questions like "what are the incentives confronting the ICT firms in China? What is the role of the state in shaping the regional characteristics and stimulating the innovation-involved strategies and activities of firms? How will firms respond to the external environment and the stimulus by the state? Why are some regions more innovative than others?" All these questions warrant further systematic studies.

In the end, the endogenous explanation of economic growth and technological innovation in a region is challenged by a number of scholars who argue that the "global pipeline" and the international linkages play a no less important role in the process of innovation than the localized clustering and networks (Bathelt, 2007; Bathelt and Gräf, 2008; Bathelt *et al.*, 2004; Simmie, 2004). In particular, the global pipeline and international linkages appear to be very significant for cases in developing countries where technological innovation is generally believed to be dependent upon advanced economies. A plethora of studies highlights the necessity for developing countries to tap in and gain access to international knowledge production as a means to enhance their competitiveness in the global economy (Kesidou and Romijn, 2008). The role played by multi-national corporations and the effects of technology transfer and global linkages have long preoccupied the research agenda concerning technological development in the developing countries that are seen as "late-comers" in the process of innovation (David, 1997; Kim and Nelson, 2000; Malecki, 1997).

The existence of competing interpretations and unsettled debates identified above have called for special efforts to be devoted to further enquiry into the actual dynamics of technological innovation in different regional contexts. Given the increasing role played by China in the globalizing world, a study of the growth dynamics and spatial pattern of the ICT industry in the Chinese economy undergoing rapid growth and profound structural changes may generate significant insights into a better understanding of the different trajectories of technological innovation in different socio-economic and political contexts.

1.4. Understanding the Uneven Innovative Performance of the ICT Industry in China

Identification of the gap between the existing theoretical models and the complicated reality in China has pushed me to establish a new conceptual framework to achieve a better understanding of the dynamics of technological innovation in China's ICT industry. In this book, I argue that most of China's ICT firms are reluctant to conduct innovation-related activities. One reason for that is related to the fact that they can still make a satisfactory profit margin without any innovation-involved investment in the transitional economy that is characterized by an immature market environment. Another reason is the fact that they have been stuck at the low end of the ICT global value chain and, without external assistance and stimulus, are unable to move up toward the segment of higher-end products and designs which has been occupied by the powerful multinationals (MNCs) for many years. In this view, the state plays a significant role in building an innovation-supportive institutional environment and stimulating the innovation-related strategies and activities of the firms. Firms only pursue profit maximization, and innovation is a significant tool for them to realize the final goal. The innovation-related strategies of firms are mainly determined by the internal resources that they possess and by the external institutional environment. Therefore, the uneven growth in technological innovation should be contingent upon how the state builds a favorable institutional structure and market environment to stimulate, encourage and support firms' innovation-related activities and how firms actively respond to the external institutional environment and strategic selectivity created by the state, according to their own resources and conditions.

Based on this understanding, this book hypothesizes that the dynamics of technological innovation in China's ICT firms is not dictated by the "clustering" explanation as suggested by the existing literature in economic geography, but instead is embedded in their actor and place-sensitive process of state-firm strategic coordination. In the new conceptual framework, the state is understood as a political entity with the capability and power to provide vision for the future that encompasses different scales of government and is full of strategic selectivity. The firm is defined as a collection of production resources that determines its innovation-related strategies and operations and is regulated and molded by its situated social, institutional and political environment. State-firm strategic coordination refers to a dynamic process in which firms' innovation-related strategies are coordinated with the strategic selectivity of the governments, which is a key to understanding the divergent dynamics and trajectory of technological innovation of China's ICT firms.

The major objective of this book is to unravel the nature and technological innovation of China's ICT industry and, more importantly, to investigate the cause-effect relationship between state-firm strategic coordination and the uneven innovative performance among individual firms and across space in an economy under transition. Specifically, it attempts to achieve four goals. First, it tries to understand the nature of China's ICT industry, especially its structural and spatial characteristics as well as innovation capability. Second, it attempts to investigate the relationship between industrial cluster and technological innovation. Third, it aims to examine the relationship between different degrees of state-firm strategic coordination and the uneven innovative performance of China's ICT industry. Finally, it tries to explore the regional variation in the degree of state-firm strategic coordination and how this difference has led to an uneven geography of innovation in China. This book also attempts to address the following questions. What is the nature and technological innovation of China's ICT industry? Does the innovative performance of the ICT firms vary from place to place? If yes, why are some regions more innovative than others? Is there any relationship between industrial cluster and technological innovation? If yes, why do some firms tend to be more innovative than others, even if both of them are located within the same industrial cluster? Is there any cause–effect relationship between state-firm strategic coordination and innovative performance of individual firms? In what manner and to what extent has state-firm strategic coordination affected the uneven innovative performance among individual firms and in different regions?

To achieve the major objective and answer the research questions, the uneven geography and structural composition of China's ICT industry is first analyzed, with special attention given to the relationship between industrial cluster and technological innovation as well as the importance of attributes, business interests and motivations of individual firms in the process of technological innovation. To evaluate the influences of state-firm strategic coordination on uneven innovative performance among individual firms within a region and in different regions, the software sector and the IC design sub-sector in Shanghai and Shenzhen are chosen for a detailed analysis and to conduct a direct comparative study between them. The analysis in this book challenges the "relational" explanations in the existing literature of technological innovation, which understands innovation dynamics as being determined by inter-firm linkages, connections and networks, without paying much attention to the attributes, nature, motivations and strategies of active actors and agents in an economy. Through detailed statistical analyses and comparative case studies, this book argues that the uneven innovative performance among individual firms and in different regions is not driven by industrial clustering and various relationships, but is affected by the actor and place-specific state-firm strategic coordination.

1.5. Terminology

Before we turn to the nature, spatial distribution and complex process of technological innovation in China's ICT industry, several terms used frequently in this book require clarification. The first term is the ICT Industry. According to the standard of national economic industry classification (GB/T4754-2002), "ICT Industry" consists of both the ICT manufacturing sector and service sector. The ICT manufacturing sector, with the industry code 4000, includes eight sub-sectors, namely manufacturing of telecom equipment (4010); radar and related equipment (4020); broadcasting and television equipment (4030); electronic computers (4040); electronic devices (4050); electronic components (4060); household audio and video equipment (4070); and other electronic equipment (4090). The ICT service sector includes the service of telecoms and other information transmission (6000), the service of computers (6100) and the software industry (6200).

Based on the definition of Porter (2000b, pp. 253–254), cluster in this book refers to a geographical concentration of a bunch of *interconnected companies with similar or complementary functions* in a particular field. By contrast, spatial agglomeration only refers to a geographical concentration of firms whose mutual linkages may or may not exist (Malmberg, 1996). It is noted that industrial cluster here is defined differently from what the Chinese literature has conceptualized. The latter mainly focuses on the phenomena of spatial agglomeration. However, this study follows the Western mainstream definition of industrial cluster.

Identification of industrial clusters involves intensive and careful research to obtain insights into the linkages existing among firms which unfortunately cannot be obtained by quantitative methods, whereas spatial agglomeration can be measured statistically using a number of indicators such as the Herfindahl index (H-index) (Fan and Scott, 2003), location quotient, growth-share matrix (Wolfe and Gertler, 2004), EG index (Ellison and Glaeser, 1997) and so on. It is argued that "[o]ne of the most common techniques employed by analysts to identify the presence of clusters within a specific geographical locale is the use of the employment location quotient." (Wolfe and Gertler, 2004, p. 1080). For comparability and data consistency, the employment location quotient is adopted as a measurement of spatial agglomeration. The formula of location quotient (LQ) is: $LQ = (E_{ij}/E_j)/(E_{in}/E_n)$; where E_{ij} is employment of industry i in region j, E_j is total employment in region j, E_{in} is national employment of industry i, and E_n is total national employment (Wolfe and Gertler, 2004). However, identifying a cluster with only quantitative methods is regarded to be insufficient by some scholars, and case studies were suggested as a good way to make up for it (Wolfe and Gertler, 2004, p. 1081). Therefore, identification of industrial clusters in this study will be based on both the statistical analysis of the employment location quotient at the provincial level with the data obtained from the 2004 economic census and the examination of the actual localized linkages among the firms with the data obtained from a questionnaire survey (for data collection, please see Appendix I).

A considerable number of scholars have made great efforts to define technological innovation (OECD and Eurostat, 2005; Porter, 1990; Simmie, 2002). Technological innovation in this study is regarded as a result of introducing new products to market or better ways to improve productivity. It can be measured by patent or patent citation (Audretsch, 1998; Feldman, 1994, 1999), patent application, patent certification and new products sales (Sun, 2002b). Technological innovation in this study will be measured by the number of granted invention patents and the output value of new products generated per enterprise. Innovative firms refer to those firms who at least hold one granted invention patent and non-innovative firms refers to those firms who are unable to achieve any invention patents.[2]

1.6. Organization of the Book

This book is organized in two major parts. The first part is devoted to theoretical and methodological development while the second part deals with empirical analyses, demonstration and explanation.

The first part includes two chapters. Chapter 2 is a systematic and critical review of the existing theoretical models and interpretations of the innovative performance of a region. Given that the numerous studies

---

[2]This study adopts the number of invention patents held by firms rather than the new products developed by the firms as the benchmark to distinguish innovators from non-innovators because the concept of "new" products is too obscure to be used. First, it is found that firms have different understandings of what is considered to be "new", which has made it difficult to adopt a standard to compare innovation across the firms. Second, it is difficult to judge how "new" a product should be in order to qualify a firm to be an innovator. OECD and Eurostat (2005) defined three kinds of new products, namely "new to the firm", "new to the market" and "new to the world" with an ascending degree of novelty. Unfortunately, the database did not provide any relevant specific information on the degree of novelty. When a firm claimed that new products have been created, it remained unknown whether the "new" product is genuinely new or just a change of appearance and whether the "new" product is only new to the firm or significantly new to the world. It would therefore be obscure and even misleading to take the introduction of new products as the indication to differentiate the innovators from non-innovators when dealing with Chinese firms.

which attribute technological innovation to industrial clusters cannot be enumerated and discussed in detail, only three influential interpretations with sophisticated theoretical engagement and rich empirical support for critical review were chosen for this study, namely the framework of the localized production network, innovative milieu and localized knowledge spillover. The review aims to highlight the core arguments and major explanatory logics in these three frameworks, pinpoint their respective and common limitations and provide an appeal for a framework which pays more attention to the motivations and strategies of active actors and agents.

The research gaps identified in Chapter 2 entail an innovative theoretical framework, which will be developed in Chapter 3. State-firm strategic coordination is understood as a mechanism to stimulate the innovation-related strategies of the firms and enlarge their pre-existing resources to be innovative. State-firm strategic coordination should be evaluated in three layers, namely the strategic selectivity of the central government, the capability and strategic selectivity of local governments and the strategic reactivity of the ICT firms. Firm-level state-firm strategic coordination can be measured by project-based, product-based and award-based state-firm strategic coordination while region-level state-firm strategic coordination can be measured by information-based, product-based and fund-based strategic coordination. It is expected that such a framework will enhance our understanding of the uneven innovative performance among individual firms and in different regions.

The second part contains five chapters (Chapters 4–8). Chapter 4 is intended to explore the nature, structural and spatial variations and technological innovation in China's ICT industry. Emphasis is placed on the relationship between industrial cluster and technological innovation as suggested in the existing literature. In addition, influential factors that differentiated the ICT innovative firms from non-innovative firms will be identified and explained.

Chapters 5 and 6 are devoted to investigate the cause–effect relationship between state-firm strategic coordination and firm-level innovative performance in Shanghai and Shenzhen. The statistical analyses will test such a relationship and information from the in-depth interview will further explain the process of different degrees of state-firm strategic coordination among individual firms within these two city-regions.

Chapter 7 is used for the direct comparison of the degree of state-firm strategic coordination in Shanghai and Shenzhen to understand how the different degree of state-firm strategic coordination has led to different levels of innovative performance between these two city-regions. It is accomplished through investigating and comparing the regional characteristics that are historically shaped by the strategic selectivity of the central government, the capability, power and strategic selectivity of local governments and the innovation-related motivation and strategies of local firms.

Finally, Chapter 8 concludes the study, summarizes the main findings of this book, discusses major theoretical and empirical implications and points out the limitations of this study and the direction of further research.

Chapter Two

INTERPRETING TECHNOLOGICAL INNOVATION THROUGH INDUSTRIAL CLUSTERING

2.1. Introduction

In the past two decades, the study of economic geography has been characterized by heightened attention paid to the "re-emergence of agglomeration", "localization of the world economy" or a "global mosaic of regional economies" (Malmberg *et al.*, 1996; Martin and Sunley, 2003). A large number of scholars have argued that the process of globalization is reinforcing rather than weakening regional economic distinctiveness (Porter, 1998; Scott, 1998; Storper, 1997, 1999). Much attention has been paid to the innovativeness and competitiveness of firms in region-based industrial clusters as the performance of industrial firms is believed to be less dependent on cost-reduction through access to cheap land use and the labor force and more determined by their innovative capabilities in a new knowledge-based global economy (Breschi and Malerba, 2001; Malmberg *et al.*, 1996; Martin, 1999; Porter, 1990, 1998, 2000a, 2000b). To Michael Porter and many of his followers, industrial clustering is the main source of national competitiveness and innovativeness, because innovation is produced in the process of inter-firm (with suppliers, customers or counterparts) and extra-firm linkages (with universities, research institutions, local governments or other organizations) (Porter, 2000b, pp. 253–254). The described relationship between industrial clustering and technological innovation has been widely addressed in the burgeoning literature identified as "new economic geography" by some and "new regionalism" by others. The focus of attention has shifted from the structural-organizational characteristics of the production linkages involved, to the social-institutional environment and more recently to the cognitive nature of the relationship (Lagendijk, 2006). More specifically, this relationship has been explicitly elucidated in three influential models, namely localized production networks, innovative milieu and localized knowledge spillovers.

There has been an ardent debate over the relationship between industrial cluster and technological innovation in recent years. Some scholars maintain that industrial clusters can intensify localized productive linkages (Porter, 1990, 1998, 2000a; Saxenian, 1994), produce innovative milieu (Camagni, 1991b, 1995; Crevoisier and Maillat, 1991; Maillat, 1995; Shefer and Frenkel, 1998) and facilitate knowledge spillovers (Keeble and Wilkinson, 1999; Maskell and Malmberg, 1999; Tödtling *et al.*, 2006), thereby leading to a higher innovative performance, while others argue that mainly focusing on local processes, interactions and relationships is far from sufficient to understand the innovative performance of a region. The accessibility to national and international knowledge as well as the capability to build global linkages and relationships is even more pivotal for innovation (Bathelt *et al.*, 2004; Simmie, 2003, 2004; Simmie and Sennett, 1999). The key issue underlying the heated debate is on what spatial scale the interactions, connections and relationships among the firms, organizations and institutions could simulate and facilitate innovation-related activities and improve the innovative performance of firms. A multi-scalar explanation rejects the singular perspectives in the existing literature and offers a more general viewpoint on the process of innovation, which further complicated the debate over the relationship between industrial cluster and technological innovation (Bunnell and Coe, 2001).

To better understand the relationship between industrial cluster and technological innovation, this chapter starts with a critical evaluation of diverse theoretical perspectives. Attention will be directed first of all to the different views of the relationship between industrial cluster and technological innovation, including that of Schumpeter and Porter, founders of the theory of innovation and cluster, respectively. This will then be followed by a critical evaluation of three theoretical frameworks that support the positive relationship between industrial cluster and technological innovation, namely localized production networks, innovative milieu and localized knowledge spillover. The framework of global and multi-scalar linkages which contradicts the described cluster-innovation relationship will be discussed subsequently. Finally, a comprehensive critique of the existing theoretical inquiries is provided.

2.2. Industrial Cluster and Technological Innovation: Is There a Relationship?

2.2.1. *The origins of innovation and cluster*

The earliest theoretical contribution to understanding the innovation of economic activities is the Schumpeterian theory of entrepreneurial innovation (Schumpeter, 1934). To the Schumpeterians, innovation could be regarded as a creative destruction of the old economic system or a new combination of the materials and forces that has been successfully introduced to the market (Schumpeter, 1934, 1942). Schumpeter (1934, p. 66) identified five different types of innovation, namely new products, new methods of production, new sources of supply, the exploitation of new markets and new ways to organize business. Following the definition of innovation proposed by Schumpeter, Porter lays much emphasis on the first two types of innovation — new products and new methods of production — what is usually called "technological innovation". Porter conceives technological innovation as an effort "to create competitive advantage by perceiving or discovering new and better ways of competing in an industry and bringing them to market" (Porter, 1990, p. 45). However, there are significant differences in the understanding of innovation between Schumpeter and Porter. Schumpeter regards cumulativeness and evolution as important features of innovation while Porter sees innovation as one of the elements of competitive advantages underlying industrial clusters, without paying much attention to its evolutionary characteristics (Baptista, 1998, p. 44).

Even more differences can be found in the understanding of the relationship between cluster and innovation between Schumpeter and Porter. To Schumpeter, neither geographical proximity nor inter-/extra-firms linkages contribute to innovation. Similar to neoclassical economics, the Schumpeterian theory employs an atomistic view to understand industrial firms. A firm is basically conceived as a productive unit which is willing to take the risk of conducting innovation-related activities in order to seek profit maximization. Furthermore, firms act in isolation from other economic agents as well as their situated social, political and institutional environment (Yeung, 2005a). Therefore, Schumpeterian innovation emerges as a result of individual effort rather than the collective efficiency of co-located actors and agents. Innovation is believed to be produced through intra-firm investment and thus has nothing to do with geographical concentration of related firms and inter-firm or extra-firm linkages. In particular, Schumpeter attributes innovation to the wise decision-making and adventurous inputs of entrepreneurs without allocating any relevance to the influence of geography or space on innovative activities (Baptista, 1998). Susskind and Zybkow (1978, p. 5) summarize with insight the Schumpeterian heroic theory about innovation: "It is the energetic entrepreneur who is willing to take risks, who amasses capital to finance the invention, who sees the idea through to actual production and introduction to the marketplace. He is the man who links together the social needs, frequently expressed in terms of profit potentialities, with the creative ideas of the inventor, thereby coupling the marketplace with the invention".

In contrast, Porter, as one of those economists who have newfound interests in geography in recent years, sees innovation through a spatial lens, highlighting the importance of geographical proximity, inter/extra-firm interactions and linkages and collective efficiency in the process of technological innovation and maintains there exists a positive relationship between industrial cluster and innovation (Martin, 1999; Simmie, 2004). It has been pointed out that "the enduring competitive advantages in a global economy are often heavily local, arising from concentrations of highly specialized skills and knowledge, institutions, rivals, related business and sophisticated customers" (Porter, 1998, p. 90). The concept of cluster was thereby coined by Porter (1990; 2000b, pp. 253–254) to refer to a "geographically proximate group of interconnected companies and associated institutions in a particular field, linked by commonalities and complementarities" which is believed to be the main source of national competitiveness and innovativeness because innovation is produced in the process of inter-firm (with suppliers, customers or counterparts) and extra-firm linkages (with universities, research institutions, local governments or other organizations). In this perspective, industrial clusters can lead to technological innovation because the localized clusters "allow rapid perception of new buyer needs; concentrate knowledge and information; allow the rapid assimilation of new technological possibilities; they provide richer insights into new management practices; facilitate on-going relationships with other institutions including universities; the knowledge-based economy is most successful when knowledge resources are localized" (Simmie, 2004, p. 1102).

Furthermore, Schumpeter contends that a monopoly is better than competition in terms of propelling the innovative activities "because a local monopoly restricts the flow of ideas to others and so allows externalities to be internalized by the innovator. When externalities are internalized, innovation and growth speed up" (Glaeser *et al.*, 1992, p. 1127). In sharp contrast to the cluster theory that advocates a free flow of ideas among co-located agents, such an opinion further suggests that innovation will not occur through an industrial cluster of related firms. Moreover, Porter argues that both cooperation and competition among different actors in particular locations are beneficial to innovation and it is the local competition, rather than local monopoly, that stimulates the new ideas and facilitates the adoption of innovation (Glaeser *et al.*, 1992).

In summary, Schumpeter believes that innovation is tightly related to intra-firm inputs and outputs, and hence is independent of factors such as geographical proximity and cooperation that Porter considered to be most significant to technological innovation. The Schumpeterian theory on innovation has been criticized by many scholars in view of its weakness in two aspects. First, the neglect of space in his theory cannot explain the recent feature that technological innovation arose in particular locations before it was adopted and transferred to other places (Sturgeon, 2003). Second, his intra-firm view on innovation has been widely questioned because of the rise of an endogenous growth theory and the effect of knowledge spillover in the age of knowledge-based economies. Feldman (1994, pp. 1–2) points out, "For students of economic development from Adam Smith to Karl Marx and Joseph Schumpeter, innovation is seen as the product of entrepreneurs who harness the resources required for innovation, profit and growth. Analysis of innovation has typically been confined to the organizational boundaries of the individual firm. However, the notion that the capacity to innovate incorporates external sources of knowledge has gained acceptance. Innovation is perhaps best characterized as an intrinsically uncertain problem-solving process which blends private knowledge with public knowledge". Audretsch (2003) adopts a similar point of view: "Early work on innovation focused almost exclusively on the unit of observation of the firm. The innovative process was considered to occur solely within the boundaries of the enterprise, resulting in a scholarly tradition consisting of theories and empirical insights focusing on innovative activity as a firm-specific activity. More recently, however, recognition of the role of knowledge externalities has led to the emergence of geographic space as a crucial platform for innovative activity" (Audretsch, 2003, p. 11).

Although the cluster conceptual framework proposed by Porter brings our attention to the importance of geographic space and the effect of external economies in the process of innovation, it has exposed several drawbacks and incurred criticism. Firstly, the geographical scale of a cluster is so vague and flexible that further clarification should be requested (Martin and Sunley, 2003). It also raises the question on how "geographically proximate", according to Porter's definition, a group should be before this so-called cluster could produce a self-reinforcing dynamics that stimulates and facilitates the process of innovation. In addition to the problem in defining the boundary of a cluster, the "chaotic concept" of a cluster either cannot clarify how strong the linkages have to be or what range of related industries and activities should be included to constitute a cluster (Martin and Sunley, 2003).

Second, Porter's theory fails to elucidate the social dimension of the formation and development of the cluster (Martin and Sunley, 2003) and underestimates the strength of the "relational assets" or "untraded interdependencies" in the process of innovation (Amin, 1999). It has been argued that it is not the geographical proximity but the social relationship that facilitates the process of innovation: "Geographical proximity is not so much an economic cause of agglomeration as a social effect of the embeddedness of economic relations in inter-individual relations" (Torre and Rallet, 2005, p. 52). The context and the position in which the clusters are placed to a large extent affected the relationship between industrial cluster and technological innovation because whether "relational assets" are able to accelerate regional development "must be theorized in relation to their complementarity and specificity to particular regions in question" (Yeung, 2005b, p. 48).

Third, Porter overlooks the various characteristics of the different types of clusters and therefore only partially understands the relationship between industrial cluster and technological innovation. It is argued that "clusters vary considerably in type, origin, structure, organization, dynamics and developmental trajectory, yet Porter's theory is supposedly intended to fit all" (Martin and Sunley, 2003, p. 15). It is also argued that local competitiveness and innovation is determined by the types of industry, the life cycle, composition of activities and locational conditions instead of the oversimplified geographical clustering (Feldman, 1999; Glasmeier, 2000b). Finally, in view of all the theoretical flaws and weaknesses identified above, it comes as no surprise that many empirical studies have found an untenable relationship between industrial cluster and technological innovation in some particular regions (Beaudry *et al.*, 2000; Harrison *et al.*, 1996; *cf.* Martin and Sunley, 2003).

Despite these drawbacks underlying Porter's cluster approach, it not only triggers the "geographical turn" of economists but also relights the passion for agglomeration economies by economic geographers (Malmberg, 1996; Martin, 1999). Especially with the advent of knowledge-based economies, innovation has been given highest priority because of its contribution to long-term economic prosperity (Davelaar and Nijkamp, 1997). The positive relationship between industrial cluster and technological innovation has been addressed in the existing literature concerning territorial innovation, which experienced three stages of transition from structuralist-organizational perspectives to social-institutional perspectives and then to cognitive perspectives (*cf.* Lagendijk, 2006). According to theoretical models included in this line of enquiry, this chapter broadly groups the huge literature into three categories: the framework of the localized production network, the framework of innovative milieu and the framework of knowledge spillovers. These frameworks are not always mutually exclusive but they offer different viewpoints on what are believed to be the most important points from their special focuses.

2.2.2. *Framework of localized production network*

Drawing its theoretical cues from the fierce debate over Fordism and post-Fordism that was triggered by the crisis of Fordism as well as the theories of agglomeration economies and transaction costs, the approach of the localized production network emphasizes the production linkages based on the division of labor and the vertical disintegration in a cluster. It is claimed that a localized production network not only increases external economies of scale and scope (Marshall, 1920), produces collective efficiency (Schmitz, 1995), but also reduces the transaction costs based on trust relationships (Grabher, 1993a). A basic assumption of this framework is that geographic proximity plays an important role from at least five aspects. First, it is generally believed that industrial firms located in the same region could share collective resources such as infrastructure, by which the production costs of individual firms could be reduced (Fan and Scott, 2003; Weber, 1929). Second, firms could benefit from the localized labor pool with specialized skills because of the agglomeration of related economic activities (Fan and Scott, 2003; Marshall, 1920). Third, geographical proximity could facilitate the interactions and linkages between local agents, and build up the trust relationships between them that in turn intensify their communications and connections (Gertler, 1995; Gordon and McCann, 2000). Fourth, geographical proximity could stimulate mutual competition, which is believed to improve the performance of local agents (Porter, 1990;

Wolfe and Gertler, 2004). Finally, firms could easily grasp useful industrial information and knowledge by being in proximity to each other, since there exists "something in the air" within the industrial districts (Marshall, 1920).

Many empirical studies have confirmed the positive relationship between a localized production network and innovative performance. For instance, Saxenian (1994, 1999) conducted a comparative study on Silicon Valley and Route 128, and illuminated how regions can be more innovative and successful through developing a network-based production system. It is very intriguing to see why Silicon Valley could get through the crisis in the 1980s and achieve a sustainable competitive edge while Route 128, in contrast, failed to control the declining trend and lagged behind, considering the fact that both electronics clusters in Silicon Valley and Route 128 were supported by a similar advantageous location, proximity to famous universities, easy access to talented people and funding support from the government. To Saxenian, the reason lies in the fact that Silicon Valley benefits from its localized network-based system and regional culture of encouraging cooperation and competition, whereas Route 128 remains stuck to the ossified organization of vertical integration, which internalizes the production linkages, fails to get useful information from others, stifles the production and organization model, retards the decision-making to the flexible and promptly changing market, and hence ultimately leads to its failure.

Porter (2000b, p. 262) analyzes the positive cluster-innovation relationship by emphasizing the localized production network of a cluster: "A firm within a cluster often can more rapidly source the new components, services, machinery, and other elements needed to implement innovations, whether a new product line, a new process, or a new logistical model. Local suppliers and partners can and do get closely involved in the innovation process, thus ensuring that the inputs they supply better meet the firm's requirements. New, specialized personnel can often be recruited locally to fill gaps required to pursue new approaches. The complementarities involved in innovating are more easily achieved among nearby participants". Bathelt *et al.* (2004) divide the linkages of the production network into horizontal and vertical dimensions and explain how the two kinds of linkages can speed up the process of innovation. Bröcker *et al.* (2003, p. 1) observe that "there are many indications that, increasingly, regional growth and innovation seem to emerge from innovative complexes of firms and organizations. It is argued that it is primarily within these geographically concentrated networks or 'clusters'".

Based on the explanation of economic and business linkages, a number of scholars seek to elaborate the dynamics and innovativeness of various types of clusters from an evolutionary and morphological perspective. Park (1996) differentiates nine types of network patterns through examining their differences in local and non-local networks, embeddedness, production systems, governance, cooperation and competition, etc. He argues that different types of clusters have their own competitive advantages in a given industrial environment at a certain period of time, but their competitive power will change over time and in the context of both the local and global economy. Furthermore, his case study on East Asia reveals very different types of networks in this region from the popular ones identified by Markusen (1996) based on Western experiences, suggesting that we should be cautious to apply these models to specific regions. Although Park's work contributes to the understanding of the dynamics and the typology of industrial clusters or industrial districts in less developed countries, he neglects the significant influence of linkages and interactions beyond the inter-firm scale in local innovativeness and competitiveness. Extra-firm interactions, such as linkages between universities, research institutions and firms which have been proven to be important to the innovation of firms, are largely overlooked in Park's research (Kaufmann and Tödtling, 2001). At the same time, Park gives special attention to the supplier–customer linkages, taking into account the firm's size, but he fails to distinguish tricky and delicate linkages between international corporations and indigenous firms from those between the same genetic firms in analyzing the dynamics of clusters and innovativeness, although he recognizes the leading position of multinational firms and their branch plants in East Asia that is largely ignored by Markusen (1996).

Walcott (2002) extends Park's Asian development topology to include an intermediary category of "bridge high technology" with an emphasis on domestically generated technology for native companies to interpret the diverse performances of China's industrial parks. Walcott brings the universities and research institutes into her framework and highlights them as a driver for local R&D activities and innovativeness. She also takes into account the multiple types of firms and various supporting structures in different locations. However, the importance of universities and research institutes in generating valuable technologies to facilitate the technological innovation of firms appears rather questionable. Furthermore, Walcott's model is only based on 39 interviews conducted in four Chinese science parks, so that more empirical evidence and cautious application to other regions are needed. Despite the flaws in Park's and Walcott's theoretical frameworks, they do bring our attention to the type of industrial network and its development stage in understanding the relationship between industrial cluster and technological innovation.

Although the framework of the localized production network offers a sound explanation of the innovative performance of a cluster, it has been widely criticized for its over-emphasis on the pure economic relationship without a serious look at the influence of social, political and cultural contexts on firms' behavior as well as external linkages of firms with other organizations and institutes. The last two decades witnessed a renaissance of the "institutional turn" in the field of economic geography, which believes that "economic activity is *socially and institutionally situated:* it cannot be explained by reference to atomistic individual motives alone, but has to be understood as enmeshed in wider *structures of social, economic and political rules, procedures and conventions*" (Martin, 2000, p. 79, emphasis in the original). In addition, the framework of a localized production network claims that innovation can be achieved in a cluster because the localized production network would enhance the collective efficiency and mutual trust between related firms. Nevertheless, whether or not, or to what extent, this mechanism could stimulate innovative activities and improve the innovative capability remains vague and controversial. Malmberg and Power (2005, p. 413) have found that the local production and service linkages failed to stimulate R&D activities and create new knowledge on the basis of a number of empirical studies.

More importantly, it is problematic to borrow the framework of a localized production network to explain China's industrial clusters and their technological innovation. One of the basic assumptions in this framework is that geographical proximity cannot only facilitate and intensify local production linkages and hence lead to a trust relationship between associated agents by iterative meetings and face-to-face contacts but also stimulate competition for innovation as Wolfe and Gertler (2004, p. 1077) have maintained: "The advantages of proximity arise from continuous observation, comparison and monitoring what local rival firms are doing, which act as a spur to innovation as firms race to keep up with or get ahead of their rivals". While this mechanism may or may not be empirically verified by the cases in the West, it cannot work in the case of China where spatial clustering of industrial firms in most regions is initiated by the Chinese government in the form of "high-tech parks" or "science parks" (Cong, 2004; Walcott, 2002). It is necessary to examine how the industrial cluster has come into being and why firms choose to locate together in certain places before jumping to the beneficial effects of geographical proximity. It is reported that there exist no close and frequent inter-firm linkages between different agents in the case of Zhongguancun in Beijing, which was one of the earliest established and most innovative parks in China (Zhou, 2005). Firms in most science parks in China are mainly tempted by favorable policies, cheap land and tax exemption, etc., instead of spontaneous concentration for convenient interactions. They normally prefer to do business with previous partners outside the industrial park rather than establish new-brand relations from scratch in their new location. With regard to multinational corporations, they have enough power to make their old suppliers locate nearby or cultivate emerging local firms to service them. A research of the Taiwan-based PC manufacturers reveals the fact that they tend to persuade their Taiwanese suppliers to come along with them to establish branches in the mainland in recognition of the insufficient technological capability of indigenous firms to meet their requirements (Hsu, 2005). To some extent, it is the relational proximity over the geographical proximity that fosters local production linkages in the case of China, which partly resonates with the recent "relation turn" in economic geography (Boggs and Rantisi, 2003).

The argument that geographical proximity permits firms to observe, compare and monitor their counterparts is untenable. In the industrial parks of China, manufacturing factories tend to isolate themselves from their neighbors through rigid surveillance to restrict the entrance of strangers. High-end technologies and product information are kept strictly secret by some employees, which other employees within the firm are forbidden to approach, let alone strangers or competitors. Therefore, it is almost impossible for their rivals to observe and monitor them. The hostility rather than amity between co-located firms is not hard to understand when taking into account the cultural and institutional environment under which those firms operate. On the one hand, high-tech firms in China are afraid of good ideas being stolen due to the lack of an effective institution to protect intellectual property rights, which, to a large extent, reduces the mutual trust in the co-located firms (Cong, 2004). On the other hand, based on the credo that "blood is thicker than water" (*xue nong yu shui*), Chinese people are inclined to cooperate with relatives and friends and do not easily trust strangers, which made the linkages that are stimulated by the geographical proximity of related firms impossible. It is no wonder that many studies in China have discovered that "*guanxi*" (relationship) is very important for the success of business in China (Su and Littlefield, 2001; Tsang, 1998; Wong, 1998). The case of China therefore confirms that relational proximity appears to be more important than geographical proximity. Moreover, whether or not observation, comparison and monitoring could have a positive effect on innovation truly depends on the nature of the industry and the attributes of firms. Interestingly, it is argued that the repetitious transactions among different agents are not necessarily leading to mutual trust or synergies among the firms. Sturgeon (2003) observes that face-to-face contacts in the electronic industry appear to be a problem rather than a factor in innovation. Also, it is argued that collective synergies are not resulting from the face-to-face contacts but are rather conditional on a similar background of interacting economic agents: "Face-to-face interaction between two actors cannot alone generate synergies; the latter can only develop between two individuals who belong to the same network or share common representations" (Torre and Rallet, 2005, p. 52).

Furthermore, the economic agents in this theoretical framework are assumed to be indigenous firms with counterbalanced power relations with others, which has been found untenable in the case of East Asia's industrial districts where the hub-spoke relationship formed by big multi-national corporations (MNCs) and small indigenous firms is rather common (Bair and Gereffi, 2001; Park, 1996). While the industrial districts of Western countries are characterized by a spontaneous and balanced relationship between co-located firms, the obviously uneven power relations between MNCs and indigenous firms existing in China's industrial clusters, without any doubt, have shaped a divergent development trajectory and innovative performance. Zhou and Tong (2003) identified both negative and positive influences of MNCs on the performance of indigenous ICT service firms in Zhongguancun in Beijing. While the easy acquisition of technological transfer from the MNCs retards the enthusiasm for indigenous innovation, the indigenous firms are able to rapidly learn a lot in both knowledge and management from MNCs in the process of interaction, which has improved the innovative performance of indigenous firms. However, the empirical research of Zhou and Tong (2003) is based on the most self-innovative area in China which is full of highly qualified talent and supportive infrastructure. Indigenous firms that are located in the rest of China may confront so many difficulties in conducting R&D activities that they have more chance to be subjected to MNCs and to become MNCs' manufacturing factories or low-end service centers without the enthusiasm and capability for technological upgrading. Such localized production linkages could never be a spur to the creation of innovation in firms.

2.2.3. *Framework of innovative milieu*

Recognizing the problems underlying the framework of the localized production network, a number of economic geographers have started to discard the purely economics-focused explanation in interpreting the regional competitiveness and innovativeness and moved toward seeking a framework that stressed the influence of cultural and social contexts on growth and innovation — a shift that has been coined as "institutional turn" or "culture turn" in economic geography (Amin, 1999; Amin and Thrift, 1999; Barnes, 1999, 2001; Boschma and Frenken, 2006; Martin, 2000; Storper, 1995). Technological change in this approach is conceived as "an inherently socio-cultural activity dependent on the institutional setting within which it takes place" rather than "some exogenous disembodied process" as mainstream economists have proposed (Martin, 2000, p. 82). Scholars explain why certain places are more technologically innovative than others by giving prominence to various local institutional settings. The framework of the innovative milieu is one of the representatives in this line of theoretical inquiries. It is argued that "certain forms of local institutional regime or 'milieu' (such as the presence of a well-developed enterprise culture, supportive regulatory and promotional agencies, research-orientated universities and locally committed financial structures) particularly appear to facilitate the emergence and development of clusters of technologically based activity" (Martin, 2000, p. 82).

Coined by the GREMI Group (Groupement Europeen des Milieux Innovateurs) in 1991, the concept of an innovative milieu interprets economic dynamics from the sociological perspective of a spatial relationship and highlights the influence of social interactions and synergies on innovative capability in a specific place (Camagni, 1991b). In this framework, economic space consists of all kinds of "relations". Interaction with the social-cultural environment, the coherent efforts, especially the collective learning process, and the sharing of the same values together determine the innovative capability. It is argued that "spatial proximity matters not really in terms of a reduction in physical 'distance' and in the related transport costs, but rather in terms of easy information interchange, similarity of cultural and psychological attitudes, frequency of interpersonal contacts and cooperation, and density of factor mobility within the limits of the local area. All these elements in fact are crucial, but particularly because they determine the local response capability to a changing external environment, its innovativeness and production flexibility" (Camagni, 1991a, p. 2). An innovative milieu is therefore defined "as the set, or the complex network of mainly informal social relationships in a limited geographical area, often determining a specific external 'image' and a specific internal 'representation' and sense of belonging, which enhance the local innovative capability through synergetic and collective learning processes" (Camagni, 1991a, p. 4). After the seminal work of the GREMI Group, some empirical studies have validated that an innovative milieu lying in the spatial clustering of related actors has a positive influence on the local economy and innovative capability (Shefer and Frenkel, 1998).

Compared to the framework of a localized productive network that places much emphasis on the economic relationship, the framework of an innovative milieu pays more attention to the social network and relationships as well as institutional regimes. Lagendijk (2006, p. 390) points out, "In stressing the social-territorial embedding of innovation, the notion of milieu does not refer to either organizational structure or environment, but to the territorially rooted elements underpinning the social-cultural, interactive and cumulative nature of learning." The milieu works mainly through two mechanisms. First, the social network is a key to the milieu. Local firms are confronted with many uncertainties when making a decision about innovation-related activities because of both the uncertain characteristics of innovation *per se* and the uncertain market information from the imperfect competition (OECD and Eurostat, 2005). The high failure odds of innovation-related activities depressed the motivation of the firms to invest in innovation. It is disclosed that "only one out of ten research projects turns out to be a commercial success, and that many patented inventions never find any direct commercial applications" (Malmberg *et al.*, 1996, pp. 89–90). The milieu, on the basis of the informal social relationships that can produce the sense of belonging as well as facilitating the circulation of market information, to a large extent mitigates these uncertainties and reduces risks.

Second, collective learning is a fundamental precondition and a result of the milieu. Collective learning happens not only among firms but also between firms and universities and other organizations. In the framework of an innovative milieu, space "is not seen merely as a 'container' in which attractive location factors may happen to exist or not, but rather as a milieu for collective learning through intense interaction between a broadly composed set of actors" (Malmberg *et al.*, 1996, p. 91). Moulaert and Sekia (2003, p. 291) point out that "the GREMI stress the concept of apprenticeship, which means that the innovative capacity of the different members of the milieu depends on the capacity of learning... the apprenticeship dynamics and the co-operative organization based on interaction constitute the core of the *milieu innovateur*". Furthermore, learning is an efficient mechanism to increase the knowledge stock (Oinas, 2000), and hence induces innovation and intensifies the innovative milieu in light of the evolutionary characteristic of innovation (Nelson and Winter, 1982). Social embeddedness in a specific region makes the collective learning much easier and keeps this process localized and self-strengthened. In this sense, an innovative milieu or cluster can also be regarded as a "learning region", which "functions as collectors and repositories of knowledge and ideas, and provides an underlying environment or infrastructure which facilitates the flow of knowledge, ideas and learning". "Learning regions are increasingly important sources of innovation and economic growth" (Florida, 1995, p. 528).

However, the milieu approach fails to identify the cause–effect relationship between milieu and innovation. This framework has been criticized because "the GREMI group has never been able to identify the economic logic by which milieu fosters innovation. There is a circularity: "Innovation occurs because of a milieu, and a milieu is what exists in regions where there is innovation" (Storper, 1999, p. 211). In addition, collective learning, as the significant element under-pinning the framework of innovative milieu, is not easy to achieve. The concept of collective learning is too abstract to deeply understand what is really going on among firms. It is no way to find out how the learning machine starts, who is learning from whom and to what extent this kind of learning facilitates innovation. With the conceptual fuzziness and methodological underdevelopment, the framework of an innovative milieu is even more problematic when applied to interpret the phenomenon of China. There exists an extreme asymmetry in the knowledge stock and technological capability between the MNCs and indigenous firms whose co-existence is a popular typology of China's industrial parks. In recognition of the technological gap with MNCs, some indigenous firms are urged to learn from MNCs, which is believed to be easier given the geographical proximity, while MNCs tend to learn from their global network and international market rather than local undeveloped agents (Zhou and Tong, 2003). The possibility of mutual learning also depends to a large extent on corporate strategies and political consideration rather than the geographical co-location. For example, MNCs are reluctant to share their knowledge unless the host country forces them to do so (Liu, 2000). The relationship based on unwillingness and conflict of interests runs against the motto of collective learning that is supposed to be produced on the basis of spontaneity, equality and mutual benefits. To make things worse, it has been found out that spatial proximity is not necessarily conducive to learning (Oinas, 2000). At the same time, it is revealed that in-house R&D efforts made by indigenous firms rather than external linkages with MNCS are the primary source of innovation in China's manufacturing sectors, and the self-dependent innovative capability of indigenous firms reduces their desire for collective learning and seeking for external assistance, especially in a non-trust environment (Sun, 2002b).

The hybrid of firms with different sources of investment in China's industrial clusters has also complicated the social relationships among them and weakened the territorial social-embeddedness. Firms invested with foreign capital have closer social connections to their headquarters, which are normally located in their motherland, while firms invested with Taiwanese capital are more likely to cooperate with Taiwanese firms who have a tendency toward geographic co-location (Walcott, 2002, p. 362; Wang and Lee, 2007). It is hard to say whether these firms really have a sense of belonging and it is debatable if synergic interactions or coherent efforts do exist between them. The framework of an innovative milieu exaggerates the "collaborative and cooperative nature" but ignores "questions of social equity and clashes of social interests" among firms (Sunley, 2008, p. 5). Besides, no quantitative methods have been developed to measure this social embeddedness or the social-cultural relationships and thereby the vagueness of the concept "innovative milieu" has been criticized by many scholars (Moulaert and Sekia, 2003). It is difficult to apply this theory in practice in view of its vagueness and non-measurability and it is almost impossible to conduct empirical research to testify whether or not and how firms can benefit from an innovative milieu and to what extent they benefit from it to facilitate technological innovation.

2.2.4. *Framework of knowledge spillover*

The recognition of the importance of collective learning, coupled with the advent of "knowledge-based" economies, has since the 1990s given rise to the theory of localized knowledge spillover in the process of industrial clustering. It is generally believed that "innovation is closely associated with knowledge. Indeed, innovation in a narrower sense may be defined as application of knowledge. Innovation does not only derive from the application of novel pieces of knowledge or a novel combination of existing pieces of knowledge, but knowledge can also be created during the process of innovation" (Fischer, 2006, p. 1). Some are convinced that the real advantages of clusters do not lie in the emergence of trust and reciprocal actions to lowering transaction costs but in the creation of knowledge and the process of learning through the horizontal and vertical dimensions of clusters (Bathelt, 2005b; Maskell, 2001b). Porter (2000b) also reveals that easy access to knowledge and information within a cluster is an important factor in making firms innovative. With the increasing complexity of knowledge and technology, it has become impossible for a firm to achieve technological innovation without access to external knowledge or networks (Lee *et al.*, 2001; van Waarden, 2005). The localized knowledge spillover in the cluster is therefore identified as a major driving force for technological innovation and regional growth (Kesidou and Romijn, 2008). Since the 1990s, a great deal of theoretical and empirical work has been done to investigate the process of localized knowledge spillover and the geography of innovation (Audretsch and Feldman, 1996; Bottazzi and Peri, 2003; Breschi and Lissoni, 2001a, 2001b; Cooke, 2001; Döring and Schnellenbach, 2006; Howells, 2002; Kesidou and Romijn, 2008; Ponds *et al.*, 2010; Porter, 2000a).

Influenced by the endogenous growth theory, the prevailing view is that the characteristics of partial excludability and non-rival knowledge allow firms to benefit from the spilled knowledge without paying any fees. Fischer (2006, p. 101, emphasis in the original) claims that "knowledge spillovers arise because, as Romer (1990) emphasized, knowledge is a partially excludable and non-rival good. *Lack of excludability* implies that knowledge producers have difficulty in fully appropriating the returns or benefits and in preventing other firms from utilizing the knowledge without compensation or with compensation less than the value of knowledge... *Non-rival* means essentially that a new piece of knowledge can be utilized many times and in many different circumstances". Here, knowledge spillover is understood as "working on similar things and hence benefiting much from each other's research" that could increase rates of innovation (Feldman, 1999, p. 7).

It has been pointed out that the knowledge base of individual firms is limited and external heterogenous knowledge is an important complement for a firm to achieve technological innovation. Fagerberg (2005, p. 11), for instance, has argued that "the growing complexity of knowledge bases necessary for innovation means that even large firms increasingly depend on external sources in their innovative activity". It has further been suggested that "firms do not innovate in isolation but depend on external sources such as other firms, customers or public institutions in the creation of new knowledge" (Tappeiner *et al.*, 2008, p. 863). In this view, localized knowledge spillover could cut down the cost of knowledge search and scientific discovery and hence, to a large extent, reduce the risk resulting from the uncertainty of innovation (Audretsch and Feldman, 2003). The importance of knowledge externalities in the process of growth and innovation has been empirically demonstrated with econometric techniques (De Groot *et al.*, 2001).

Geographical proximity has been greatly highlighted in this line of theoretical inquiry. Baptista and Swann (1998, p. 527) maintain that geographical proximity becomes vital for innovative activity because of knowledge spillover, since knowledge is seen as some localized asset which firms outside the region find difficult to reach (Simmie, 2004, p. 1098). It is generally believed that geographic proximity plays a significant role in speeding up the knowledge spillover, stimulating various forms of learning-by-doing, learning-by-using and learning-by-interacting, and increasing the stock of knowledge for innovation, which in turn attracts more firms to locate together (Malmberg, 1996; Maskell and Malmberg, 1999; Porter, 1990, 2000a). Moreover, the knowledge-based economic activities are inclined to geographical clustering because knowledge can be produced much more easily and transmitted more efficiently in a cluster while the formal and informal interactions between co-located firms induces the formation of innovative milieu that further stimulates the process of knowledge exchange and spillover (Audretsch, 1998; Shefer and Frenkel, 1998).

In the process of exploring the relationship between knowledge spillover, innovation and cluster, knowledge usually is divided into two forms: codified knowledge and tacit knowledge, whose ceaseless interaction creates new knowledge and accelerates the process of innovation. However, tacit knowledge is regarded as more difficult to understand, assimilate and apply than codified knowledge since the former involves know-how that needs certain background knowledge to make full use of it (Howells, 2002). It is believed that the more tacit the knowledge is, the higher the transfer cost will be (Powell and Grodal, 2005). In this view, tacit knowledge is more valuable than codified knowledge in the process of innovation and can be best transmitted and absorbed through face-to-face contacts (Audretsch and Feldman, 2003). Therefore, tacit knowledge tends to be restricted to the local cluster while codified knowledge can freely flow in the world (Malmberg *et al.*, 1996). As Acs and Varga (2002, p. 140) maintain, "new technological knowledge (the most valuable type of knowledge in innovation) is usually in such a tacit form that its accessibility is bounded by geographic proximity and/or by the nature and extent of the interactions among actors of an innovation system". The empirical research on Hsinchu of Taiwan, China, illustrates that spatial proximity of firms strengthens the flow of high-tech talents and that is one of the most effective ways for knowledge spillover and hence promotes innovative activities (Hu *et al.*, 2005).

While the framework of knowledge spillover has been widely deployed to interpret the innovation of a cluster, there are at least five theoretical flaws and problems underlying this framework. In the first place, it fails to explain where new knowledge originates and how firms achieve their core technology. It assumes that there exist two types of firms in a cluster. One type is characterized by the potential ability to create new knowledge that is pursued by another type of firm to facilitate the process of technological innovation. However, this is not always true. It has been found that indigenous firms in developing countries acquire their new knowledge through either their in-house R&D activities or technology license from multi-national corporations. This kind of new knowledge that is generated through either internal innovative activities or purchase has been demonstrated to be rigidly restricted within the boundary of the firm in China (Liu and Buck, 2007; Lu, 2000; Sun, 2002b; Walcott, 2002; Wang and Lin, 2008; Young and Lan, 1997). Therefore, spatial proximity of competitors to some extent could lead to hostility and knowledge closure rather than knowledge spillover or circulation. It could be very misleading to discuss knowledge spillover without a clear clarification of the sources of valuable knowledge or an understanding of how knowledge is generated and circulated.

Second, localized knowledge spillover assumes that individual firms could benefit from spilled knowledge without examining their absorptive capability (Howells, 2002, p. 879). This framework believes that firms are able to absorb and take advantage of the spilled knowledge that must be a perfect complement for them to be innovative. However, even if new knowledge does exist and could be spread in a region, a firm could never benefit from the new knowledge if it lacks the background knowledge to fully understand and absorb the newly advanced knowledge: "The expected economic value of new knowledge to a firm is shaped by what is termed as the core competency of the firm" (Feldman, 1999, p. 19). Also, it is argued that "information exchange is hindered when the parties have differential levels of absorptive capacity, that is the ability to recognize the value of new information, assimilate it and apply it to commercial ends" (Powell and Grodal, 2005, p. 77). Giuliani (2005, p. 269) insists that "the dynamic growth of a cluster depends on its absorptive capacity and therefore on the capacity of firms to absorb external knowledge and diffuse it into the intra-cluster knowledge system". To Giuliani, the absorptive capability of a cluster depends on the level of the firm's knowledge base and absorptive capability. In order to accelerate knowledge share and technological cooperation, as well as taking better advantage of the spillover knowledge, the knowledge base of a firm should be neither the same as, nor totally different from, but similar and complementary to that of other firms in a cluster, which has been badly ignored in the framework of knowledge spillover. Furthermore, firms with limited absorptive capability fail to benefit from the free knowledge resources in a cluster. Howells (2002, p. 879) summarizes that "virtually all of the knowledge spillover studies fail to acknowledge the role of knowledge demand and consumption and the ability (and cost) of firms to absorb such knowledge".

Third, there is no evidence to show that tacit knowledge is more valuable than codified knowledge for innovation. The capability to absorb tacit knowledge varies from firm to firm, so it is hard to say that tacit knowledge is still valuable if the firm failed to grab, absorb and apply it. A number of scholars also raise questions over the model of "tacit = local" versus "codified = global" (Bathelt *et al.*, 2004; Hakanson, 2005). They challenge the perceived notion that tacit knowledge is confined to the local milieu which is impossible or hard to access by agents outside the cluster. Instead, tacit knowledge that is contained in the human body can be footloose in the wide world (Malmberg *et al.*, 1996). In addition, knowledge spillover does not always deliver desirable outcomes. On the assumption that spilled knowledge increases the stock of the knowledge base and generates more knowledge spillover, the framework of localized knowledge spillover is criticized for neglecting the fact that knowledge-produced firms may not be able to exclusively enjoy the rewards achieved from their innovative activities. Instead, they could benefit from external spilled knowledge even without any R&D activities. Therefore, they may turn out to be reluctant to invest in their own innovative activities but rather to reap fruits from others' hard work (Hall, 2002). A possibly negative outcome is that localized knowledge spillover depresses the motivation of local firms for investment in innovation.

Fourth, it is problematic that proximity could propel and facilitate the process of knowledge spillover. The "fetishing of proximity" in terms of knowledge spillovers has been criticized by scholars (Taylor, 2005). Martin and Sunley (2003, p. 17) warn that not only is the binary division of knowledge, such as the tacit and codified, less than clear cut, but it is also too arbitrary to impose a certain form of knowledge upon one form of geographical concentration or any one scale of social relationships. Feldman (1999, p. 21) contends, "There is evidence that there are geographic limits to the extent to which knowledge may spill over. However, this is not to say that location is important to innovation in all circumstances. There is further evidence that the degree to which location matters to innovation depends upon the type of activity, the stage of the industry life cycle and the composition of activity within a location". Glasmeier (2000a) conveys similar information that the benefits of geographical clustering are sensitive to certain industries at a certain stage of development in certain places under certain conditions. The empirical research conducted by Watts *et al.* (2003) demonstrates that spatial proximity does not lead to knowledge transfer between local buyers and suppliers and there is no important advantage from face-to-face contacts for learning and trust relationships among the agents within the Sheffield metal-working cluster. No knowledge spillover has been found in the biotechnology sectors of the UK, where firms are inclined to be close to each other, possibly because larger firms internalized any knowledge spillover (Martin and Sunley, 2003, p. 23).

Finally, the issues of why and how knowledge is spilled remain unknown (Audretsch and Feldman, 2003). There may be two forms of knowledge spillovers. One is the intended knowledge spread and another is unintended or unconscious knowledge spillover. The former can also be explained as technology transfer that tends to happen on the basis of traded-interdependency. The latter is built up on the basis of untraded-interdependency that is much more subtle and complicated and thus much harder to track and identify. Job-hopping and chatting in a restaurant or café may lead to unintended or unconscious knowledge spillover but, again, these forms of knowledge spillover are very tricky and hard to identify and measure. The reasons why and how knowledge spills over may vary from firm to firm, from industry to industry and from region to region. Besides, it is extremely difficult to quantify knowledge spillovers. It remains unknown whether or not and how much a firm can benefit from knowledge spillovers and to what extent this kind of knowledge spillover contributes to the economic growth and innovative performance. Krugman (1991, p. 53, cited from Feldman, 1999) points out there is no way to measure knowledge spillovers because "knowledge flows are invisible, they leave no paper trail by which they may be measured and tracked". Although

Feldman (1999, p. 10) argues that "the relationships between the originating patents and the citing patent are used to identify knowledge spillovers", it is far from enough to measure knowledge spillovers by only calculating the patent-citations because much useful knowledge may never be patented. Also, it is not a short time after a firm applies for the patent that this

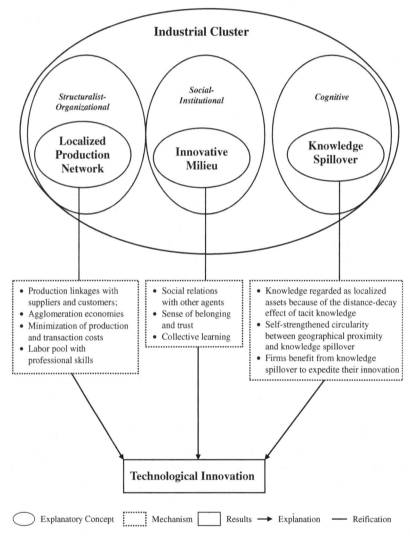

Figure 2.1.   The evolution of theoretical frameworks in explaining the relationship between industrial cluster and technological innovation.

patent is granted. This kind of knowledge could spill over in the meantime, which cannot be measured by patent-citation. Therefore, more theoretical and methodological research should be conducted regarding these problems in order to better understand the process of knowledge creation.

Putting all the flaws and problems aside, it is still questionable whether the framework of knowledge spillover can be applied to cases in developing countries where technological innovation is believed to be dependent on global knowledge and technology transfer from advanced economies, rather than localized knowledge spillover. In recognition of the limitation of localized knowledge spillover, scholars have started to emphasize the significance of the "global pipeline" and international linkages in the process of knowledge acquisition and creation within a cluster in recent years (Bathelt and Gräf, 2008; Bathelt *et al.*, 2004). An appeal to discard the singular scale approach and turn to a multi-scalar examination of economic activities and innovation has also been emerging in the recent literature (Bunnell and Coe, 2001).

2.2.5. *A critique*

While the aforementioned frameworks uphold the positive relationship between cluster and innovation from economic, social and cognitive aspects (Fig. 2.1), a number of scholars have tried to "cool down the cluster fever" by drawing attention to a broader spatial scale. The cluster theory has been criticized for overstating the role of local processes at the expense of the important global linkages in the process of innovation. Maskell *et al.* (2006) reveal that inter-firm linkages outside a cluster are important sources of firms' growth and local innovation. To them, the concept of "temporary cluster", which means temporarily but intensified geographical concentration of international experts, entrepreneurs and engineers to exchange state-of-the-art knowledge and experiences in the form of trade fairs, conferences and exhibitions, etc., greatly highlights the importance of global communication and international knowledge in the process of innovation. Bathelt and Schuldt (2008) also illustrate that the international trade fairs, viewed as "temporary clusters", are important events that facilitate interactive learning and knowledge creation. Research on six opto-electronics clusters in the U.K., U.S. and Germany suggests that national and international relations are more frequent and important than localized ones because of the diverse markets and the complex technologies in this field (Hendry *et al.*, 2000). Saxenian and Hsu (2001) argue that

Table 2.1. The relationship between cluster and innovation described in the existing literature.

Discourse	Local production network	Innovative milieu	Knowledge spillover
Main Argument	Geographical proximity facilitates cooperation and competition on the basis of production relations as well as producing external economies of scale and scope; and repetitious transactions among economic agents can strengthen mutual trust and shape a benign circle of cooperation and competition	Informal social relationships induced by geographical proximity enhance the local innovative capability through synergetic activities and collective learning processes	Spatial clustering speeds up the circulation of knowledge and co-located firms would greatly benefit from knowledge spillover, especially the spillover of tacit knowledge, thus increasing the stock of knowledge and inducing the creation of new knowledge
Causal Explanations	• Production linkages with suppliers and customers • Agglomeration economies • Minimization of production and transaction costs • Labor pool with specific skills	• Social relations with other agents • Sense of belonging and trust • Collective learning	• Knowledge regarded as localized assets because of the distance-decay effect of tacit knowledge • Self-strengthened circularity between geographical proximity and knowledge spillover • Firm benefit from knowledge spilover to expedite their innovation

(*Continued*)

Table 2.1. (*Continued*)

Discourse	Local production network	Innovative milieu	Knowledge spillover
Criticism	• Over-emphasis on the inter-firm economic linkages at the expense of the untraded-interdependencies as well as extra-local connections • Problematic assumption that proximity could facilitate the inter-firm linkages and induce mutual trust	• Failure to identify the economic logic by which the milieu fosters innovation • Lack of explanation of incentives of the synergetic activities and collective learning • Neglect of the barriers to social synergetic and collective learning from different sources of investment • Conceptual vagueness and methodological problem	• Lack of explanation of where original knowledge comes from and neglect of individual firm's absorptive capabilities • Problematic assumption that tacit knowledge is more valuable than codified knowledge and geographical proximity induces and facilitates knowledge spillovers, especially tacit knowledge • Lack of explanation as to how and why knowledge spills over and to what extent it facilitates the process of technological innovation

the boom in the cluster in Hsinchu Science Park of Taiwan, China, is largely dependent on the "brain-drain" from the U.S. and the frequent communications between Hsinchu and Silicon Valley, rather than localized interactions. Also, Grabher (1993a, 1993b) argues that non-local ties play an even more significant role in regional innovation, and turning to global (or external) linkages is more and more valuable in order to avoid "lock-in" or "path-dependency". Tödtling (1994) maintains that metropolitan areas are important "innovation poles" because those areas are the nodes of communication and transportation at both the national and international level. For less developed countries, the non-local linkages and interactions are conceived as being even more important for local innovation because the local agents with limited innovative capability still rely on foreign companies for technology upgrading (Bair and Gereffi, 2001, p. 1887).

A growing number of studies have laid much emphasis on the ability of local firms to access national or international knowledge for innovation. According to Simmie (2003), knowledge is a key resource for innovation and the most innovative firms turn out to be those with great capability to access international sources of knowledge (ref. his study of South East England, U.K.). To Simmie, innovative firms need to transfer and share knowledge from the local to international level, and the metropolitan area as the interactive node of both local and international knowledge is the best location for firms to be innovative. In his later research, Simmie (2004) further challenges Porter's main arguments concerning the perceived relationship between local clusters and technological innovation. He argues that "national and international linkages are as significant for innovation as are more local networks. This provides at least a *prima facie* case suggesting that innovation must be understood in terms of trading nodes in an international system that encompasses both local and international knowledge spillovers and multilayered economic linkages extending over several different spatial scales" (Simmie, 2004, p. 1103). Bathelt (2005a) suggests that creation of new knowledge in a cluster can be completed if cluster firms have linkages with external markets and employ a mix of local and trans-local transactions. A discussion on "knowledge and geography" inspired by the *Journal of Industry and Innovation* also starts to re-evaluate the interplay between local and global forces in the process of knowledge-creation (Lorenzen, 2005).

The perceived relationship between cluster and innovation is further challenged by a number of scholars who contend that the production of innovation lies in articulated multi-scalar interactions and linkages, in recognition that economic activities would never be restricted on either a local or a global scale (Brenner, 2001; Bunnell and Coe, 2001; Sheppard, 2002). Bunnell and Coe (2001) point out that privileging one particular spatial scale is not appropriate any more for understanding the process of technological innovation. More attention should be paid to the relationships between and across different geographical scales because "to understand technological change, it is crucial to identify the economic, social, political and geographical context in which innovation is generated and disseminated. This space may be local, national or global. Or, more likely, it will involve a complex and evolving integration, at different levels, of local, national and global factors" (Archibugi and Michie, 1997, p. 2, cited from Bunnell and Coe, 2001). In a similar vein, Wolfe and Gertler (2004, p. 1079) suggest that "clusters can be seen as nested within, and impacted by, other spatial scales of analysis, including regional and national innovation systems, as well as the kind of global relationships and forces... each of which adds an important dimension to the process of knowledge creation and diffusion that occurs within the cluster. Various elements of each of these spatial levels of analysis may have significance for the innovation process".

Besides the problem of overemphasizing the local process and geographical proximity, these frameworks of the localized production network, innovative milieu and knowledge spillover also simplify the relationship between cluster and innovation that may be more complicated than what has been described (Wang and Lin, 2008). Abundant empirical research indicates that clusters located in different regions present various innovative capabilities and performances. The relationship between cluster and innovation may work somewhere (e.g. Silicon Valley) but not elsewhere (e.g. high-tech parks in China). It is an indeterminate, situational relationship between industrial cluster and technological innovation, which cannot be truly understood without situating the industrial cluster in a specific background and context.

Second, even if there exists a correlation between industrial cluster and technological innovation, their cause–effect relationship in the existing literature is rather vague and confused. The logic in this line of inquiry is that an industrial cluster leads to a higher innovative performance through synergic and mutually beneficial localized activities. However, innovation-related activities *per se* appear to have a strong inclination to cluster in specific places (Audretsch and Feldman, 1996; Feldman, 1994). The question is whether it is a cluster *per se* that attracts more firms to co-locate to become more innovative through the mechanisms of a localized production network, innovative milieu and knowledge spillover, or whether innovation-related activities are accidently produced in specific places first, and only subsequently does geographic innovation attract more related firms or institutions to locate together to finally become an industrial cluster. Moreover, empirical research on clusters has shown a noticeable bias toward those regions that are already innovative, competitive, advanced and successful, which makes it harder to explain what these economies originally looked like before becoming innovative and successful (Lin, 2009b). The regional-level examination appears to be limited to the explanation of the cause–effect relationship between cluster and innovation.

In addition, focusing on a regional-level examination of innovation, the existing literature fails to explain why certain firms are more innovative than others within an industrial cluster. This problem exists despite the recent call in economic geography to reconsider firms instead of the region as central actors in the process of innovation and economic development because "their individual behavior may influence the meso-level conditions that eventually contribute to firms' innovation" (Giuliani, 2007, p. 143). Furthermore, the existing literature ironically investigates innovation through laying emphasis on external linkages, networks and interactions outside the boundary of the firms, but ignores the internal nature and dynamics and the role played by actors and agents beyond the fashionable concepts of networks and relations. Martin and Sunley (2003, p. 17) point out, that "the cluster literature, including Porter's own approach, lacks any serious analysis or theory of the internal organization of business enterprises. Instead, it emphasizes the importance of factors external to firms and somehow residing in the local environment". The prevailing "new economic geography" has tended to privilege some elusive and loosely defined "networks", "linkages" and "relations" at the expense of solid, bounded and grounded actors, agents, nodes and territorial entities that have different natures, positionality, interests and motivations within different institutional and regional contexts. After an obsession with Granovetterian sociology, it may be a good time for geographers to make a sober re-evaluation of how structure, agency and territory have actually reshaped the new economic geography of different world regions beyond the "loose and ubiquitous" network that "explains everything and nothing" (Sunley, 2008, p. 8).

Third, these frameworks place a common emphasis on technology and knowledge but downplay the role played by capital investment in innovative activities. O'Sullivan (2005) has noticed that the relationship between financial resources and innovation has been largely overlooked in the innovative literature. Knowledge and technology are unquestionably important for innovation. However, there are many other factors that would affect the process of innovation, one of which is financing for innovation-related activities. An ignorance of capital mobilization would cripple the cluster theory when it is applied to the regional economies in less developed countries where the capital problem becomes more serious in the process of technological innovation. Even in the developed countries, the financial constraints on firm-level technological innovation and economic growth have been quite obvious, which has been examined and confirmed by a number of studies (Carpenter and Petersen, 2002; Hall, 2002; Himmelberg and Petersen, 1994; Hyytinen and Toivanen, 2005; Santarelli, 1995). Recent research has revealed that innovation-related activities of small high-tech firms in the U.K. were severely hampered by the financial factors (Canepa and Stoneman, 2008). It is highlighted that "capital constraints appear to limit research and development expenditure, especially in smaller firms" (Lerner, 1996, p. 3). Many small high-tech firms have to commit themselves to R&D activities in order to keep their competitive advantage. However, those small firms cannot afford the costly expenditure in technological innovation with a long cycle of investment and return. To make things worse, small firms have difficulties raising funds from external sources. It is a well-known fact that "many small companies — even companies with promising growth opportunities — find it extremely difficult or impossible to raise outside capital on reasonably favorable terms" (Butters and Lintner, 1945, p. 3) and that most small firms finance their growth almost exclusively through retained earnings" (Carpenter and Petersen, 2002, p. 298).

Fourth, these frameworks tend to assume that every firm in a cluster would like to engage in innovation without taking into consideration the motivation of firms for innovation and the institutional environment under which innovation takes place. Technological innovation is "the outcome of the interaction between (a) capabilities and stimuli generated within each firm and within industries and (b) broader causes external to the individual industrials" (Dosi, 1988, p. 1121). Before a firm launches a research project, it must take a long time for the firm to make innovative strategies and finance R&D activities (Lazonick, 2005). Rogers (2003) elaborates that there are five stages that a firm has to experience before an innovation is put into practice. Knowledge acquisition is a necessary but insufficient condition for innovation. After obtaining the initial knowledge, the firm has to experience the stages of persuasion, decision, implementation and confirmation to complete an innovation (Rogers, 2003, p. 168). In addition to financial constraints, there are many other considerations under which firms are reluctant to engage in innovation-related activities.

There is also a tendency for the existing literature to only stress the benefit of innovation but ignore the huge risk that innovators would have to take (Meeus and Oerlemans, 2005). It has been noticed that the return from innovation is expected to be much more than the investment in innovation, including compensation for the considerable risks that the firm would take (Dorfman, 1987, p. 32). It is not always true that innovation-undertaking firms will obtain a considerable return because investing in innovation is fraught with uncertainty and can easily end up in failure (Christensen, 1997). Many R&D investors tend to suffer a loss from an immature market and an unfavorable institutional environment. As a result, the imitators or competitors generally obtain greater economic returns from the innovation than the innovators (Teece, 1986). In an immature market environment, a satisfactory profit could be made without any investment in innovation. In view of the flaws and problems that these theories have suffered from, there is a need for a better theorization of the geography of technological innovation by taking more seriously the motives and behavior of individual firms as well as the institutional settings that shape the firm-level strategies and behavior.

In recent years, the phenomenal growth of China's high-tech industry has attracted much attention from the world. A few Chinese scholars have made a great contribution to our understanding of China's high-tech industry and the relationship between industrial clusters and technological innovation (Wang and Tong 2005; Wang *et al.*, 2001; Zeng, 1997, 2006; Zeng and Wen, 2004; Zhang *et al.*, 2009). However, as Yeung and Lin (2003) have pointed out, studies on economic geographies of Asia are mainly limited to the application and modification of Western theories. Also, it is noted that research on regional development in China is "increasingly influenced by Western theories of economic geography and regional development... they often draw on Western literature, not necessarily testing Western theories but using such theories as research frameworks, especially for work on globalization, institutions, regional inequality and industrial districts" (Wei, 2007, p. 30). Following the Western theory on industrial clusters and networks, many Chinese scholars tend to believe that a positive correlation exists between industrial clusters and technological innovation as well as regional development, without any empirical validation (Gai, 2002; Wang *et al.*, 2001; Wei, 2003; Wei *et al.*, 2006; Zeng *et al.*, 2006; Zeng and Wen, 2004). The notion of clusters and networks is basically used as a criterion to estimate the success of a region and as a panacea for advising policy-makers on regional growth and innovation without a critical examination of the theoretical frameworks. As two of the earliest scholars who showed an interest in China's industrial clusters, Wang and Wang (1998) opened an era of industrial districts/clusters research in China. They explained the new-tech agglomeration in Beijing with the concept adopted from the industrial district school and at the very beginning made the emerging high-tech districts in China known to the world. In spite of their great contribution, they failed to give a theoretical implication based on the case of Beijing. This problem has confronted many Chinese scholars. Numerous Chinese researchers merely advised applying the cluster theory to China's industry after a simple introduction of different Western theories of regional development, or a detailed elaboration of experiences and policies that have been taken by Western countries, without any theoretical and empirical contributions (Liu, 2005; Luo and Shi, 2003; Wang *et al.*, 2006; Wei *et al.*, 2002).

While most of the Chinese literature mainly focused on the application of the framework of industrial clusters to China's reality, the literature in English on China's high-tech industry started to question the perceived relationship between industrial clusters and technological innovation and placed more emphasis on factors such as the role of the state and the MNCs in explaining growth and innovation in China (Wang and Lin, 2008). For example, the earlier study of Shanghai's semiconductor industry revealed a significant role played by both the central and local governments in the growth and innovation of China's high-tech industry (Simon and Rehn, 1988). The technical standard-setting strategies adopted by the central government has been recognized to exert a far-reaching influence on the technological development of China (Naughton and Segal, 2003; Zhou, 2006). Segal (2003) demonstrated how the growth of high-tech enterprises that occurred in different geographical locations such as Beijing, Shanghai, Xi'an and Guangzhou has been stimulated and guided by local governments. In explaining the innovativeness of Zhongguancun in Beijing, Zhou (2008) brought the state into her theoretical framework. Lu (2000) pointed out the fact that several emerging electronic giants, such as Stone, Legend and Founder owed their great success to their relations with the state sector and the accessibility to valuable research results generated by the state.

Meanwhile, the role played by multinational corporations has long preoccupied the research agenda concerning technological development in China that is seen as a "latecomer" in the process of innovation. Despite the popular notion that MNCs have little incentive to transfer their core technology to the developing countries, recent research has shown that successful technological catch-up could be achieved if developing countries adopted sound policies toward investment in human capital, exports and industrial development (He, 2002; Lu, 2000; Miao *et al.* 2007; Naughton, 1997; Sun, 2002b; Wei *et al.*, 2009; Zhou and Tong, 2003). It is contended that the key for developing countries to catch-up is the effective forging of links between capacity building, technology transfer, investment inflows and competitiveness, through which foreign technology is best utilized to develop domestic technological capability (Lall, 1993). Many empirical studies have therefore been conducted to investigate how the interaction between MNCs and local firms has contributed to the advancement of technological innovation (Wei *et al.*, 2009; Zhou and Tong, 2003). In contrast to the framework of industrial clusters, the emphasis is thereby not placed on the region as a base of endogenous and self-sustained knowledge production but rather on the process of external connections and the mechanism of technology transfer, although a few studies contend that technological upgrading can also take place in developing countries through self-dependent R&D rather than technology transfer (Lu, 2000; Sun, 2002b; Zhou, 2008).

Although a plethora of studies existed to explain the growth and innovation of China's high-tech industry, most of them are built on empirical research without developing a systematical theoretical framework acceptable to all. Being aware of the theoretical inadequacy regarding this subject, this book is intended to fill the theoretical gap between Western popular theories and China's complicated reality.

2.3. Summary

The recent decades have witnessed the popularity of "new economic geography" and a "relational turn". One of the hottest topics in this line of theoretical enquiry is the relationship between spatial clustering and technological innovation. As a founder of innovation theory, Schumpeter attributes innovation to intra-firm efforts and entrepreneurial spirit, without giving credit to the geographical proximity and external linkages outside the boundary of firms. However, Porter explicitly claims that spatial clustering, geographical proximity and inter-firm linkages to a large extent contribute to the technological innovation and hence there exists a positive relationship between industrial cluster and technological innovation. After Porter, a large number of studies have been generated to explore the relationship between industrial clusters and technological innovation, from which three influential theoretical frameworks emerged. The framework of localized production networks mainly focuses on economic relations among co-located firms and suggests that geographical proximity can intensify production linkages, build up the trust relationship and stimulate competition. The framework of an innovative milieu pays much more attention to social relations and institutional settings and contends that geographical proximity can lead to informal social networks and collective learning that are believed to be able to reduce the risks resulting from innovation, while the framework of knowledge spillover implies that geographical proximity can facilitate the flow and circulation of knowledge that is indispensable for innovation.

Although these theories shed significant light on the issue of why some regions happen to be more innovative than others, they have received wide criticism. Focusing on the economic links and relationships, the localized production network neglects the untraded-interdependencies and informal interactions between firms. The assumption behind this framework that geographical proximity will lead to desirable cooperation and mutual trust also appears to be very problematic. The framework of an innovative milieu places much emphasis on the social relationships, institutional settings and collective learning in the process of innovation. Nevertheless, it fails to identify the economic logic by which a milieu fosters innovation, overstates the synergetic activities and collective efficiency, and ignores the conflict of interests among firms. In recognition of the importance of knowledge in the technological innovation, the framework of localized knowledge spillover maintains that knowledge spillover could increase the stock of knowledge and encourage the creation of new knowledge. However, this framework never clarifies where new and original knowledge comes from and who will benefit from spilled knowledge. It also is exposed to criticism due to the assumption that geographical proximity could facilitate knowledge spillover.

In addition to the problems identified in each framework, all of these theoretical frameworks overemphasize the localized interaction and links at the expense of the networks and connections to other spatial scales. More recently, these theories have been criticized for neglecting the situation in which the clusters have been placed in explaining the relationship between cluster and innovation. Also, it is impossible to find out the cause–effect relationship between clustering and innovation by only focusing on the regional-level examination without a detailed investigation of the strategies and behavior of individual firms. Ignoring the motives and behavior of individual firms because of a bias toward the benefits from innovation but neglecting its risks, these theories are unable to explain why some firms turn out to be more innovative than others, even though they are in the same cluster. At the same time, these theories pay much attention to knowledge and technology but underestimate other factors that affect innovation, such as financial constraints and the external institutional and market environment. It has been suggested that studies in economic geography should no longer privilege relations, networks, linkages and ties over agents and nodes, whose nature is the key to understanding economic activities and innovation. A brief review of the existing literature on China's high-tech industry further pointed to a theoretical inadequacy because of the obvious gap between Western experiences and Chinese practice. Since the existing theoretical frameworks fail to offer a satisfactory explanation of the geography of technological innovation in China, a new theoretical framework should be established with more emphasis placed on firm-level attributes, motivation, behavior and strategies, in order to profoundly understand how and why firms embark on a path to innovation.

Chapter Three

UNDERSTANDING CHINA'S TECHNOLOGICAL INNOVATION THROUGH STATE-FIRM STRATEGIC COORDINATION

3.1. Introduction

In recognition of the theoretical weakness in the existing literature reviewed in Chapter 2, this chapter attempts to develop an alternative conceptual framework for a better understanding of the uneven innovative performance of the ICT firms across China through examining their different degrees of strategic coordination with the state in consideration of the importance of the state in stimulating and facilitating the process of technological innovation. By viewing the state as an important component rather than an outlier of the economic system, this chapter highlights the significant role of the state as a vision provider for the future by releasing industrial policies to guide economic activities and technological development in general and selecting certain potential firms to promote in particular. The firm is viewed as the basic unit of production and technological innovation that can be distinguished by its heterogeneous combination of different resources. Innovation is so fraught with uncertainty and risk that some firms are reluctant to invest in innovation-related activities in an immature market environment. The low motivation for innovation-related investment may be inspired by the state. This chapter develops a new conceptual framework through identifying the innovation-related strategic selectivity of the state as well as the strategic response and selectivity of the firms to explain the uneven innovative performance of China's ICT industry.

This chapter is organized into four parts. Section 3.2 is devoted to the definitions of major concepts, including state, firm and state-firm strategic coordination, which are central to the new theoretical model. It is then followed by a theorization of state-firm strategic coordination and how it affected the innovative performance of firms, which is the theoretical basis for this book. Section 3.4 discusses how state-firm coordination in China has changed over time and space. The last part summarizes the main points of this chapter and highlights the significant features of the new conceptual framework.

3.2. Defining Major Concepts: State, Firm and State-Firm Strategic Coordination

The first major concept in the new conceptual framework is the state. Although much effort has been exerted on the state theory, no consensus on the definition of the state has been reached in the academic field (Brenner, 2004; Jessop, 1990; Mann, 2003; Painter, 2002). Conventional definitions of the state emphasized the homogeneous, unified, coherent and territorially sovereign characteristics, which "is a story told by the state itself, and thus not to be taken on trust. Instead the state should be understood as a political project in a continual process of formation, deformation, and reformation. States are complex and heterogeneous and are never fully coherent" (Painter, 2002, pp. 360–361). Conceptualizing the state should give adequate attention to the relations between different scales of states as well as between the state and other social and economic entities. In the existing literature, the state has been conceptualized from different angles in order to highlight certain salient points which usually varied from scholar to scholar. In the field of economic geography, the strategic-relational approach to the state theory proposed by Jessop (1990) and the qualitative state paradigm by Block (1994) have generated great insights into understanding the nature and the role of the state in the economy.

Jessop views the state as a social relation which can be analyzed as "the site, generator and the product of strategies" (Macleod and Goodwin, 1999, p. 516). The concept "strategic selectivity" proposed by Jessop is used to "analyze the role of political strategies in forging the state's institutional structures and modes of socio-economic intervention" (Brenner, 2004, p. 87; Jessop, 1990, p. 9). On this point, Jessop echoed what Offe has hypothesized, that "the state is endowed with selectivity — that is, with a tendency to privilege particular social forces, interests, and actors over others" (Brenner, 2004, p. 87; Offe, 1984). According to the strategic-relational approach, first the tendency of the state to select certain economic agents over others is spatially and temporally contingent upon the actions and strategies of participated agents. Second, the state is oriented toward a range of social and economic goals and tries to bring coherence among diverse activities through creating a series of strategies (Macleod and

Goodwin, 1999). Finally, the present structure and behavior of the state is inherited from and affected by the past strategies (Brenner, 2004).

A more important and controversial issue about the state theory is the role of the state in the economy. The debate over the role of the state has been heated since the upsurge of neoliberalism that advocates the virtues of an unregulated market and upholds "deregulation, opening-up and privatisation" (Chang, 2003, p. 1). According to Chang (2003), when it comes to the role of the state, the neoliberal views consider, firstly, that any extension of the role played by the state beyond the "night-watchman" is morally unacceptable. And if there were a clash between economic efficiency and individual freedom, it is the latter that should be guaranteed (Chang, 2003). Second, neoliberal economists argue that state intervention eventually will fail because the spontaneous order of the market determines the economic efficiency and any planning by the state is misguided (Chang, 2003). Finally, the capability of the state to guide its economy is questionable since state intervention very possibly leads to inefficient allocation of resources, rent-seeking waste instead of a correction for market failure (Chang, 2003). Hence, the more constrained the state is, the better it is for the economy (Chang, 2003). However, the neoliberal view of the state's role has been challenged by the fact that neoliberal policies have increased income inequality and economic instability and failed to generate faster growth (Chang, 2003). As Chang (2003, p. 2) has pointed out, the *per capita* income in the world grew at only 2 percent during the neoliberal period of 1980–2000, even lower than that of the "bad old days" of 1960–1980 and the growth of *per capita* income of developing countries had decelerated from 3 percent to 1.5 percent from 1980 to 2000. He also stressed that the 1.5 percent growth rate of those countries would be impossible without the growth of distinctively non-neoliberal China and India.

In addition to the failure in practice, there exist several theoretical drawbacks to the neoliberalism view of the role of the state. First of all, the assumption that the spontaneous order of the market is the only effective tool to economic growth is problematic (Chang, 2003). It is argued that constructed orders are associated with organizations, networks and state intervention, and the latter played as equally important a role as the spontaneous order of the market in establishing property rights and other market institutions (Chang, 2003, p. 50). Second, there is no adequate evidence to show that state intervention would lead to a corrupting influence on the management of the economy as the neoliberal economists have claimed

(Chang, 2003). The neoliberal theories have a deep mistrust of the state but an obsession with trust in individual entrepreneurship (Chang, 2003). While individual entrepreneurship failed to produce collective effects and therefore incurred the wasting of resources, the state could furthest satisfy the public interest and create a benign environment for the individuals (Chang, 2003). Moreover, many studies have demonstrated that "an explicitly political management of the economy may or may not produce a desirable outcome depending on things such as the influence of institutions and ideologies on the determination of the public agenda, the autonomy of the state *vis-a-vis* interest groups in setting and executing such an agenda, and the forms of interest group representation and its impact on the process and outcome of state intervention" (Chang, 2003, p. 50).

The qualitative state paradigm even goes further in criticizing the neoliberalism regarding the role of the state in the economy. The qualitative state paradigm "begins by rejecting the idea of state intervention in the economy. It insists instead that state action always plays a major role in constituting economies, so that it is not useful to posit states as lying outside of economic activities" (Block, 1994, p. 696, cited from O'Neill, 1997, p. 294). Therefore, the new paradigm rejects evaluating the role of the state by measuring its degree of intervention because it regards the state as a composition rather than an outlier of the economy. O'Neill (1997, p. 294, emphasis in original) further elucidates four major characteristics of the qualitative state that are summarized by Block (1994): "[F]irst, (an) *economy* is necessarily a combination of three events: markets, state action and state regulation. A corollary of this constitution is that there is an infinite number of ways in which an economy can be organized. Second, although economic efficiency is dependent on markets, markets are state-constrained and state-regulated and thereby incapable of operating in a *laissez-faire* environment. Third, neither capital nor the state is capable of achieving its goals simultaneously or independently. Finally, it should be recognized that any coherence that exists about the idea of *economy* derives essentially from our cultural beliefs, which (in Anglo cultures at least) have led to constructions of an economy being overlain with the dichotomy of *planned versus market*, which, in turn, has had the effect of denying the existence of multiple forms of economy". Painter (2002, p. 363) contends that these characteristics of the qualitative state have great implications for the economic geography: "[T]he nature of the combination between markets, state action and state regulation varies geographically (most notably from state to state). Markets also operate in spatially uneven ways and this geography influences and is influenced by state regulation. Cultural beliefs about the economy and thus about state-economy relations vary significantly from place to place".

Based on strategic-relational understandings and the qualitative state approach, this book takes the state as a political entity with capability and power to provide vision for the future that encompasses different scales of government and is embedded in the regional economy. Being a generator of policies and developing diverse interconnectedness and interdependency with other socio-economic agents, the state is an important component of the economy and is "constituted by continuous administrative, legal, bureaucratic and coercive systems that not only build relationships between the state and other groups in society, but also heavily influence relationships within and between these groups" (O'Neill, 1997, p. 296).

This book adopts an institutional view of the role of the state. It is believed that "the market is only one of the many economic institutions and not necessarily the primary one" and there is no need to identify the state-market dichotomy because there are no clear boundaries between different institutions (Chang, 2003, p. 51). The role of the state is as the "designer, defender and reformer of many formal and informal institutions, while taking seriously the political constraints on the effective exercise of such a role" (Chang, 2003, pp. 51–52). In realizing this role, the state should be able to provide the vision for the future and build new institutions. For example, the central state can "drive private agents into a concerted action without making them spend resources on information gathering and processing, bargaining and so on" (Chang, 2003, p. 53). Furthermore, the state also should be able to encourage private sectors through "socializing risk" to invest in high-risk activities which normally private sectors are reluctant to do (Chang, 2003). Therefore, state capacity refers to the ability to provide the vision for the future, to make policies, rules and regulations to guide industrial development as well as to upgrade and transform the industrial economy in cooperation with selected economic groups.

The state in this study is broken down to two scales, the national state and local state. It has been described that the state is undergoing fundamental restructuring and there is a tendency to "hollowing out" of the national state with the state capacity being reorganized on a super-national, national, regional, local and trans-local level (Jessop, 1994, p. 251, 2000). Swyngedouw (1997b, 2000, p. 52) conveys a similar message through coining the concept of "glocalization" to indicate a "contested restructuring of the institutional level from the national scale both upwards to supra-national and/or global scales and downwards to the scale of the individual body, the local, the urban, or regional configurations". However, the "hollow-out" metaphor and "glocalization" process indicate the shift rather than the diminution of the role played by national states with complex power relationships continuously structured and restructured across different geographical scales (Bathelt, 2003; O'Neill, 1997, p. 293). The national state power "permeates almost all aspects of social and economic life (and by extension social and economic geography). That is not to say that social and economic life are state-controlled, but they are affected by the state in remarkably deep-seated and enduring ways" (Painter, 2002, p. 362). As Weiss (1998, p. 7) argued, "By providing the infrastructure, socializing the risks and encouraging cooperation, the state is in a position to orchestrate more nationally effective responses to technological competition".

Meanwhile, it has been argued that the local state plays a no less critical role than the national state in regional development and innovation (Segal, 2003). Countries in the transitional economy are experiencing rapid economic and social restructuring and this process presents geographical unevenness within the national boundaries. One of the salient character-istics of China's transition is decentralization of decision-making which has given local governments more incentives and freedom to stimulate local development (Lin, 2002). The spatially uneven economic development reflects the different capability of local states to regulate economic activities and guide regional development. Along with the rise of regional economies, local scale has been the focus of the scholars and policy-makers. Regional development at some level is the result of competition and interaction between the national and local governments. Nevertheless, the local and national governments are not engaged in a zero-sum game but the local government operates in the institutional environment created by both the national and local governments (Segal, 2003, p. 8).

The second major concept in need of clarification is the firm. It is fundamental to highlight the conception and characteristics of the firm in order to thoroughly understand the dynamics of innovation in an economy. Unfortunately, the conceptualization of the firm has remained vague and under-theorized in the field of economic geography (Maskell, 2001a). Classical and neoclassic economics consider firms as a set of input and output units with clear-cut boundaries and full of rationality, which cease-lessly adapt themselves to the ever-changing market demand and external environment (Yeung, 2005a). The basic assumption of this approach is that the firm is a rational economic unit which follows the rules of the market and targets profit maximization. Following the neoclassical view of the firm, neoclassical economic geography takes the firm "as a self-contained and homogenous 'black box' capable of producing economic outcomes in space" (Yeung, 2005a, p. 308). However, the neoclassic view of the firm cannot explain why some firms input more resources in production and innovation than others when facing the same market demands and under the same institutional environment on the one hand, and fails to identify the distinctiveness of individual firms on the other hand. Instead of defining firms in terms of outputs that they produce in the conventional economic analysis, a resource-based view of the firm regards the firm as "a collection of productive resources" and hence distinguishes individual firms from others according to the heterogeneous combination of resources they hold (Bathelt and Glückler, 2005; Penrose, 1959; Seth and Thomas, 1994, p. 176). In this definition, it is understandable why some firms are more able, and would be more likely, to invest more resources in production and innovation than others because their heterogeneous resource base to a larger extent determines their input capability and affects their investment strategies.

Both neoclassic economics and resource-based views highlight the intra-firm economic characteristics at the expense of the influences of the external institutional environment on firms' motivations and strategies. This "under-socialized" explanation of a firm has been criticized and supplemented by a socioeconomic perspective in recent years (Michael Taylor and Asheim, 2001). An institutionalist perspective conceives that "the economy emerges as a composition of collective influence which shapes individual action and as a diversified and path-dependent entity moulded by inherited cultural and socio-institutional influences" (Amin, 1999, pp. 367–368). Therefore, it has been widely accepted that firms cannot be understood any more by divorcing them from their situated social, political and institutional background which significantly shapes them and is concomitantly shaped by them (Bathelt and Kappes, 2009). A number of scholars have started to explore the relationship between firms and the territories where they are located. They particularly focused on the "firm-territory nexus" in order to profoundly comprehend the nature and behavior of the firm, because territory not only is a container of diverse economic and social processes but also can shape the strategies and behavior of the firm through the geographical effects on social actors (Bathelt, 2006; Dicken and Malmberg, 2001, p. 346; Yeung, 2005a, p. 319).

The book tries to focus on the conceptualization of the firm through combining the resource-based view and institutionalist perspective, building upon the existing literature. On this note, the book rejects the understanding of the firm as an atomized unit that is separated from its situated place, since the strategic choices of firms are strongly affected by the external market and institutional environment under which they operate. The firm in this study is defined as a collection of productive resources that determines its strategies and operation, and is regulated and molded by its situated social, institutional and political environment. In this definition, the firm is firstly viewed as a collection of productive resources. Resource is understood as "anything which would be thought of as a strength or weakness of a given firm", which includes capital, employment of skilled personnel, machinery, knowledge and technology, brand-name, channels to external information, etc. (Wernerfelt, 1997, p. 119). Individual firms are not homogeneous productive units but are distinguished by their heterogeneous combination of resources. Firms target certain segments of the market and invest in production according to their existing resources and continuously adjust their production function and corporate strategies according to their external environment, such as market demand, local and national regulations and policies, etc.

Second, the resource that the firms hold determines what and how they are going to produce. The market needs can be conceptually demarcated into high-, middle- and low-end demands, based on the technological complexity of the products involved. The diversity of market requirements has given firms many choices regarding the market segments in which they wish to compete. An important issue with which the firms have to deal is to seek a strategic resonance between their strategic decision and market needs in which the resources the firms hold play a significant role (Brown and Fai, 2006). Some firms insist on investing in innovation-related activities, considering the potentially enormous rewards as well as their capability and resources to cover all kinds of possible trouble, whereas others would prefer to adopt less risky strategies to avoid risks and unfavorable outcomes because of their poor and limited resources (Meeus and Oerlemans, 2000). Wight (1997, p. 31) estimates that "[t]wo firms facing the same environment will often follow different strategies and innovation paths. Certain conditions constrain a firm in its decision to experiment, to acquire a new process or product, or to change organizational practices in general". Firms with advantageous and valuable resources tend to be more likely to invest in the high-risk and meanwhile high-reward activities to further explore more potential resources and keep competitive. At the same time, the resource that the firm holds normally leads to different routines adopted by the firm: "Some firms may be inclined towards innovation, while others may prefer the less demanding (but also less rewarding) imitative route. If a routine leads to an unsatisfactory outcome, a firm may use its resources to search for a new one, which — if it satisfies the criteria set by the firm — will eventually be adopted" (Fagerberg, 2005, p. 17).

Finally, the firm is not an isolated entity in its situated environment but is regulated and molded by its social, political and institutional framework. It has been claimed that all economic activities are necessarily placed or situated in particular geographic space, which is fundamental to maintaining these activities themselves (Swyngedouw, 1997a). A firm is located in a particular geographical space which is made up of given institutions, routines, norms and so on. The territory-bounded and thus the local state-led factors regulated and influenced strategies and behavior of the firms. Fagerberg highlights that "A central finding in the innovation literature is that a firm does not innovate in isolation, but depends on extensive interaction with its environment" (2005, p. 20). Sternberg and Arndt (2001) identify three groups of factors that impact firms' innovative behavior, namely location-specific factors, extra-region general environment and innovation and technology policies. They argue that "the regional environment can help firms to realize their existing, but sometimes unexploited, innovation potential. In particular, the R&D environment that the region (and the other firms based there) offers an innovating firm is certainly capable of influencing a firm's innovation behavior, even independently of firm-related features" (Sternberg and Arndt, 2001, p. 379). In situations where the market is immature, the motives of firms to innovate would be depressed. Gerstenfeld and Brainard stress that "indeed if non-innovation investments for a firm offer a higher rate of return than innovation (when all factors are considered), then firms may indeed choose to invest less in innovation activities. It is perhaps through industry-government cooperation that this situation can be ameliorated" (Gerstenfeld and Brainard, 1979, p. 1).

The innovative capability of a firm refers to the ability of the firm to create new knowledge to improve productivity or produce new products. The innovative performance is affected by both internal and external factors. The former includes the innovative-related strategy made by the firm, resources that the firm holds for innovative inputs and the ability of the firm to fully utilize these resources, while the latter includes the industrial policies, market environment and institutional framework built by the state. The strategies of the firm refer to a set of objectives, policies and plans that define the scope of the firm and its approach to survival and success (Rumelt, 1998). According to Rumelt *et al.*, strategies generally include "the selection of goals; the choice of products and services to offer; the design and configuration of policies determining how the firm positions itself to compete in product markets (e.g. competitive strategy); the choice of an appropriate level of scope and diversity; and policies used to define and coordinate the work... It is the integration (or reinforcing pattern) among these choices that makes a set of strategies" (Rumelt *et al.*, 1994, p. 9).

The last concept in the new conceptual framework is state-firm strategic coordination. When it comes to technological innovation, firms no doubt play a significant role as a basic production unit with a rather high sensitivity to market needs. However, firms might turn out to be very reluctant to invest in innovation-involved activities since their terminal goal is the maximization of profits rather than technological innovation that is only a tool to realize the goals and requires long-term commitment but may bring back nothing. As aforementioned, the innovation-related strategies made by the firms are affected not only by their internal resources and capability but also by their external institutional and market environment that can be shaped and reshaped by the state. For the state, the pressing need to improve the national innovative capability and catch up with advanced countries forces it to release innovation-related regulations and policies in general and select potential firms in particular to encourage and stimulate innovative activities in the whole society. Essentially, there exists an evident difference in terms of innovation-related considerations between the state and the firm. Nevertheless, through constructing an innovation-supportive environment in which the innovators could achieve the considerate profits that they deserve while non-innovators could no longer reap where they have not sown, there will emerge a strategic coordination between the state and the firm in the process of technological innovation.

The concept of state-firm strategic coordination refers to a dynamic process in which firms' innovation-related strategies are coordinated with the "strategic selectivity" of the central or/and local governments. As the important actors in economic development and technological innovation, certain firms are selected by the local or central state to develop their technological capability. At the same time, selected firms are not totally passive in their interaction with the state because they have their own interests and strategic considerations. State-firm strategic coordination is therefore a mutually selective process rather than a process unilaterally induced by the state. The emphasis will be placed on how the governments shape the regional environment which is crucial to stimulating the innovation-related motivation of firms and boosting their innovative performance and how firms with different resources and capability respond to the regional milieu and coordinate with the strategic selection of the state. It is noted that state-firm strategic coordination is particularly important in the transition from a state-dominated to a market-oriented economy. With the maturity of the market and institutional environment, the importance of state-firm strategic coordination may decline.

State-firm strategic coordination differs from strategic alliance, strategic fit and strategic partnership. Strategic alliance refers to a formal relationship between two parties who pursue a set of agreed goals in order to secure common interests. First, state-firm strategic coordination is not based on common interests and agreements. Instead, state and firm essentially pursue different goals as the former dedicates itself to regional innovation and economic development and the latter simply chases profit maximization. In this view, strategic coordination is also very different from strategic fit that is "likened to a jigsaw where all parts fit together" (Brown and Fai, 2006, p. 61). Second, strategic coordination does not point to a formal relationship between the state and the firm but an informal coordination that is dynamically contingent upon the changing of the interests and strategies of the two parties. Due to the different goals and interests of these two parties, parts of their strategies may reach a state of coordination in certain contexts and at certain stages. However, this kind of coordination may be broken when the strategies of any party have been altered, since this coordination is not restrained by any form of contract or documents. Therefore, strategic coordination differs from strategic partnership that is usually formalized by one or more business contracts to bind the different parties together. Unlike a strategic alliance, strategic partnership and strategic fit which work in a static form, strategic coordination is based on a dynamic two-way choice. To realize its innovation strategies, the state tends to select certain economic agents over others on the one hand and tries to forge a favorable institutional structure and market environment on the other hand, which are frequently adjusted according to the effects and results of these strategies (Jessop, 1990; Brenner, 2004). Firms establish their business models and strategies according to their own interests, capabilities and resources to survive in market competition and eventually make profits. They have to constantly adjust their strategies to adapt to the changes in institutional structure and market environment. With the state's selectivity and firms' reactivity, the state and certain firms manage to achieve a strategic coordination from which the potential innovation of firms could be triggered, their internal resource base be enlarged and their capability be promoted. It is very important to note that state-firm strategic coordination does not put the major emphasis on the relationship between the state and the firm. Instead, it highlights the importance of motivations, interests and strategies of the active agents and actors that are the key to understanding the formation of any kind of economic and social relationship among actors, the evolution of these relations and innovation-related behavior and performance of the firms.

3.3. Theorizing the Innovative Performance of Regions and Firms: A State-Firm Strategic Coordination Framework

By looking at the firm as a heterogeneous entity distinguished by the resources it holds and the state as an institutional builder and vision-provider for the industry and economy with a strong strategic selectivity, a new conceptual framework has been constructed with a focus on innovation-involved strategies (Fig. 3.1). In this framework, two theoretical propositions can be made to understand the differentiated innovative performance among China's ICT firms. The first proposition deals with the relationship between innovation-related activities and performance of firms and the degree of state-firm strategic coordination.

Proposition 1. *Difference in the firm-level innovative performance can be attributed to various degrees of state-firm strategic coordination.*

1. *The dynamics of state-firm strategic coordination reflect the active motivation of firms to invest in innovation*

The dynamics of state-firm strategic coordination can be scrutinized through a close look at the strategic selectivity of both the state and the firms respectively. The degree of state-firm strategic coordination reflects the determination, power and capability of the state to construct an innovation-supportive environment and to stimulate and encourage individual firms to invest in innovation-related activities as well as firms' motivation, interest and will to conduct such activities.

(1) Strategic selectivity of the state: In recent years, the important role played by the central and local governments in shaping the institutional environment and technological development, and particularly in affecting

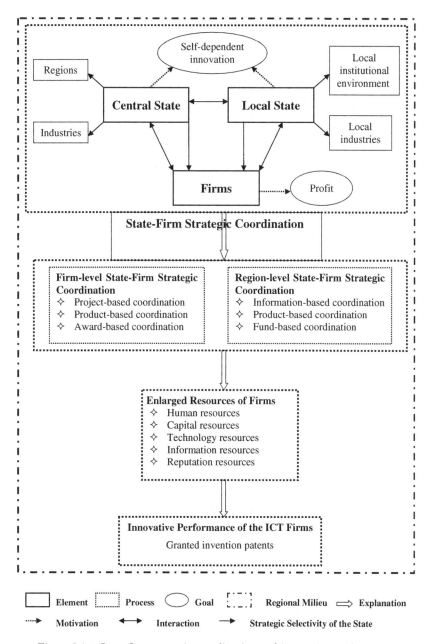

Figure 3.1.   State-firm strategic coordination and innovative performance.

the strategies and behavior of firms in developing countries, has been studied by a large number of scholars (Block, 1994; Evans, 1995; Lin, 2009b; Naughton and Segal, 2003; O'Neill, 1997; Schneider and Maxfield, 1997; Segal, 2003; Sun, 2002a). Lu (2000, p. 183) maintains that the state could stimulate firms to invest in innovation and shape their resource structure by taxation, local schemes and other administrative tools. The "governed interdependence" approach proposed by Weiss (1998, p. 39) rejects the notion of a state's imposition on firms but stresses the ability of the state to "use its autonomy to consult and to elicit consensus and cooperation from the private sector" and highlights the coordination, cooperation and interdependence between government and firms. For instance, firms may rely on the state to enlarge their resources, obtain valuable information and establish relations with other agents for improving their capability to occupy the market, whereas the state depends on firms to maintain economic development and increase wealth.

Although there is a growing body of literature on the role played by the state in the process of innovation, much attention has been paid to state policies without looking more closely at the strategic selectivity of the state. There are three fundamental levels of the strategic selectivity of the state (especially the central government) to encourage and stimulate the innovation-related activities of firms. At the macro-level, the state tends to select certain regions and industries to give special support through releasing a series of regulations and policies, etc. At the meso-level, the state could act like a supervisor to organize and coordinate economic actors to complete significant research projects such as technical standard-settings that are related to national interests and security. Also at the micro-level, the state selects certain firms to provide necessary support and assistance in expectation of several of them becoming internationally competitive. Concretely, each region has occupied a strategic position in the national economy assigned and coordinated by the central government, resulting in certain firms in some regions receiving more support from the central government or enjoying more preferential policies than other firms elsewhere. Similarly, the central government appears to favor certain industries over others because different industries make a differential contribution to the whole economy. Due to resource restraints, the central government cannot evenly distribute its resources across the whole country or the whole economy. The central government tends to be forced to select certain regions and industries to give special support in expectation of them being able to drive the growth of other regions and industries. At the regional level, strategic selectivity of the central government is mainly based on the prospect of catching up with the advanced economies in the world through exploiting certain regions' advantages to the most. It is an interactional process of strategic selection by the central government and the characteristics of the regions. Normally, the strategic position of a region presents a feature of "path dependency". The characteristics of a region, such as history, location, institutions, growth trajectory, etc., affects the strategic selectivity of the central government, and, in reverse, the strategic selectivity of the central government will, to a larger extent, strengthen and shape the regions' characteristics. At the industry level, the state tends to select industries with high-tech and security-involved characteristics to improve its innovative capability and get rid of the technology control of multinational corporations (MNCs).

A significant effort made by the central government in addition to the release of innovation-related policies to stimulate the indigenous innovative activities and industrial growth would be the launch of research projects concerning technical standard-setting in certain ICT fields. The state is able to mobilize the nationwide S&T resources, such as the most promising firms and well-developed research and development institutes, to concentrate on specific research projects for significant technological innovation. By involving these significant research projects, firms can have more chances to communicate with, and learn from, other excellent participants in this field. There is evidence that Chinese manufacturing firms which participated in state-launched projects and obtained support from the government perform better than others (Guan *et al.*, 2009). The state can also coordinate different interest groups at the national level to cooperate on large-scale research projects and technological breakthrough. It is claimed that "State coordination, in principle, is vital to induce firms to engage in activities where the risk level would be so great as to deter firms acting alone. Such cases arise whenever investments are not only large scale but interdependent and, therefore, need to be made concurrently ... the state can resolve many important problems of coordination better than the market by virtue of reducing 'transaction costs' in the wider economy" (Weiss, 1998, p. 6). In particular, the state always aims at nurturing some domestic firms that are able to achieve international competitive advantages in certain high-tech fields. In this case, the state will not only provide capital support through various ways such as government procurement and research-funding distribution, but also help them enlarge their existing resource base and establish extensive channels to obtain important information.

With regard to local governments, some of them invest more than others to support the innovation of their firms or select certain firms in some industries over those of other industries for innovation-related promotion. This is the strategic selectivity of local governments. The power of the decision-making has been decentralized to local governments in recent years, making them play a significant role in local economic development. Segal and Thun (2001, p. 558) point out that "although national institutional characteristics provide the overall framework for growth and regulate the overall process, variation in developmental outcome is the result of the specific characteristics and abilities of local institutions . . . local governments do not simply try to reproduce and catch up with development efforts initiated by the central government, but are often the actual architects of growth, designing and implementing development policies that are conducive to local institutional frameworks and specific development needs." Also, Nee (1992) elaborates how market pressure could urge local governments and private firms to form a cooperation relationship to protect themselves against an uncertain environment (Segal and Thun, 2001). To Nee, local governments may "provide the backing and resources needed by entrepreneurs to compete effectively in an economy characterized by partial reform, in which the still-dominant redistributive institutions interact with market forces in a manner that subordinates market institutions" (Nee, 1992, p. 4).

(2) Strategic selectivity of the firm: As the huge body of literature has validated, technological innovation is the major source of competitive advantage and economic rewards, leading to the assumption in the existing literature that firms are very likely to invest in innovation without taking into account the risk of innovation investment and the barriers to the success of innovation-related activities (Meeus and Oerlemans, 2005). Activities of technology innovation are full of uncertainty. On the one hand, technological innovation requires a long-term and continuous investment without immediate reward. These activities are highly risky because they could end up with nothing. On the other hand, even though innovative inputs could be successfully transformed into new products, it is still unknown whether these kinds of new products will be accepted by the market and whether the innovators can fully and exclusively enjoy the rewards from innovation-related investment in the end because imitators sometimes could make more profits than innovators. Therefore, innovation requires a risk-taking spirit, accurate and useful information about market demand, a benign market environment, supportive state policies as well as abundant resources for innovative inputs such as adequate capital and a highly qualified workforce. As a matter of fact, in an immature market environment, a satisfactory profit could be made without any investment in innovation-related activities. Firms usually confront the dilemma of innovation. The fierce competition compels them to invest in innovation to achieve a long-term competitiveness while at the same time they are intimidated by the huge risk that results from innovation-related activities because they cannot afford the huge economic loss which could easily happen in an immature environment.

In view of this dilemma facing firms, it is pivotal to investigate the innovation-related strategies and considerations to understand the innovative performance of firms. The innovation-related strategic decisions made by firms are affected by their internal resources and external institutional environment. Resources required by the innovation-related investment mainly include human resources, technology resources, capital resources and information resources. Firms do not invest in the research and development of a new product, even though it might be likely to yield considerable economic rewards if they do not hold enough resources to realize the innovative projects. Likewise, even though the firms hold abundant resources for innovation-related activities, they do not apply innovation-related strategies if they operate in an innovation-averse market and institutional environment. In a word, innovation is only a tool rather than a terminal goal for firms and therefore the innovation-related strategies are sensitive to the internal resources of firms as well as to the external institutional and market environment and the strategic selectivity of governments.

2. State-firm strategic coordination enlarges the resource base of firms and thereby improves their innovative performance

At the level of individual firms, the better the coordination between individual firms and governments, the more innovative the firms will be. Here, three types of state-firm strategic coordination that are specific to China's undergoing market transition can be identified, namely project-based, product-based and award-based coordination (see Table 3.1). Project-based coordination refers to a relationship in which the state initiates a research project and the firm is chosen as one of the participants, or the firm drafts a product/project proposal and obtains direct financial support from the state. Project-based state-firm coordination can be measured by the number of the government-funded (both national and local) research projects in which the firm participated. Since the research project involves several participants, the cooperation between them will increase their knowledge

Table 3.1.   Mechanisms of strategic coordination in innovation of firms.

Type of strategic coordination	Resources enlarged by the coordination
Firm-level coordination	
Project-based	Capital resource and technology resource
Product-based	Capital resource and reputation
Award-based	Capital resource and reputation
Region-level coordination	
Information-based	Information resources
Product-based	Capital resource and reputation
Fund-based	Capital resources

stock. It has been demonstrated that firms with close relations to the state have benefited from accessibility to the R&D resources of national labs, which significantly enriches the knowledge base of the firms and directly leads to their success after commercializing these mature R&D projects (Lu, 2000). Project-based coordination also enlarges the capital resource base of firms with access to government-initiated research funds. Product-based coordination refers to a relationship through which the state purchases products and services from the firm. It can be measured by the variety (i.e. the number of types) of products that the firm has provided to the central or local governments. This kind of coordination not only enhances the financial capability and capital stock of firms but also reduces the risk of conducting innovation-related activities. Award-based coordination refers to the fact that a firm receives awards from the government to stimulate and encourage innovative activities of firms. It can be measured by the number of awards that the firm has received from government. Once the firm receives an award from the state, it will be exempted from a certain percentage of taxation and enjoy other favorable policies while, at the same time, it has to meet certain state requirements. Award-based coordination not only enlarges the capital stock of firms but also helps firms build up or promote their reputation that will increase the trust of their customers, which is a key resource for innovation and success.

At the regional level, state-firm strategic coordination is evaluated on product-based, fund-based and information-based state-firm strategic coordination.[1] Product-based strategic coordination at the regional level

---

[1]The reason why the measurements of the region-level state-firm strategic coordination are different from those of the firm-level state-firm strategic coordination will be explained in detail in Chapter 4.

is measured by the share of government procurement to the total sales revenue. Again, this kind of strategic coordination enlarges firms' resource base in both technology and capital. Fund-based coordination is measured by the absolute amount of innovation funds initiated by local governments and the ratio of innovation funds to total financial expenditure of local governments. Fund-based coordination that reflects the capability, determination and power of local governments to push innovation-related activities of local firms enlarges the capital resource and promotes the reputation of the firms. Information-based strategic coordination refers to the exchange of innovation-related information between local governments and firms. It is argued that closer interaction based on information exchange between state and firms could allow officials to ensure that the right information will get to the right managers and provide the security to firms that their innovation-related investments will receive particular governmental support (Schneider and Maxfield, 1997, p. 8). Furthermore, in the process of innovation, firms have to obtain all possible information to make the right decisions to meet the market demands that sometimes are dependent on state strategies in transitional economies and take advantages of state policies. Meanwhile, the central and local governments need to adjust their strategies and selectivity according to the feedback from firms to better support the innovation-related activities in a region.

The measurement of firm-level state-firm strategic coordination is different from that of region-level state-firm strategic coordination for three reasons. First of all, the region-level strategic coordination is not simply a sum of the firm-level state-firm strategic coordination because of the different objectives on which they focus. The firm-level state-firm strategic coordination pays much attention to the internal strategies and motivation of individual firms, while the region-level state-firm strategic coordination lays much emphasis on the strategies and capability of local governments as well as the coordination between local governments and the specific sectors rather than individual firms. Second, it has to be admitted that the measures of firm-level state-firm strategic coordination are not good enough because they are based on the unit number (i.e. the number of projects, types of products and awards) that may lead to an inaccurate comparison. For example, the government may purchase five types of products from one firm with a 1 million *yuan* payment and purchase only one type of product from another one for 1.2 million *yuan*. For the enlargement of the capital resource, the latter obviously benefited more than the former from government procurement. However, the former has a much better coordination with the government than the latter according to my measurement. While this problem cannot be solved because of the extreme difficulty in obtaining ideal firm-level data, the region-level examination can be based on more scientific measurements. Finally, this study selects a small-scale high-tech sub-sector to closely scrutinize each firm's strategies and motivation to understand the firm-level state-firm strategic coordination for data availability. However, the region-level analyses should be established on the basis of a larger-scale sector if the data allow me to do so in order to strengthen the representativeness of this study.

Proposition 2. *State-firm strategic coordination is embedded in the regional institutional and market environment and thus varied from region to region, leading to a regional difference in innovation. Furthermore, under the same regional institutional environment, the degree of strategic coordination varies between firms and thus leads to a divergent innovative performance within a region.*

This proposition concerns two facets of state-firm strategic coordination that separately stress the influence of the external institutional environment and internal resources in the process of state-firm strategic coordination. The characteristics of a region, including its industrial traditions and culture, S&T environment and financial system as well as the capability, power and determination of local governments, affects the innovation-related strategies and behavior of firms and leads to a regional difference in the degree of state-firm strategic coordination.

First of all, the foundation and advantages of certain sectors in a locality could shape state-firm strategic coordination through affecting the strategic selectivity of both local governments and firms. Local governments are inclined to give a high priority to those sectors that have historically performed well to improve the city's or region's image and reputation. Furthermore, past development has influenced the training of technical staff and accumulated related technologies and valuable experiences in this field, which again could attract more firms to be innovatively active. When firms select such a region for their location, they expect to enjoy the well-established "hard" and "soft" environment so as to have a good business start. They expect to have a better chance of enlarging their technological resources than others elsewhere.

Second, it is generally agreed that the traditions and culture of a locality largely affect economic activities although traditions and culture are very hard to quantify. It is pointed out that "institutions shape and are shaped by the local culture, the shared understandings and practices that unify a community and define everything from labor market behavior to attitudes toward risk-taking" (Saxenian, 1994, p. 7). Likewise, Segal (2003, p. 44) observes that "institutions and local actors operate within and are shaped by distinct local cultures". Local governments tend to seek shared understandings and routine practices to define and act on problems in the process of development and innovation, particularly when they are not sure how to develop new sectors and are not sure how rapidly changing technologies will develop in the future (Segal, 2003). The traditions and culture of a locality also influence the way firms think and act. For instance, a locality that advocates a business culture of "short-term, cheap and quick" will not produce many innovative firms. Firms might select to conduct much less risky business activities when they locate in a region where people generally believe that innovation-related investment probably ends up with nothing while investment in low-end technologies and production and the establishment of expeditious distribution channels may allow them to make considerable profits.

The regional S&T environment includes innovation-related policies released by local governments and the S&T resources that a region holds such as the existence of universities/R&D institutes and S&T personnel. The S&T environment can be shaped and promoted by local governments through a series of investments in education and science and technology. Various capabilities and determination of local governments to do so aggravate regional differences. Firms select a region to start their business based on numerous considerations. Choosing a locality with a better S&T environment reflects the innovation-oriented strategies of firms, though mechanisms that help utilize local resources and help the firm benefit from the milieu vary from firm to firm. In recognition of the importance of capital in the process of technological innovation, firms located in a region with a better financial system will be provided with more opportunities to get a loan to support their innovative activities. Generally, firms in such localities will presumably generate a higher degree of state-firm strategic coordination than that of others elsewhere.

Regional characteristics shape the behavior of local governments and meanwhile are reshaped by local governments. The difference in economic wisdom and power of local governments results in distinct degrees of state-firm strategic coordination across the nation. Although national policies set a general tone for industrial development and innovation, it is the way local governments respond to and implement those policies that makes a huge difference in the development of regional economies. The economic wisdom of local governments on how to deal with challenges and problems in their development, how to select industries for promotion, how to enhance the local image and attract more high-tech firms, how to encourage firms to engage in innovative activities, how to provide vision and how to forge an institutional and market environment have led to diverse trajectories of regional development and various degrees of state-firm strategic coordination across geographical space. For example, local government acts very differently in retaining highly qualified talent in Shanghai compared to Shenzhen, with the former implementing a much more relaxed *"hukou"* system than the latter. The determination and power of local governments to carry out strategies and plans also varies. Some local governments may have a strong determination and more power to guide and push their firms while others simply adopt a *laissez-faire* attitude to their economy and industry. In summary, distinct characteristics of regions shape different degrees of state-firm strategic coordination that is further reinforced by differences in the wisdom of local governments and their determination and power. At the regional level, the more the local government is committed to building a better institutional environment, the higher the degree of state-firm strategic coordination that will be reached and the more innovative the regions will be.

Even under the same regional institutional and market environment, firms will make very different strategic choices according to their internal resources and the evaluation of their capabilities. When firms operate in an innovation-supportive environment, some of them might not select to apply innovation-related activities as long as they can survive through imitation or in other ways, particularly if their resources do not allow them to make a long-term commitment to innovation. In like manner, some firms will still insist on investing in innovation-related activities even though they operate in an innovation-averse institutional environment, if they hold enough resources for innovation-related investment and have positive expectations for the market response to their new products. No matter the strategic selectivity of the state, the firms can stick to their own strategic choices based on a comprehensive analysis of their internal resources and external environment, leading to various degrees of state-firm strategic coordination within a locality.

3.4. Explaining the Innovative Performance of China's ICT Industry through State-Firm Strategic Coordination

The theoretical framework proposed above has illustrated how state-firm strategic coordination can take place, how it varies from region to region and from firm to firm and how it affects the innovation of firms. This section proceeds to explain how such a framework can contribute to our understanding of the different innovative performances of China's ICT firms over time and space.

3.4.1. *State-firm strategic coordination before the reform and opening-up in China*

(1) Strategic Selectivity of the State and the National Innovation System

Since the foundation of the People's Republic of China in 1949, the development of science and technology had been given a high priority. The central state was devoted to restoring the Chinese Academy of Sciences (CAS) and establishing a set of new R&D institutes. It expected to improve the national innovative capability through an S&T structure in which the CAS housed the basic research institutes and the industrial ministries were in charge of applied research institutes, while universities focused on training rather than research (Simon and Rehn, 1988). Lu (1997) further identified three levels of research institutions in China in that period. The highest level was the CAS that was founded in November 1949 following the Soviet model. This institute took charge of most S&T activities and managed more than a hundred institutes nationwide in China (Pecht, 2006). The middle level consisted of the research institutes and labs under the various industrial ministries. The lowest level consisted of the local R&D institutes. In the planned system, the main body of innovation was not initiated by firms but by research institutes. The innovation process was not embedded in market-based relationships but determined by the top-down process of decision-making and project selection of the state. All R&D activities, including basic research, applied research and new products development were "controlled and funded by governments at various levels and carried out by scientific and technology institutes separated from industrial enterprises" (Shi, 1998, pp. 35–36). It has been summarized that "in planned systems, innovation tends to be part of a larger administrative hierarchy whose R&D efforts are more the product of highly directed resource mobilization than a response to market signals", although this planned system had indeed achieved significant technological breakthroughs in certain fields (which will be elaborated in Chapter 4) and had produced many valuable research results through mobilizing the national resources for several important projects (Simon and Rehn, 1988, p. 2). There were at least three problems in this S&T system.

First, research and development (R&D) activities in China were separated from industrial enterprises and restricted to the institutions that were built up and supported by the state in the planned economy system. This not only depressed the initiatives of enterprises to a large extent but also impeded the commercialization of research outputs (Lu, 2000). The fruits of research were normally left unused in the lab even if they were very valuable for commercialization. The central government decided what was to be researched and how to distribute research funds without taking into account the market demand. Furthermore, the research institutes allocated the received funds according to the budgetary allocation rather than the technological performance of groups or individuals (Simon and Rehn, 1988). Given that the research funds were allocated to the research institutes each year, there was no need for them to worry about whether their research success would result in any business returns to the country. The unreasonable funds-allocation system and incentive mechanisms failed to induce the growth of innovation.

Second, S&T activities in this period concentrated on military-use research and made little practical contribution to economic construction (Pecht, 2006). It is noted that "the government's strategy was to focus the Academy's resources on advanced technical problems rather than on (general economic) modernization" (Dean, 1979, p. 29). The industrial orientation of the state that underestimated the needs of society went against economic development and social well-being. At the same time, an ideology that undervalued technological knowledge and incentives to innovate severely constrained S&T development (Simon and Goldman, 1989; Wang and Lin, 2008, p. 164).

Along with the military-oriented strategies, China's ICT industry developed mainly in response to military requirements and to meet defense standards (Simon and Rehn, 1988). It is documented that a systematic approach to developing the indigenous ICT industry could be tracked back to the mid-1950s. A few significant research projects were conducted and achieved success through mobilizing the national manpower, materials and financial resources under the planned system. However, these achievements made by the research institutes could not be successfully commercialized in view of the existence of very few ICT firms in China before 1978. The strategies that selected research institutes over firms to develop technological innovation not only heavily separated research results from economic applications but also did not leave many choices and incentives for firms to be innovative. The following section will further examine the innovation-related behavior and reaction of firms under the planned economy.

(2) Passive Reaction of Firms

In the planned economy, the ownership-types of enterprises were confined to the state-owned enterprises, collectively-owned enterprises and rural collectives, among which state-owned enterprises accounted for about 80 percent of the industrial gross output before the economic reform launched in the late 1970s (Lu and Tang, 1997). The resources for production input, such as raw materials, were allocated by the government or relevant administrative ministries and the output of enterprises was distributed by the state as well. Even capital and labor were manipulated by the government. Enterprises operated according to the planned production targets rather than the market signals. All earnings and profits of the enterprises had to be handed to the state. Since the state controlled the input-output system, labor system and the flow of capital to the enterprises, the latter were not responsible for their profit and loss. Therefore, enterprises were not independent entities but pure production units without any economic autonomy and interests.

As a consequence, firms were neither capable nor motivated to invest in innovation. Shi (1998, p. 36) claims that "most industrial enterprises, except for a few large firms, had no technology development departments. The function of engineers and technicians in industrial enterprises was mainly to guarantee the operation of equipment and the production of existing products according to relatively unchanged technical coefficients". Furthermore, industrial managers and engineers appeared to be risk-averse and reluctant to invest in innovation because they were under pressure to complete state-set quotas while experimental activities, for them, only delayed the production process (Shi, 1998). It is revealed that "it was not the cost of experimental development but rather the risk to production that deterred the chief engineer from introducing innovation. From management's point of view, any experimentation that involved production facilities was a risk to output and to the fulfillment of production quotas in the state plan. Pressure to meet production quotas even caused management to avoid the trial-production assignments that were included in the state plan, and were accompanied by allocations of state funds to cover the additional costs involved, and for which adjustment could be made in the enterprise's production plan" (Dean, 1979, p. 58, cited from Simon, 1988, p. 10).

In summary, no state-firm strategic coordination existed during that period since the firms were treated as non-independent units without any autonomy. Firms had no power to decide the inputs for innovation since the entire input–output system was manipulated by the state. Nor were they motivated to pursue innovation due to their lack of responsibility regarding profit or loss. Under this planned system, there was no real market competition or cooperation among firms. The state-firm relationships were not based on innovation-related strategies but were "largely confined to bargaining with administrative organs for more favorable treatment over material allocation, resources and planned output quotas and also to forming 'formal' linkages and relationships with a range of organizations in order to reduce uncertainties resulting from the inefficient functioning of the plan" (Conroy, 1992, p. 30). Although the hierarchical innovation system had generated significant technological breakthroughs in certain fields through mobilizing limited national resources to significant research projects, it is believed that this system completely downplayed the role of firms in the process of innovation and often failed to produce economic value because most of the research results were largely left on the shelf and were never commercialized.

3.4.2. State-firm strategic coordination after the reform and opening-up in China

(1) The Rise of China and State Strategies for Technical Standard-Setting

Since the 1978 economic reform, China has embarked on a road of rapid economic growth. With products "made in China" sold everywhere in the world, China has gained the reputation of being the "world's factory". After three decades of development, China, with an increasing stock of knowledge, technology and a highly qualified workforce has accumulated substantial experience and gradually laid a foundation for indigenous innovation in the ICT-related field.

However, the state increasingly realized that there was no large profit margin left for domestic firms after the high patent and royalty payments despite the increase in the manufacturing capability of the nation. MNCs had much greater bargaining power in the market with control of core technologies while indigenous firms suffered from a thin profit margin resulting from low value activities of processing and assembly. The state has learnt a bitter lesson from the dispute over DVD player exports in 2004. China at that time produced over 80 percent of the world's DVD players and became the largest DVD maker in the world (Zhou, 2008, p. 151). When China tried to export its DVD players to Western markets, the Chinese DVD manufacturers were charged up to $22 patent fee per unit, leaving a negligible profit for Chinese manufacturers (Suttmeier and Yao, 2004). This event led to a large number of China's DVD player manufacturers closing down.

In recognition of the importance of gaining access to core technology, a number of domestic firms started to move toward higher-end products with more value-added technologies. Unfortunately, it is extremely difficult for domestic firms to avoid using certain patents of MNCs who had applied for as many patents for protection as they could. This led to the fact that the more higher-end products the indigenous firms were involved in, the greater the royalties they had to pay — a "patent trap" that they could not escape from without external assistance. It has been argued that when domestic firms "strive to raise their technological position, these firms have found that international technical standards can act as a check on their advance. Following the global mainstream standards is much like trying to set up your own shop in a crowded shopping mall where all the spaces have already been taken or reserved" (Zhou, 2008, p. 152). There is a popular saying referring to the significance of standard-setting and the awkward position of Chinese firms in the world economy: "First-class companies set standards; second-class companies develop technology and third-class companies manufacture products" (*yiliu de qiye zuo biaozhun, erliu de qiye zuo jishu, sanliu de qiye zuo chanpin*).[2]

In this situation, the state intended to set up its own technical standards to help indigenous firms get rid of the costly patent and royalty fees and shake off dependence on the core technology of MNCs, given the improvement in the national technological capability and increasing ability to succeed in setting these new technical standards. The role of the state

---

[2]This is a popular saying in Chinese business circles revealing that China has lagged behind its counterparts in advanced economies because most Chinese firms are only able to manufacture products, following the technologies of others and operating under rules set by others. See also Suttmeier and Yao (2004).

in developing homegrown technical standards is critical because only the state can invest in such huge projects, mobilize the nationwide resources, distribute tasks to various actors (firms, universities, research institutes, related organization) across administrative levels and coordinate their conflicts of interest. Among all indigenous technical standards, China's third-generation (3G) wireless communication standard has obtained strongest support from the state. The state has mobilized the most promising and innovative firms, universities and research institutes in the field of the telecommunications industry to develop a technical standard for the third-generation mobile telephony: TD-SCDMA (time division synchronous code division multiple access). It is the first technical standard that was entirely created by China in the field of mobile communications and it is the third technical standard in the field of telecommunications that was accepted in the world, equivalent to the GSM standard established by Europe and WCDMA in the U.S. This action opened up a new technological path and new opportunity for indigenous firms to be innovative and to be independent of their foreign counterparts. Technical standard-setting strategy is one of many strategies that show the resolution of the state to spur on its firms to move from a labor-intensive to an innovation-centered stage. In addition to the standard-setting strategy, the state released a series of innovation-related policies to provide special support to a number of "pillar" industries and offer all possible assistance to encourage and facilitate the innovation of potential firms.

(2) Strategic Selectivity, Reaction of Firms and Regional Differences in State-Firm Coordination

After the 1978 economic reform, the participation of foreign capital and private capital in the economic construction led to a diverse ownership-structure of firms that organize and produce, mainly in response to market signals rather than decision-making by the state. The S&T system reform aimed at linking research results to the industrial economy highlighted the role of firms in the process of innovation and reinforced the connections between research institutes and firms. A series of measures has been introduced by the state to build up horizontal linkages between research labs and industrial enterprises to facilitate the diffusion of technological results into industry. Three approaches have been adopted to restructure the S&T system, namely "merging R&D institutions into existing enterprises; spinning-off new technology enterprises from R&D institutions and transforming entire individual R&D institutions into manufacturing or engineering corporations with intensive in-house R&D and design" (Gu, 1999, p. xxiv).

Over the past two decades, Chinese firms have gradually learnt that the benefit of technological cooperation with MNCs has become more and more limited (Zhou, 2008). They have to build up their own technology base to survive in the fierce competition and catch up with their foreign counterparts. For years, they have been trapped at the low end of the global value chain and acted only as followers of their Western counterparts, suffering from the dual difficulties of both lack of finance and lack of highly qualified human resources (Segal, 2003). Despite a large number of people returning from overseas with advanced knowledge and years of experience in developed countries, their enthusiasm for innovation has been depressed by not only the lack of capital and highly qualified homegrown talent, but also by their disadvantageous situation with respect to MNCs having monopolized the high-end market leaving them no space to fill. Furthermore, the disorderly market environment and immature institutional system in many city-regions made firms very reluctant to commit themselves to high-risk investments since they were able to obtain a satisfactory profit from the existing huge market demands and diversified market segments. There is a well-accepted concept in business circles in China which jokingly reveals the popular attitude of indigenous firms to innovation: Not to invest in innovation is waiting to be killed, but engaging in innovation is seeking to be killed (*bu chuangxin jiu dengsi, chuangxin jiu dengyu zhaosi*).

Through engaging in homegrown standards, those indigenous firms who are unhappy about the slimmer profit margins from lower-end operations as well as high patent and royalty payments show their desire to improve their innovative capability and move towards high-end production and R&D. However, many other indigenous firms still choose to adopt conservative strategies that are determined by their business interests and internal resources and thus fail to actively match the innovation-related plans of the state. As such, strategic coordination varies across the country because local governments with varying power and strategies shape a distinct institutional and market environment. Shanghai and Shenzhen are two typical examples that show the difference in the degree of state-firm strategic coordination.

The Shanghai municipal government is well known as a strong government which energetically supervises its economy and development. Already from the 1950s onward, Shanghai has established its ICT technology base and paved the way for the innovation of its ICT firms (Simon and Rehn, 1988). Considering its strategic position in China, the central government selected Shanghai as a location to develop the national IC (Integrated Circuit) industry, which further reinforced the IC industrial foundation of Shanghai. Also, the Shanghai municipal government released a set of policies to retain talent, foster start-ups and stimulate innovation-related activities of firms. Given the presence of many MNCs and stringent supervision by the local government, the market environment in Shanghai is more orderly and disciplined than elsewhere. In view of the high cost of locating in such an international metropolis as Shanghai, firms that intend to reduce production costs will normally not choose Shanghai as their location. However, Shanghai will be the first choice for firms that seek technology support, new talent and a better innovative environment. In this institutional and market environment, a high degree of state-firm strategic coordination in Shanghai can easily be accomplished.

In sharp contrast, the Shenzhen municipal government is much more reluctant to supervise its economy and regulate its market environment. As a small border town before the 1978 economic reform, Shenzhen, without any technology base or highly qualified human resources, grew rapidly through attracting a great deal of foreign direct investment (FDI), especially labor-intensive investment from Hong Kong (a Special Administration Region of China now, whose sovereignty was transferred by Great Britain to China on the 30th June 1997). With low negotiating power at the beginning, the Shenzhen municipal government had to make its peace with a disorderly market, severe environmental issues and many other problems caused by low-end manufacturing activities. Although the flexible and *laissez-faire* policies adopted by the Shenzhen municipal government have spawned a large number of small ICT firms and resulted in the cluster of related firms, the developmental pattern is harmful for long-term technological innovation. A salient feature of Shenzhen's business circle is that most firms have to occupy the market as soon as possible at the cheapest price and with the shortest production cycles, which is against the nature of innovation that requires long-term investment without instant rewards. Without strong supervision and regulation of the local government over its industry and economy, Shenzhen's economic activities often focus on copycat products that make the non-innovators more profit than the innovators and hence further deteriorate the local competitive environment. Consequently, there exists a much lower degree of innovation-based state-firm strategic coordination in Shenzhen.

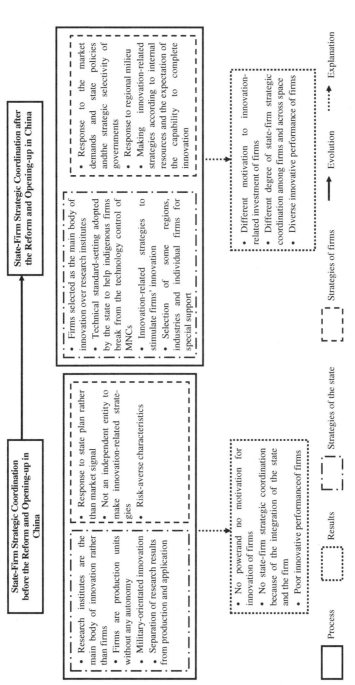

Figure 3.2. Evolution of state-firm strategic coordination in China.

3.5. Summary

The concept of industrial clusters did not provide a satisfactory explanation of the uneven innovative performance of China's ICT industry and the Western-centric understanding of a firms' innovation in the existing theories of economic geography failed to appreciate the incentives and constraints confronting high-tech firms. To overcome these theoretical limitations, this chapter has developed a framework that integrates both internal resources of firms and the external institutional and market environment with special emphasis on the strategic selectivity of the state and the strategic reaction of firms to an individual and place-sensitive model.

In this new framework, the state is defined as a political entity with the capability and power to guide economic development and provide a vision for the future. The firm is understood to be a collection of productive resources, including capital, employment of skilled personnel, machinery, knowledge and technology, brand-name, channels to external information, etc. State-firm strategic coordination refers to a dynamic process in which firms' innovation-related strategies coordinate the "strategic selectivity" of the central or local governments, which not only concerns the strategies, capability and determination of the state but also considers how firms make innovation-related strategies according to their internal resources and external environment.

Building upon this framework, the innovation-related activities and performances of China's ICT firms are affected by both their internal resources and external environment that can be greatly shaped by the state. Although the strategic selectivity of the central government has, to a large extent, stimulated the motivation of innovation-related activities, enlarged the internal resources and hence led to a better innovative performance of the chosen ICT firms, the local milieu and local governments' strategies and actions played a no less significant role than that of the central government. At the individual level, firms chose whether they liked to, and were able to, match the state's strategic selectivity according to their internal resources and the evaluation of their own capability, which led to a different degree of state-firm strategic coordination among individual firms. At the regional level, the strategies and selectivity of ICT firms were affected by the regional institutions and milieu that are shaped by local governments, leading to a different degree of state-firm strategic coordination among regions. Firm-level state-firm strategic coordination can be evaluated by project-based, product-based and award-based strategic coordination, and the region-level state-firm strategic coordination can be broken down into information-based, product-based and fund-based strategic coordination. All the types of state-firm strategic coordination not only reflected the pre-existing innovation-oriented strategies of the firms but also enlarged and enriched their internal resources, such as capital, information, technology and reputation, and so on, to make them more innovative.

No state-firm strategic coordination existed before the 1978 economic reform since firms were dependent entities without any power to make production and innovation-related decisions. At the same time, innovation-related activities were conducted by the research institutes with their research outputs not connected to economic demands. This economic system has experienced profound reforms since 1978 when China strived for transformation from a planned economy to a combination of state and market economy. After over two decades of rapid growth, the Chinese government intended to help its firms get rid of the technology control by MNCs and move toward the upper-end of the global value chain. The series of innovation-related polices and the strategic actions related to technical standard-setting taken by the central government provided great opportunities for indigenous firms to become innovative and catch up with their foreign counterparts. Due to diverse regional milieu and various levels of power, determination and capability of local governments, the degree of state-firm strategic coordination varies by region, which is well demonstrated in the cases of Shanghai and Shenzhen.

This new framework differs from the existing frameworks in three aspects. First of all, it stresses the importance of the role played by the active actors and agents and moves beyond the fashionable concepts of networks and relationships. As has been pointed out in Chapter 2, the prevailing frameworks tend to privilege "networks", "linkages" and "relations" over actors and agents. This new framework does not deny the importance of networks, linkages and relationships in innovation, but contends that it is the actors and agents that determine whether or not to build their "networks", "linkages" and "relations", and with whom and how. It is pointed out that any analysis in economic geography should be based on an understanding of "the intentions and strategies of economic actors and ensembles of actors and the patterns of how they behave" (Bathelt and Glückler, 2003, p. 125). Without taking into account the attributes of actors and agents, it is impossible to understand the formation and characteristics of inter-firm relations and their influence on innovation-related activities. By taking a serious look at the active actors and agents such as the governments and firms, this new theoretical framework suggests that the entities, not the relationships, should be the key units of analysis. Second, the new framework highlights the importance of motivation and strategies of actors and agents in the process of technological innovation. While the existing frameworks placed much emphasis on knowledge and technologies in understanding the creation of innovation, they neglected to examine the innovation-related motivations, interests and strategies of firms. It is argued within this new framework that the innovation-related motivation and strategies of firms that are affected by their internal resources and external environment determine whether or not they will commit themselves to innovation, before moving on to pursue the valuable knowledge and technologies for innovation. The strategic considerations and choices of firms are diverse and not necessarily related to innovation. It is not possible to deeply understand technological innovation without probing into the interests, motivation and strategies of the firms. Finally, the new framework brings the state into the analytical framework rather than simply explaining technological innovation by focusing exclusively on firms and their business linkages. When the existing frameworks paid more attention to the synergic effects between firms within the industrial clusters, they tended to underestimate the significant role played by the state not only in establishing an institutional environment but also in its strategic selectivity towards certain potential firms. The new framework suggests that the state, as a part of the economy, could make a significant contribution in stimulating the innovation-related motivation and removing certain obstacles confronting the firms in their process of innovation at this specific historical juncture, as China is still in the midst of economic transition that is characterized by a disordered and immature market environment.

Finally, it needs to be stated here that the new framework developed in this chapter is not intended to falsify or replace the existing frameworks reviewed in Chapter 2, but serves as a new supplement to them by explicitly emphasizing the innovation-related strategies and behavior of both the state and the firms in the Chinese context in which firms are confronted with many more constraints than incentives in their process of technological innovation. The relational approach serves its own purpose well. It is surely true that the linkages, networks and relationships on different geographical scales more or less contribute to technological innovation, but it is too imprecise and a generalization to sufficiently explain the innovation-related incentives and constraints facing the firms. It is not argued in this book that relations on different spatial scales are not important for technological innovation in the Chinese context. However, the theoretical framework emphasizes that we should not privilege those relations over active actors and agents. Specifically, it highlights that state-firm strategic coordination that gives a special focus to innovation-related motivation and strategies of both the state and firms is a critical factor for technological innovation in the transitional economic system.

Chapter Four

THE GEOGRAPHY
OF TECHNOLOGICAL INNOVATION
IN CHINA'S ICT INDUSTRY

4.1. Introduction

As one of the most important high-tech industries, the ICT industry can be seen as a thermometer to reflect the level of technological capability and innovation in a region. Despite its importance to economic growth, China's ICT industry did not achieve rapid growth until the 1990s when the Chinese government started to give it a high priority and global capital was shifted to China in order to reduce the production costs and chase a higher profit margin. Within a time span of less than 10 years, China's ICT industry has experienced a dramatic expansion so that it has now occupied an important position in the world economy. At the end of 2004, the ICT manufacturing sector contributed approximately 12 percent of sales revenue to the whole manufacturing sector with only 5 percent of employment and less than 9 percent total assets (CSSB, 2005a).[1] The OECD (2005) identified China as the leading exporter of ICT goods in the world, ahead of Japan and the European Union since 2003 and overtaking the U.S. since 2004. At present, China is ranked number one in the world in both the production and consumption of electronic products (Pecht, 2006).

The dramatic growth of the ICT industry in China has been the subject of great scholarly interest. However, it is no easy task to fully understand the nature and the dynamics of the growth and innovation of the Chinese ICT sector. The difficulty is the result of a number of long-lasting problems. First of all, the concept of the "ICT industry" has actually involved a large number of sectors and sub-sectors and there is, unfortunately,

---

[1]According to the standard of national economic industry classification (GB/T4754-2002), "manufacture" in the 2004 economic census refers to all industries except the mining industry, the electricity and gas production and supply industries, and construction in secondary industries. It includes 13 sections, 30 divisions, 169 groups and 482 classes.

no standard definition and classification of the industry. Researchers defined the ICT industry according to their understanding and collected data from different official or unofficial statistics, which led to not only confusion and misunderstanding, but also false comparison. For example, Amighini (2005) divided ICT products into office machines, IT products, telecom products and semiconductors. In contrast, Meng and Li (2002) analyzed China's ICT industry as the electronics industry, which included electronic components, communications equipments, computer products and software products. The report conducted by the International Finance Corporation focused on ten sub-sectors: telecommunications equipment, the IC industry and fabless (fabrication-less) chip design, the software industry, security services, mobile data, online gaming, e-commerce, digital media applications, software outsourcing and IT services, and handset design (Khalil and Hamid, 2005).

Second, research on China's ICT industry has been hampered by the lack of accurate and consistent data (Katsuno, 2005). According to Katsuno, there are three main sources of official ICT statistics in China: the Ministry of Information Industry, the National Bureau of Statistics and Chinese Academy of Sciences. He notes that there are great discrepancies between data from different sources: "There are some coherency problems between the disaggregated data of the Ministry of Information Industry and those supplied by the National Bureau of Statistics. Similar problems exist within the various statistics reported by the Ministry of Information Industry itself" (Katsuno, 2005, p. 17). Moreover, it is questionable whether China's ICT statistics are comparable to those OECD countries because of the different systems of classification (Breidne, 2005).

Third, most of the existing studies have taken China's ICT industry as a whole and have never examined the spatial variation of this industry at a disaggregated provincial or county level (Amighini, 2005; Breidne, 2005; Katsuno, 2005; Meng and Li, 2002). In recognition of the importance of the ICT industry, Chinese local governments have committed themselves to the establishment and development of a local ICT industry. However, as a high-tech industry that requires a more demanding industrial environment than more traditional industries, its development has inevitably been unevenly distributed.

Finally, the technology level and innovative capability of the ICT industry remains unknown. As Katsuno (2005, p. 8) has pointed out, China's ICT sector is a strategic sector for which the Chinese government expects to not only attract foreign direct investment but also develop its own technology base. It has been documented that China has established its own innovative capability and has started to develop its own technical standards in selected fields, such as third-generation (3G) mobile telephony and the TDSCDMA (Time Division Synchronous Code Division Multiple Access) standard (Suttmeier and Yao, 2004). However, it has also been contended that "China's ICT industry today has largely been stuck at the lowest level of the high-tech value chain" (Breidne, 2005, p. 11). Furthermore, the technology landscape and innovative capability of China is highly uneven because of the "considerable difference in local resources, culture and institutions, as well as in the positions in MNCs' global or China strategies" (Zhou and Tong, 2003, p. 149).

What are the status, internal structure and dynamics of China's ICT industry? Has China's ICT industry reached a higher technological level or is it still stuck at the low end of the global value chain? Does the spatial clustering lead to a better economic and innovative performance as the conventional wisdom would expect? If not, what factors have contributed to the innovative performance of China's ICT firms? This chapter attempts to examine the growth, structure, spatial distribution and performance of China's ICT industry with special attention given to the relationship between industrial clustering and technological innovation. To make this point, this chapter is organized in four parts. It begins with an historical examination of the science and technology environment and innovation system to understand the growth and innovation of the ICT industry since the foundation of the People's Republic of China. Afterward, it examines the recent growth, structural composition and different performance among enterprises invested by three types of capital, namely domestic, foreign and Hong Kong, Macao and Taiwan capital investment in the ICT industry. Attention is then turned to the uneven spatial distribution of the ICT industry with a focus on the relationship between spatial clustering and economic as well as innovative performance. The influential factors on innovative performance of the ICT manufacturing firms are then identified. The last part is a summary of research findings.

4.2. Historicizing the Growth and Innovation of China's ICT Industry

China is a latecomer in developing the ICT industry. When the first electronic computer was produced in the U.S. in 1946, China was still in the midst of domestic turmoil and civil war. It was only after the mid-1950s when a new approach was adopted by China to develop the electronics industry in its 12-year plan promulgated for improving national science and technology (Simon and Rehn, 1988). The growth and innovation of China's ICT industry cannot be separated from the changing political and economic environment in China. To understand China's ICT industry, it is necessary to examine the historical background, changing political contexts, state policies and plans pertaining to science and technology (S&T) and the ICT industry that have been introduced at different stages.

After the foundation of the People's Republic of China in 1949, the Chinese leadership was confronted with not only a disordered national economy but also the threat of the subversion of state power by Western countries, especially the U.S. It was in this unstable political context that the Chinese leadership decided to devote itself to sophisticated weapons with the belief in "grasping nuclear technology to restrain nuclear attack" (*yihe zhihe*) in spite of the financial limitations and the poor national economy (Liu *et al.*, 2004). Although the military-oriented industrial strategies had been criticized by many scholars who claimed that this strategic selectivity depressed the development of the civilian industries, widened the gap between R&D and production, and led to the separation between researchers and end-users, the pattern of R&D and innovation that is characterized by the hierarchical structure in response to administrative commands during that period indeed achieved an astonishing success in certain top-end technology fields.

A typical case was the success in developing the atomic and hydrogen bombs, and a satellite (these projects later came to be called two bombs and one satellite, *Liangdan Yixing*). In the turbulent international environment, the development of the atomic bomb was put on the agenda in 1955, when the national economy started to revive and the S&T resources had been expanded. The number of research institutes had increased to 380 with more than 9000 technical staff compared to less than 40 research institutes with only 600 people before 1949 (Liu *et al.*, 2004, pp. 37–38). Almost without any external assistance, China shocked the world by successfully developing its first atomic bomb through mobilizing worldwide talents and nationwide resources in the mid-1960s. More striking is the pace with which China developed its hydrogen bomb. It only took China less than three years, much shorter than the U.S. (over seven years), the Soviet Union and Britain (four years) and France (more than eight years), to introduce their first hydrogen bomb (Liu *et al.*, 2004, p. 130). Afterward, the fact that China successfully introduced its first and second satellite in 1970 and 1975 had struck the imagination of politicians and scientists in the Western world and made China the fifth country that could independently launch a satellite after the U.S., Soviet Union, France and Japan (Liu *et al.*, 2004). In addition, several achievements in the medical sciences also showed the technological strength of China: the creation of artificially synthesized crystalline bovine insulin and the first introduction of the chemical artemisinin to the world was hailed as a milestone in the history of malaria research by the international community.[2] Another technological innovation during this period that exerted a far-reaching influence on China and even the world was the creation of hybrid rice, which was honored as "The Fifth-Largest Invention" after the great four inventions in ancient China (Ministry of Science and Technology, 1999, p. 83).[3] In terms of the ICT industry, the National Project 748 (standing for initiation in August 1974) gave birth to the significant invention of the Chinese characters laser photo-typesetting system that laid a foundation for the later computerization of the news and publishing in China. Many valuable research results achieved during the period played a critical role in the later growth and innovation of several well-known electronic enterprises such as Legend, Founder and Greatwall (Lu, 1997).

All of these significant innovations pointed to the undeniable advantages of the hierarchical innovation system under the planned economy, namely the highest degree of concentration of the scarce resources into the strategic sectors, and the assembly of an elite corps of highly talented scientists and engineers with clear missions, despite many of the drawbacks identified in Chapter 3. For instance, the project of "two bombs and one satellite" involved "a whole industrial ministry, respectively the ministry of atomic energy for the two bombs, and the ministry of aerospace for rockets and satellites — and dozens of industrial research labs under each ministry, with the heavy involvement of top scientists from the research institutes under the CAS. All resources necessary for carrying out the projects, including finance, manpower, materials, scientific instruments, were guaranteed from the state

---

[2]Li, Xiaohong, 7 April 2005. Cong Fufang Haojiami Kan Woguo Xinyao Yanfa. (New drug R&D and the Compound Artemether.) *People's Daily.* Available at: http://scitech. people.com.cn/GB/41163/3301415.html, accessed 26 March 2010; *People's Daily*, 18 September 2009. Xinzhongguo Dangan: Woguo Shouci Rengong Hecheng Jiejing Niuyidao su Danbai (New China Files: China's first artificial synthesis of crystalline bovine insulin-like protein). *People's Daily.* Available at: http://scitech.people.com.cn/ GB/10077203.html, accessed 26 March 2010.

[3]See also the online report by *People's Daily* titled "Shijie Zajiao Shuidao Zhifu Yuanlongping Jianli (Father of Hybrid Rice: the Resume of Yuan Longping)", 21 May 2007, http://scitech.people.com.cn/GB/25509/55787/158474/158485/9484879.html accessed 26 March 2010.

budgets" (Lu, 1997, pp. 4–5). It is also reported that the invention of the atomic bomb from 1962 to 1964 involved 26 ministries and over 900 factories, research institutes and colleges and universities from 20 provinces, municipalities and autonomous regions (Liu *et al.*, 2004, pp. 73–74). Project 748, like many other large-scale projects, was completed under the joint efforts of many ministries and organizations (Lu, 1997).[4]

The great achievement of the technological breakthroughs of that period showed that the strategies, determination and power of the state could to a large extent improve the technological level of a country even though this country suffered from an extreme shortage of finance and talents. As a matter of fact, the irreplaceable role played by the state in the development of high-tech industries and technological innovation has been well-proven by the success of Silicon Valley (U.S.). The Federal Government's support through military purchase, the initiation of electronics-based programs and tax provisions for microelectronics firms was critical for the formation of Silicon Valley (Castells and Hall, 1994). According to Castells and Hall, the Defense Department and the National Aeronautics and Space Administration (NASA) intended to purchase the most innovative and thus the most risky technologies at very high prices in order to reduce the risks taken by the innovators and provide the financial support for the infant electronics industry. In addition, the dramatic expansion of military demands for electronic devices in the late 1950s and the 1960s provided a great opportunity for the growth of small electronics firms. It is documented that "in 1959 Fairchild was awarded a $1.5 million contract to provide the transistors for the Minuteman missile, and in 1963 the integrated circuits for the *Apollo* spacecraft's guidance computer. In the late 1950s the share of military markets in the total shipment of semiconductors reached the 70 percent level, and it oscillated around 50 percent during the 1960s, with the defense market being concentrated in the higher layers of the technology" (Castells and Hall, 1994, p. 17).

Unfortunately, most of the technological breakthroughs and research results only stayed in the research labs without any chance to be commercialized. Furthermore, the continuous political campaigns in this period

---

[4]It is documented that the ministries and organizations that participated in Project 748 generally include "the Fourth Ministry of Machine Industry, the First Ministry of Machine Industry, the Ministry of Post and Telecommunications, the Ministry of Fuel and Chemical Industry, the Ministry of Light Industry, the Chinese Academy of Sciences, the Official Xinhua News Agency, and the State Bureau of Publishing Affairs and other related ministries, bureau or state institutions" (Lu, 1997, p. 161).

interrupted economic development and deteriorated the environment under which the high-tech activities were taking place. During the 1950s and 1960s, the two campaigns of the "Great Leap Forward" (1958–1960) and the "Cultural Revolution" (1966–1976) brought an unprecedented disaster to the country. China not only suffered from a retrogressive economy and unstable political environment but also lost a large number of talented people including scientists, academicians and professors. This significantly encumbered S&T activities and harmed the development of the innovative system. Therefore, the ICT industry did not have any significant growth during that era. The military-oriented strategies in this period also engendered a bias in R&D and production within this industry, such as giving a high priority to the operational speed and memory size of the electronic computer but undervaluing the development of software and peripheral equipments (Simon and Rehn, 1988).

The economic reform initiated in 1978 was a turning point for China's economic development and inevitably influenced the innovation system as well as the growth of the ICT industry. The Third Plenum of the Eleventh Congress of the Communist Party of China in March of 1978 turned out to be a watershed, which ushered in a shift of emphasis from class struggle to economic development and the focus on "four modernizations", namely the modernization of agriculture, industry, S&T and the military. In this plenum, the late Deng Xiaoping put forward the significant argument that science and technology are the primary productive driving forces (Pecht, 2006). In addition, the plenum proclaimed the "open-door" policy to permit foreign direct investment and accept technology transfer. Students were encouraged to study abroad and return to their motherland with advanced knowledge and technology.

The focus of the strategic selectivity of the Chinese government has been shifted from heavy and military-oriented industries to the electronics industry since the early 1980s, when the State Council Leading Group for the Revitalization of the Electronics Industry (*Guowuyuan Dianzi Zhenxing Lingdao Xiaozu*) was established to directly guide the development of the electronics industry, in recognition of the importance of the electronics industry as the "hallmark of a country's level of modernization" (Simon and Rehn, 1988, p. 59). The then Chairman Liu Shaoqi highlighted the strategic role played by the electronics industry in the whole economy: "[The] development of a modern electronics industry will bring about a big leap forward for our industry, and it will be a starting point for a new industrial revolution in the history of China. The rapid popularization of modern electronic technology will make China the first newly industrialized socialist power with first-rate electronic technology" (Simon and Rehn, 1988, p. 47). In order to remove the hierarchical administrative barriers to ensure the smooth progress of significant projects, the central government assigned the then Premier Li Peng to lead this group. Many other members in this group came from the leading government commissions and key ministries. The leading group was under the supervision of the State Council and its policy was implemented by many commissions and ministries (Fig. 4.1). The great power given to this leading group not only eliminated the confusion and inconsistency of the decisions made by different commissions and ministries involved in the electronics industry, but also coordinated those different organizations and departments to realize the short-term and long-term goals of the electronics industry.

Although the leading group was not in charge of the funds for project allocation, it worked to ensure that ample funds could be channeled toward priority projects or be available for technology imports through commanding and supervising the State Planning Commission and other high-level government bodies (Simon and Rehn, 1988, p. 59). It is revealed that among the 550 key projects in the machinery and electronics industries that were funded by the State Economic Commission during the Sixth Five-Year Plan (1981–1985), 148 of them were focused on the electronics industry (Simon and Rehn, 1988). Around 60 percent of key technology import projects in this period were related to the electronics industry (Simon and Rehn, 1988, p. 59).

A significant contribution to the development of the electronics industry made by this leading group was the formulation and release of the document titled "The Strategy for the Development of China's Electronics and Information Industries" that set the framework for the goals of the electronics industry during the Seventh Five-Year Plan (1986–1990) which exerted a far-reaching influence on the future development of this industry. In the mid-1980s, the electronics industry was regarded as a priority sector leading the development of other industrial and economic sectors and identified as a significant sector that was required to take serious actions to improve product quality and technological capability to meet international requirements (Simon and Rehn, 1988). Since then, the electronics industry continued to be the priority area into the construction of which the state has put much effort and capital. In the period 1978–1991, both ICT manufacturing and service sectors started to germinate. At the end of 2004, the government invested over 13 percent of the capital that was funded

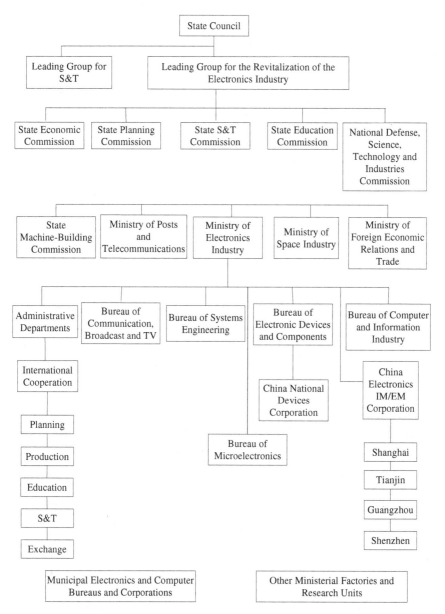

Figure 4.1.   Organization of China's electronics industry, 1987.
Source: (Simon and Rehn, 1988, p. 54).

for supporting the S&T activities of industrial firms to the electronics industry, much higher than other manufacturing sectors except the sector for transport equipment (CSSB, 2005a).

The principle that "S&T are the primary productive driving forces" was reiterated during the "Southern tour" of the late Deng Xiaoping in 1992. Since then, unprecedented attention has been focused on technological innovation and the high-tech industries. Considering the limited resources of capital and talent, the state continuously focused on the development of the ICT industry during the period of its national Ninth Five-Year Plan (1996–2000) and Tenth Five-Year Plan (2001–2005) (Pecht, 2006). According to Pecht (2006, p. 50), major development goals in the Ninth and Tenth Five-Year Plans included "[f]ocusing on the development of integrated circuits (ICs), new devices, new computers and telecommunication equipment to provide economic and social development with up-to-date information systems, and creating preferential policies to support IC development; developing microchip devices, new displays and photoelectric devices, and establishing production and export bases for computer and accessory devices; developing and producing digitally programmed exchanges, mobile communications and optical communications equipment; improving the electronics industry's technical level and international competitiveness". The S&T funds from the government to the ICT large- and medium-sized enterprises was only 270 million *yuan* in 1995. However, this number increased to 1330 million *yuan* in 2006 (CSSB and MOST, 1996, 2007). Meanwhile, the ICT firms have been aware of the importance of innovative activities and have devoted more money to developing new products. They already spent 7799 million *yuan* on their development of new products in 2006, almost six times more than that of 1995 (CSSB and MOST, 1996, 2007). The share of expenditure on developing new products out of total expenditure in the ICT manufacturing sector greatly increased from 49 percent to 77 percent during the period 1995–2006 (CSSB and MOST, 1996, 2007).

Three important national S&T programs have contributed to the development of the ICT industry and technological innovation in China. The first one is the 863 Program launched in 1986 aiming to promote S&T research in the medium to long term with a high priority given to the ICT industry (Qin, 1992). Its main objective includes "breakthroughs in the key technologies of the new generation of large stored program control (SPC) switching systems, high performance computers, information technology-based commercial and trade equipment, high definition TV (HDTV), digital audio broadcasting (DAB), Chinese information software platforms, and so on" (Sigurdson, 2005, p. 40). In order to realize this objective, the central government had allocated 5.3 million *yuan*, with another 17.6 million *yuan* financed by local governments during the Ninth Five-Year Plan to support innovation (Sigurdson, 2005, p. 40). The program also built up several centers to train selected scientific and technical personnel other than giving financial support to technological development (Qin, 1992, p. 1128). The 863 Program laid a foundation for the establishment of the Chinese indigenous 3G technical standard and, since then, the ambition of China to nurture an independent innovative capability has grown (Sigurdson, 2005, p. 145).

Compared to the 863 Program that placed much emphasis on research, the second significant program, Torch Plan, initiated in 1988, was more concerned with the commercialization of research results (Qin, 1992, p. 1128). The state intended to build up the national high-tech manufacturing capabilities with special emphasis on the R&D and the commercialization of new technologies in state-owned enterprises (Naughton and Segal, 2003, p. 167). Torch Plan not only provided the required equipment and other inputs for high-tech enterprises, but also offered a series of services taking the form of "incubators" for small and medium enterprises (Sigurdson, 2005, p. 46). Preferential policies regarding "taxes, finance, imports and exports, pricing and personnel policy" were also released in the expectation of facilitating the development of high-tech enterprises (Naughton and Segal, 2003, p. 167). For facilitating the commercialization and industrialization of the R&D products, enterprises are allowed to raise their funds for S&T activities not only from the central and local governments but also from bank loans and foreign funds (Sigurdson, 2005). Under this program, numerous high-tech development zones and economic development zones have been created since 1988 and a number of enterprises in those zones in the eastern coastal regions have been able to grow (Qin, 1992; Sigurdson, 2005).

The third significant national program is the recently-launched National Basic R&D Program — 973 Program (standing for initiation in March 1997) that was designed to "stimulate the activities of original innovation, to solve significant scientific issues in the development process of the economy and society with the aim of providing scientific support for the future development of China" (Sigurdson, 2005, p. 49). The expenditure on the 973 Program reached 2500 million *yuan* during the Ninth Five-Year Plan with the ICT industry being a significant sector to be supported and promoted (Sigurdson, 2005). A successful research project in the ICT field under this program was related to the production of a new generation of processor chips that integrated the capability of various chips and could be applied in a wide range of areas (Sigurdson, 2005, p. 50). In addition to these important S&T programs, one of the significant strategies adopted by the state was the indigenous standard-setting of wireless telecommunications. Developed by well-known SOE Datang Telecom in cooperation with a research institute under the former Ministry of Information Industry, the TD-SCDMA standard was sanctioned as one of the international standards for 3G mobile telecommunications by the International Telecommunications Union in May 2000 (Naughton and Segal, 2003, p. 185). It is regarded as a significant technological breakthrough in the history of telecommunications in China and will definitely impact the development of the entire ICT industry.

4.3. Growth and Nature of China's ICT Industry

Within the political context and S&T structure identified above, it is not difficult to understand that the growth of China's ICT industry has been a recent phenomenon. Not until the 1990s did the ICT industry experience a rapid growth. There were few ICT manufacturing start-ups before 1991, but the number grew during the 1990s and experienced a dramatic increase in the period 2000–2004 (Fig. 4.2). The temporal development of the software sector is somewhat different from that of the ICT manufacturing sector.[5] There were only 137 software firms before the 1990s, but the period 2000–2004 witnessed an extremely rapid expansion of the software sector with nearly five times as many start-ups as there had been in the 1990s (Fig. 4.2).

A close examination of the ICT manufacturing sector during the period 1990–2006 reveals a lasting growth in terms of not only the industrial scale but also S&T activities and technological innovation.[6] Employment in the ICT large- and medium-sized enterprises in 1990 was less than

---

[5]This research only examines the software sub-sector (6200) rather than the whole ICT service sector because the other two ICT service sub-sectors, namely the service of telecommunications and other information transmission (6000), the service of computers (6100) involved too much state capital and are basically monopolized by the state in China currently.

[6]Most of the research mainly focuses on the ICT manufacturing sector because data on the innovative activities of the service sector are unavailable in Chinese statistics.

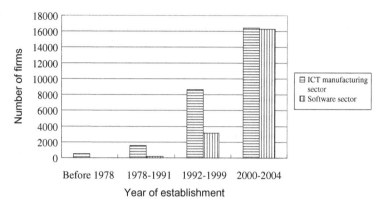

Figure 4.2. The ICT manufacturing and software start-ups in China at different stages. *Source*: (CSSB, 2005a).

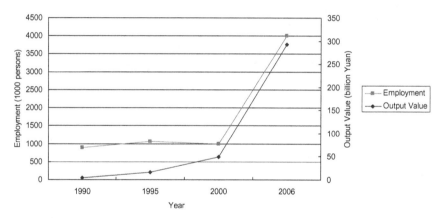

Figure 4.3. Employment and output value of the ICT large- and medium-sized enterprises in selected years.
Source: (CSSB and MOST, 1991, 1996, 2001, 2007).

0.9 million but it rose to more than four million in 2006.[7] Correspondingly, the output value of these ICT enterprises enlarged 64 times during the period 1990–2006 (Fig. 4.3).

---

[7]Large- and medium-sized enterprises refer to the enterprises with more than 300 personnel in employment, more than 30 million *yuan* in sales revenue and over 40 million *yuan* in total assets. Available at: http://www.stats.gov.cn/tjbz/t20061018_402369829.htm, accessed 26 June 2008.

It is interesting to note that the ratio of ICT manufacturing firms with tech-activities gradually descended from 1990 to 2006 despite a substantial increase in the number of firms from 1990 to 2006. Likewise, although the absolute amount spent in developing new products was expanded, expenditure on developing new products as a percentage of total sales revenue showed a significant decrease from 1996 to 2006. Furthermore, the share of sales revenue of new products out of total sales revenue in 2006 was only 24 percent, much lower than that of 1990, in spite of a sharp increase in both sales revenues of new products and total sales revenue during the period of 1990–2006 (Table 4.1). This pattern suggests that more and more ICT manufacturing firms were reluctant to devote themselves to innovative activities during this period. The declining interest in tech-activities and innovation may have been the result of increasing pressure on firms to

Table 4.1. Economic indicators of the ICT large- and medium-sized enterprises in selected years.

Year	1990	1995	2000	2006
Number of firms	611	855	887	2511
Number of firms with tech-activities	404*	—	567	1076
Ratio of firms with tech-activities to total ICT firms	66.12%	—	63.92%	42.85%
Sales revenue (billion *yuan*)	4.02	14.17	47.11	293.19
Expenditure on developing new products (million *yuan*)	557.96	1362.35	8659.85	7799.40
Expenditure on developing new products as a percentage of total sales revenue	13.88%	9.61%	18.38%	2.66%
Sales revenue of new products (billion *yuan*)	1.38	2.56	21.59	70.58
Ratio of the sales revenue of new products to all products	34.38%	18.08%	45.83%	24.07%
Total funds for S&T activities (million *yuan*)	1119.08	2996.25	16916.38	54537.88
S&T funds raised from government (million *yuan*)	160.00	269.52	474.11	1329.68
Ratio of S&T funds from government to total S&T funds	14.30%	9.00%	2.80%	2.44%
S&T funds self-raised by enterprises (million *yuan*)	677.16	2382.59	14093.73	47727.62
Ratio of enterprise-raised S&T funds to total S&T funds	60.51%	79.52%	83.31%	87.51%

*Refers to the number of firms with tech-development institutes, which should be larger than that of firms with tech-activities.
Source: (CSSB and MOST, 1991, 1996, 2001, 2007).

raise most of their S&T funds by themselves. The ratio of S&T funds from government to total S&T funds was more than 14 percent in 1990, but the percentage dropped to 2.8 percent in 2000 and further decreased to 2.4 percent in 2006. In contrast, the ratio of self-raised funds by ICT firms to total S&T funds increased from 61 percent in 1990 to 88 percent in 2006 (Table 4.1). Apparently, the state is no longer interested in providing direct financial support to firms for technological innovation.

Despite the declining interest in the innovation-involved activities of ICT manufacturing firms, a disaggregate analysis of the sectoral composition of China's ICT manufacturing revealed that this developing economy has in recent years made significant progress toward increasing the sophistication of its ICT manufacturing. Table 4.2 lists the structural composition of the ICT manufacturing sector in terms of output value and profits for the year 2007. Three sub-sectors appeared to lead the way in the production of ICT goods, namely electronic computers, electronic components and telecoms equipment. These three sectors held nearly 70 percent of total output value and 65 percent of the total profits generated by the ICT industry. By contrast, manufacturing of household audio and video equipment, which used to dominate China's electronics industry, only accounted for less than 8 percent of the total output value and 5 percent of total profits of the industry. A similar pattern can be identified from the exports of ICT goods. Among all the ICT goods produced for export in 2007, the leading sector has been the production of electronic computers which accounted for 41 percent of the total value of exports. The second

Table 4.2. Output value and total profits of eight ICT manufacturing sub-sectors, 2007 (billion *yuan*).

ICT sub-sectors	Output value	Percent of total	Total profits	Percent of total
Telecoms equipment	884.22	17.88	26.74	15.52
Radar and related equipment	15.06	0.30	0.93	0.54
Broadcasting and television equipment	31.51	0.64	1.57	0.91
Electronic computers	**1628.58**	**32.94**	**45.23**	**26.24**
Household audio and video equipment	386.82	7.82	9.28	5.38
Electronic devices	586.71	11.87	21.37	12.40
Electronic components	909.2	18.39	41.56	24.12
Other electronic equipment	502.35	10.16	25.66	14.89
Total	4944.45	100	172.34	100

Source: MII, 2008.

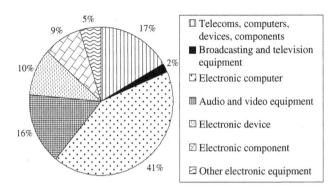

Figure 4.4.   China's ICT exports by sub-sectors, 2007.
Source: Calculated from MII (2008).

and third sectors were telecoms equipment (17 percent) and audio and video equipment (16 percent) (Fig. 4.4). This pattern suggests that China has started to produce and export more sophisticated ICT goods than the simple consumer electronics that had dominated its ICT manufacturing during the 1980s (Breidne, 2005; Naughton, 1997; Ning, 2009a).

Although China's ICT industrial capacity has experienced dramatic expansion, it has functioned primarily as a latecomer to technological advancement with a low level of innovation and a position at the lower end of the global value chain. Table 4.3 evaluates the economic and technological performance of China's ICT firms according to the sources of capital, namely domestic, Hong Kong–Taiwan–Macao, and foreign countries.[8] A quick glance at the data listed in Table 4.3 can easily identify the leading position held by foreign-funded enterprises which generated 60 percent of the total ICT manufacturing output, 72 percent of the exports of ICT goods,

---

[8]Domestic funded firms include state-owned enterprises (*guoyou qiye*), collectively run enterprises (*jiti qiye*), shareholding co-operative enterprises (*gufen hezuo qiye*), affiliated corporations (*lianying qiye*), companies with limited liability (*youxian zeren gongsi*), companies limited by shares (*gufen youxian gongsi*), private enterprises (*siying qiye*) and other domestic-funded enterprises. Hong Kong–Taiwan–Macao funded firms include joint ventures with Hong Kong–Taiwan–Macao (*gang-ao-tai hezi jingying qiye*), co-operative enterprises with Hong Kong–Taiwan–Macao (*gang-ao-tai hezuo jingying qiye*), wholly Hong Kong–Macao–Taiwan owned enterprises (*gang-ao-tai duzi qiye*), as well as companies limited by shares with Hong Kong–Taiwan–Macao capital (*gang-ao-tai touzi gufen youxian gongsi*). Foreign funded firms include sino-foreign joint ventures (*zhongwai hezi jingying qiye*), sino-foreign co-operative enterprises (*zhongwai hezuo jingying qiye*), wholly foreign owned enterprises (*waizi qiye*) and companies limited by shares with foreign capital (*waishang touzi gufen youxian gongsi*). See (CSSB, 2005b).

Table 4.3. Economic performance of China's ICT manufacturing firms by ownership, 2007.

	Domestic funded enterprises	HK, Taiwan and Macao funded enterprises	Foreign funded enterprises	Total
Output value (billion *yuan*)	1114	874	2956	4944
Percent	22	18	**60**	100
Value of export goods (billion *yuan*)	311	561	2231	3103
Percent	10	18	**72**	100
Profits (billion *yuan*)	46	31	95	172
Percent	27	18	**55**	100
Output value of new products (billion *yuan*)	350	158	503	1012
Percent	35	15	**50**	100
Labor productivity* (million *yuan*/person)	0.5	0.4	**0.9**	—
Capital profitability* (percent)	4.96	5.39	**6.40**	—

*Calculation based on the data of above-scale enterprises.
Source: Calculated from MII (2008).

55 percent of the total profits, and 50 percent of the output value of new products. Furthermore, the foreign-funded enterprises have achieved a much better economic performance with labor productivity almost twice that of the other two sources of investment and capital profitability ranking first among these three sources of capital. This pattern suggests that China's ICT manufacturing has been heavily reliant upon foreign capital.

This high degree of financial and technological dependence upon foreign sources has also been evident from the composition of ICT exports. Of the total output of ICT exports in 2007, the lion's share (70 percent) was held by goods processed with imported materials (MII, 2008). Another interesting point can be seen when the data listed in Table 4.3 are further scrutinized. The ICT manufacturing firms established by Hong Kong, Taiwan and Macao contributed only 15 percent of the total output value generated by new products, which is even lower than domestic firms (35 percent). Foreign-funded ICT firms held 50 percent of the total output value of new products, but this share was lower than their contributions in all other indicators. It suggests that the purpose for Hong Kong, Taiwan, Macao and foreign countries to set up ICT firms in the mainland was not so much the introduction of new products or technological innovation but instead the application of Western technology and manufacturing at a lower cost. As such, the technological advancement of China's ICT industry will have to be made through the mobilization of indigenous resources rather than counting on external support.

A detailed examination of the data obtained from the 2004 national economic census further revealed a severe reliance of China's ICT industry upon the advanced economies in terms of technologies and innovation. On average, domestic firms invested on average much less capital in innovation-involved activities than foreign-funded firms (CSSB, 2005a). The disregard of innovation-involved activities by domestic firms may have been the result of their limited capability to mobilize the necessary capital for innovation-related activities. While the foreign-funded firms predominately took the lead in every economic indicator of the ICT industry such as output value, exports and profits as identified above, they contributed only little to the localized technological activities and innovation since they preferred to import core technology and knowledge rather than conduct localized research and development. It is interesting to see that the foreign-funded firms spent much more money on technology import than domestic firms. Table 4.4 shows that foreign-funded firms spent nearly 73 percent of their total expenditure on technology import, in sharp contrast to the 11 percent of domestic enterprises. Furthermore, foreign-funded enterprises showed a strong inclination to co-operate with other enterprises in terms of S&T

Table 4.4.   Comparison of expenditure on S&T activities of above-scale enterprises by sources of investment, 2004.

Sources of investment	Domestic capital	HK, Macao and Taiwan capital	Foreign capital
Ratio of intramural expenditure to total	95.32%	95.36%	80.64%
Ratio of extramural expenditure to total	4.68%	4.64%	19.36%
Ratio of expenditure on co-operating with R&D institutes/universities to total extramural expenditure	24.66%	23.49%	0.40%
Ratio of expenditure on co-operating with other enterprises to total extramural expenditure	35.87%	64.19%	62.41%
Ratio of technological renovations	83.72%	65.25%	20.14%
Ratio of technology import	11.38%	30.62% •	72.70%
Ratio of absorption and digestion of technology	2.33%	1.00%	6.94%
Ratio of purchasing domestic technology	2.56%	3.12%	0.22%

Source: (CSSB, 2005a).

activities while domestic enterprises spent more money on in-house research and development. As shown in Table 4.4, foreign-funded enterprises spent nearly 20 percent of total S&T expenditure on external cooperation, in sharp contrast to only 5 percent for firms invested with domestic and HK, Macao and Taiwan capital. Meanwhile, domestic enterprises spent 84 percent of total expenditure on technological renovations, much higher than the 20 percent of foreign-funded enterprises. The universities and research institutes that are normally regarded as playing a significant role in creating cutting-edge knowledge and technology turned out to be invaluable for foreign-funded enterprises. This is not surprising because foreign-funded firms seldom conducted localized innovative activities in China and obtained their technology mainly through import. Around 62 percent of the extramural expenditure on S&T activities of foreign-funded enterprises mainly went to other enterprises while expenditure on R&D institutes or universities only accounted for 0.4 percent of the total extramural expenditure (Table 4.4).

Interestingly enough, the software sector presented a very different capital structure from that of the manufacturing sector. Domestic software enterprises kept ahead of their counterparts invested by foreign countries and Hong Kong, Macao and Taiwan through producing 67 percent of sales revenue and 71 percent of total profits with 73 percent of employment and 72 percent of total assets in 2007 (MII, 2008). Two reasons can be identified to explain the intriguing fact that the well-known technology-laggard indigenous software firms were able to take a leading position in China. On one hand, the boom in domestic software enterprises owed a lot to the determination of the central government to develop the national software industry and indigenous technological capability to narrow the gap in software technologies with developed countries. A significant and effective action taken by the central government for the growth of the software industry was the release of the "No. 18 Document" in June 2000 that covered a series of preferential policies, including investment and financial policies, taxation policies, export policies, revenue allocation, accreditation of software enterprises, etc. The plan was to enable domestically produced software products to satisfy most of the domestic market demand and to be exported in large quantities after 5 to 10 years' effort. Since then, the expansion of the indigenous software industry has taken place in selected regions. On the other hand, although foreign firms took a fancy to the potentially huge market in China, they were cautious to invest in China's software industry and to conduct substantive R&D activities due to the limited technological capability and extreme lack of highly qualified software talents as well as the protection of indigenous software firms by the government.

4.4. Spatial Distribution, Clustering and Technological Innovation

4.4.1. *Spatial agglomeration and economic and innovative performance*

Geographically, the growth of China's ICT industry has been characterized by an extreme regional variation and unevenness. The first national economic census conducted in 2004 made available some of the most interesting and valuable information on the location of ICT manufacturing activities not only at the provincial and municipal level but also on a finer scale by county and urban district. Judging by the employment location quotient, the ICT manufacturing sector was mainly clustered in five regions, Guangdong, Tianjin, Jiangsu, Shanghai and Fujian and the software firms concentrated in four regions, Beijing, Shanghai, Guangdong and Liaoning (Table 4.5). All of them are eastern coastal city-regions in advantageous locations with an abundance of highly qualified human resources and high levels of capital accumulation. Although the employment location quotient was as high as nearly nine, Beijing was not a favorite place for ICT manufacturing firms to locate. Guangdong and Shanghai were the only two city-regions where both manufacturing and software activities flourished. Figures 4.5 and 4.6 respectively mapped out the spatial distribution in the ICT manufacturing and service sectors.

At the county-city level, the unevenness of China's ICT industrial geography is even more striking. An analysis of the spatial distribution of output value (Fig. 4.7(a)), employment (Fig. 4.7(b)) and exports (Fig. 4.7(c)) has identified a consistent pattern in which three small areas of high concentration stand out to dominate China's ICT industrial landscape, namely the Shenzhen–Dongguan–Guangzhou corridor of the Pearl River Delta in the south, the Shanghai–Kunshan–Suzhou corridor of the lower Yangtze River Delta in the east, and the Beijing–Tianjin city-region on the North China Plain (Fig. 4.7). There were 2862 county-level units in China in the year 2004.[9] The output value and exports

---

[9]County-level units include counties, county-level cities and urban districts of prefecture-level and provincial-level cities. *Source*: http://www.xzqh.org/yange/2004.htm, accessed 15 August 2007.

Table 4.5.   Spatial distribution by the ICT manufacturing sector and the software sector, 2004.

Region	Manufacturing sector		Software sector	
	Employment	Location quotient	Employment	Location quotient
North				
Beijing	125,500	0.72	127,900	**8.86**
Tianjin	133,600	**1.60**	6,000	0.86
Hebei	3.29	0.15	4,600	0.25
Shanxi	12,900	0.09	2,500	0.21
Inner Mongolia	5,100	0.08	600	0.12
Shandong	179,800	0.41	10,100	0.28
Northeast				
Liaoning	85,100	0.43	18,300	**1.10**
Jilin	13,100	0.16	4,700	0.68
Heilongjiang	7,400	0.06	4,100	0.42
East				
Shanghai	271,000	**1.10**	65,700	**3.19**
Jiangsu	790,200	**1.60**	19,000	0.46
Zhejiang	287,300	0.69	28,900	0.83
Anhui	29,900	0.22	3,300	0.29
Central				
Jiangxi	31,500	0.32	2,600	0.32
Henan	24,200	0.09	6,300	0.29
Hubei	32,900	0.22	5,400	0.43
Hunan	30,100	0.19	10,400	0.81
Southeast				
Guangdong	2,082,900	**3.44**	58,300	**1.16**
Guangxi	12,100	0.15	2,400	1.94
Hainan	1,200	0.06	1,100	0.61
Fujian	172,400	**1.04**	8,300	0.60
Southwest				
Chongqing	10,800	0.11	3,800	0.47
Sichuan	98,800	0.51	7,900	0.49
Guizhou	13,900	0.26	800	0.18
Yunnan	1,900	0.03	2,700	0.44
Tibet	0	0	—	—
Northwest				
Shaanxi	74,900	0.77	7,400	0.92
Gansu	13,900	0.22	1,900	0.36
Qinghai	0	0	200	0.18
Ningxia	1,000	0.05	400	0.26
Xinjiang	0.25	0.06	1,300	0.39

Source: CSSB (2005a).

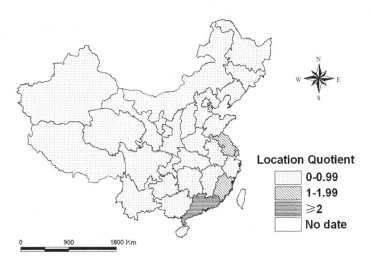

Figure 4.5.   Spatial distribution of the ICT manufacturing sector by employment in 2004.

Source: Calculated from data obtained from CSSB (2005a).

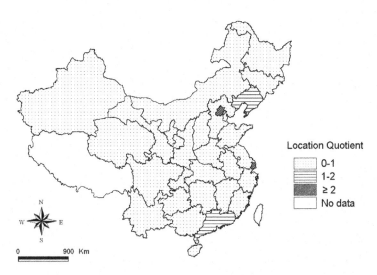

Figure 4.6.   Spatial distribution of the software sector by employment in 2004.

Source: Calculated from data obtained from CSSB (2005a).

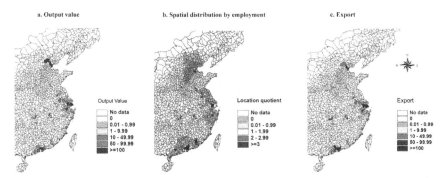

Figure 4.7.   Output value, employment and export of China's ICT manufacturing industry at the county level, 2004.

Note: Figure 4.7(a) is calculated on the basis of the average output value at county-level units which is equal to 0.79 billion RMB. The interval 1–9.99 in the legend means the values are 1–9.99 times larger than the county-level average. Figure 4.7(c) is measured on the basis of the average value of exports at the county-level units which is equal to 0.483 billion RMB. The interval 1–9.99 in the legend means the values are 1–9.99 times larger than the county-level average.

Source: Calculated from CSSB (2005a).

of ICT manufacturing generated in Tianjin, Shanghai, Suzhou, Dongguan and Shenzhen were more than 100 times larger than the national average. The extremely uneven geography of China's ICT industry unfolded here has simply presented a real case to contest the notion that "the world is flat" and reinforces the point highlighted in the latest *World Development Report 2009* concerning the unevenness of a "reshaping economic geography" in the globalizing world (Friedman, 2005; World Bank, 2009).

Is there any significant association between spatial agglomeration of ICT manufacturing activities and a better economic performance as conventional wisdom would expect? In the absence of detailed and comparable data for the software sector, Figs. 4.8 and 4.9 analyze the regional variation in labor productivity and capital profitability of China's ICT manufacturing at the provincial level.[10] As shown in Table 4.5, China's ICT manufacturing activities are highly concentrated in Guangdong Province whose location quotient was as high as 3.44. This was followed by Jiangsu

---

[10]The degree of spatial concentration is measured by location quotients calculated on the basis of employment. Labor productivity is defined as the output value generated per worker. Capital productivity is defined as total profits generated per dollar (RMB) of capital investment. Data are derived from the first national economic census conducted in 2004.

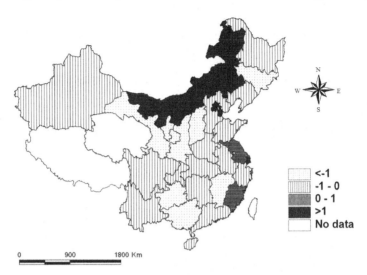

Figure 4.8.   Labor productivity of the ICT manufacturing sector, 2004 (measured by standard deviation).

Note: The interval 0–1 in the legend means the values are within 1 standard deviation of the mean.

Source: CSSB (2005a).

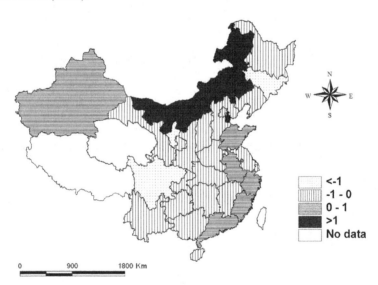

Figure 4.9.   Capital profitability of the ICT manufacturing sector, 2004 (measured by standard deviation).

Note: The interval 0–1 in the legend means the values are within 1 standard deviation of the mean.

Source: CSSB (2005a).

Province and Tianjin Special Municipality, both with an employment location quotient of 1.6. Interestingly enough, a high concentration of ICT manufacturing activities in Guangdong and Jiangsu does not lead to high labor productivity or capital profitability. As shown in Fig. 4.8, high labor productivity occurred in Beijing, Shanghai, Tianjin and Inner Mongolia, whereas labor productivity in Guangdong was actually below the national average. In a similar manner, high capital profitability was found in Tianjin and Inner Mongolia, but capital profitability of ICT manufacturing in Guangdong was not far above the national average. In general, there is a mismatch between spatial agglomeration of ICT manufacturing activities and economic performance: Guangdong Province, with a high degree of spatial concentration of the ICT industry, does not seem to perform well in terms of both labor productivity and capital profitability. By contrast, Inner Mongolia without any concentration of ICT production appeared to score highly in labor productivity and capital profitability.[11] In the case of China, it appears that spatial agglomeration may not necessarily lead to higher productivity or profitability, but high productivity and profitability can occur without spatial agglomeration.

The Pearson correlation analyses further illustrate there is no significant relationship between spatial agglomeration and economic performance measured by both capital profitability and labor productivity in the ICT manufacturing sector. Given that data on ICT enterprises were not available for Tibet and Qinghai, these two regions were excluded from the analyses. The Pearson correlation coefficients between location quotient and both capital profitability and labor productivity were low and insignificant (Table 4.6). This finding appears to contradict the normal theoretical expectation that agglomeration results in reduced transaction costs and therefore higher productivity.

Does spatial agglomeration bring about a better innovative performance as the prevailing theories would expect? The data from the national economic census provided no evidence of this relationship either. It is

---

[11]There are two main reasons for the high labor productivity and capital profitability found in Inner Mongolia. First, Inner Mongolia managed to attract several entrepreneurial and productive firms, such as TCL and Skyworth, whose output value accounted for over 90 percent of the total output generated by the region. These firms occupied the leading positions in the national market with great efficiency in production. Second, production costs (i.e. labor, land and utilities) were much lower here than elsewhere. For instance, the cost of electricity was half that in Guangdong and one-third of that in Beijing. Lower production costs have significantly contributed to a high profitability.

Table 4.6.   Pearson correlation results between location quotient and economic performance, 2004.

		Capital profitability	Labor productivity
Location quotient	Pearson correlation	0.146	0.346
	Sig. (2-tailed)	0.450	0.066
	Number of observations	29	29

Note: Tibet and Qinghai are not included here because of the lack of data.
Source: CSSB (2005a).

revealed that there was an extremely spatial variation in the innovative performance of China's ICT industry at the national level.[12] Judging by the number of granted invention patents, Beijing, Hubei, Guangxi where ICT manufacturing activities were not very active took the lead in the innovative performance while Guangdong, as the most agglomerated region, was not very innovative with its number of granted invention patents only slightly over the national average (Fig. 4.10). In a similar manner, Guangdong performed even worse than the national average in the output value of new products while several other eastern coastal areas such as Tianjin, Fujian and Shanghai showed better innovative performance (Fig. 4.11). This shows that the highest level of agglomeration does not necessarily lead to the highest innovative output. The Pearson correlation results further reveal that there exists no correlation between spatial agglomeration and technological innovation. As shown in Table 4.7, the correlation coefficients between location quotient and innovative performance measured by both new products and granted invention patents are rather low and insignificant.

4.4.2. *Localized linkages, knowledge exchange and technological innovation*

If the spatial agglomeration failed to bring about a better economic and innovative performance of ICT firms, then do the localized linkages and connections based on production and knowledge exchange contribute to the innovative performance of ICT firms? The data from the economic

---

[12]Innovative performance is measured by two indicators: the output value of new products and the number of inventive patent certifications. Data on output value of new products in 2004 are available for 25 administrative units; thus the analysis in this section is based on data from these units.

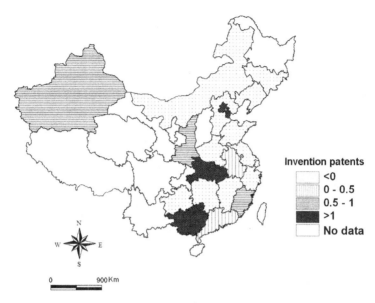

Figure 4.10. Spatial distribution by granted invention patents, 2004.
Source: AHSB (2005); BJSB (2005); CQSB (2005); CSSB (2005a); FJSB (2005); GDSB (2005); GXSB (2005); GZSB (2005); HEBSB (2005); HLJSB (2005); HANSB (2005); HENSB (2005); HUBSB (2005); HUNSB (2005); IMSB (2005); JLSB (2005); JSSB (2005); JXSB (2005); LNSB (2005); SDSB (2005); SSB (2005a); SAXSB (2005); SAAXSB (2005); TJSB (2005); XJSB (2005); YNSB (2005); ZJSB (2005).

census did not provide detailed information about inter-firm linkages and knowledge exchange, which had been completed by the data from the questionnaire survey conducted in Beijing, Shanghai, Suzhou, Shenzhen and Dongguan which have had the lion's share of total output value, exports and profits in China. The sampled firms were divided into two groups of innovative and non-innovative firms using the number of granted invention patents as a yardstick. Innovative firms were those that have been granted at least one invention patent. These two groups of firms were systematically compared in terms of their extent of production linkages and knowledge exchange with local firms to further examine whether localized linkages and exchange, or the industrial cluster, can lead to a better innovative performance. The results of the comparison are listed in Table 4.8.

Firms in the two groups reported different extents of localized production linkages as indicated in the different share of local purchases to domestic purchases, percentage of local customers, percentage of local contractors and local subcontractors. These differences are not, however,

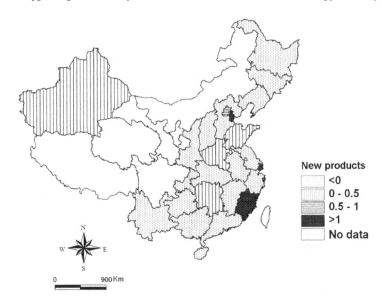

Figure 4.11.   Spatial distribution by the output value of new products, 2004.

Source: AHSB (2005); BJSB (2005); CQSB (2005); CSSB (2005a); FJSB (2005); GDSB (2005); GXSB (2005); GZSB (2005); HEBSB (2005); HLJSB (2005); HANSB (2005); HENSB (2005); HUBSB (2005); HUNSB (2005); IMSB (2005); JLSB (2005); JSSB (2005); JXSB (2005); LNSB (2005); SDSB (2005); SSB (2005a); SAXSB (2005); SAAXSB (2005); TJSB (2005); XJSB (2005); YNSB (2005); ZJSB (2005).

Table 4.7.   Pearson correlation results between location quotient and innovative output, 2004.

		Average output value of new products per enterprise	Average number of invention patent certifications per ten enterprises
Location quotient	Pearson correlation	0.390	0.086
	Sig. (2-tailed)	0.054	0.726
	Number of observations	25*	19#

*Inner Mongolia, Sichuan, Tibet, Gansu, Qinghai and Ningxia are not included because of the lack of data on output value of new products.
#Shanxi, Heilongjiang, Shanghai, Hainan, Chongqing, Sichuan, Guizhou, Yunnan, Tibet, Gansu, Qinghai, and Ningxia are excluded because data on the number of invention patent certifications is not available.
Source: CSSB (2005a).

statistically significant according to the results of the T-test. The only exception lies in the percentage of local subcontractors, in which the two groups of firms showed a difference that is statistically significant. Even here, the result of the comparison took us by surprise: non-innovative firms reported a percentage of local subcontractors higher than that for innovative firms. In fact, non-innovative firms reported an extent of local production linkages slightly higher than that for innovative firms in three of the four indicators (Table 4.8). This peculiar pattern suggested that

Table 4.8. T-test results of localized relations between innovators and non-innovators.

	Mean			
	Non-innovators	Innovators	T-value	P-value
Production linkages				
Share of local purchases *(2hrs) in domestic purchases	47.88%	45.14%	0.785	0.433
Percentage of local customers[1]	2.92	2.95	−0.281	0.779
Percentage of local subcontractors in 2*hrs	55.62%	43.58%	2.205*	0.030
Percentage of local contractors	60.72%	51.78%	1.412	0.160
Knowledge exchange[2]				
Importance of domestic alliance in technology development	0.69	1.22	−4.021**	0.000
Importance of domestic cooperation in technology development	0.79	1.49	−4.886**	0.000
Frequency of technology transfer from domestic firms	0.45	0.83	−5.018**	0.000
Frequency of technology advice from domestic firms	0.71	1.34	−5.436**	0.000
Frequency of personnel exchange with domestic firms	0.80	1.52	−5.567**	0.000
Frequency of information exchange with domestic firms	0.77	1.61	−5.971**	0.000

[1] Percentage of local customers is not measured by the actual percentage but by the ratio interval: 1 — 0%; 2 — 1–25%; 3 — 26–50%; 4 — 51–75%; 5 — 76–100%.
[2] The importance or frequency is ranked from 0 to 4, with 0 meaning no such linkages and 4 referring to most important or most frequent.
*The mean difference is at the 0.05 significance level.
**The mean difference is at the 0.01 significance level.
Source: Questionnaire survey.

the local production linkages built by these firms, or industrial clustering, had little to do with innovative activities and that innovative firms have managed to obtain their granted invention patents by other means than local production linkages.

If local production linkages cannot explain why some firms turned out to be more innovative than others, can one turn to the factor of knowledge exchange as a possible source of innovation? Here, the results of the comparison appear to be closer to normal theoretical expectation, but overall the evidence found looks rather weak. The overwhelming majority of the surveyed firms reported either the non-existence or unimportance of the formation of a partnership, cooperation and exchange with other local firms in the process of technological innovation. Nonetheless, innovative firms did show a higher frequency than the non-innovative firms in giving an "importance" response to the questions concerning knowledge exchange with other local firms (Table 4.8). Although an overwhelming majority of the firms, innovative or non-innovative, did not consider localized knowledge exchange to be important to their technological development, innovative firms appear to have a stronger desire and more positive attitude toward knowledge exchange than the non-innovative ones.

4.4.3. *Beyond clustering: Attributes, motivation and strategies of firms, state-firm strategic coordination and technological innovation*

If the industrial clustering did not seem to be significant enough to explain why some firms are more innovative than others, then what are the factors that really make a difference in the process of technological innovation for the Chinese ICT firms? Further probing into the responses to the questionnaires yielded some important insights into the special dynamism of technological innovation in the Chinese anomaly. Table 4.9 presents the internal characteristics of innovative and non-innovative firms. The analysis focuses on those attributes that are considered to be statistically significant according to the results of the T-test.

First, the regional setting appears to make a significant difference to the innovative performance of the firms. A Chi-square test confirmed that there exists a significant regional difference between innovative and non-innovative firms among these five city-regions, namely, Beijing, Shanghai, Suzhou, Shenzhen and Dongguan (Chi-square $= 68.456$, $p = 0.000$). Although there is little "local buzz" through which localized production

Table 4.9. *T*-test results of comprehensive strength and R&D strategies between innovators and non-innovators.

	Mean			
	Non-innovators	Innovators	*T*-value	*P*-value
Workers monthly income (*yuan*)	1611	2057	4.888**	0.000
R&D workers monthly income (*yuan*)	3621	4291	3.015**	0.003
Percent of R&D expenditure in total expenditure	13%	20%	4.012**	0.000
Share of R&D workers among total employees	12%	19%	2.747**	0.006
Share of professional managers among total employees	14.20%	18.21%	−2.877**	0.005
Share of marketing workers among total employees	7.61%	13.91%	−4.841**	0.000
Rank of market share of core products[#2]	2.6	2.1	4.934**	0.000
Product-based state-firm strategic coordination (measured by the government purchase as percent of total sales of the firm)	3.62%	12.98%	−3.963**	0.000

[#1]Profit is measured by several intervals: 1 — profit margin is larger than 10%, 2 — profit margin is ranged from 5–10%, 3 — profit margin ranged from 1–4%, 4 — profit margin is smaller than zero.
[#2]1 — top 5, 2 — top 6–10, 3 — below top 10.
**p-value is at 0.01 level.
Source: Questionnaire survey.

networks and knowledge spillover would supposedly bring about innovation for Chinese firms, a "local base" with a rich supply and accumulation of human resources, innovative cultural tradition, and institutional supports has clearly been conducive to technological innovation. Given the special nature of the Chinese political economy, the strategic position held by the region in the national economy and its coupling with the interests of the state have also been instrumental in the incubation and growth of innovative activities. Conversely, a regional setting taken to serve as an outlet of labor-intensive manufacturing in the global pipeline has proven to be detrimental to the pursuits of technological innovation (Sun, 2002b; Wei *et al.*, 2009; Zhou *et al.*, 2010).

Second, the pre-existing resources that the firms hold and the ability of the firms to mobilize capital, including venture capital and floating assets, stand out as other important factors explaining why some firms are more innovative than others. Of the two groups of firms, those with a better performance in innovation were able to mobilize capital and pay their workers, particularly R&D workers, a monthly salary significantly higher than what was paid by the non-innovative firms (Table 4.9). Given the fact that innovative activities are usually long-term and risky investments that may not bring about instant return, the pre-existing resources and the mobilization of venture capital has naturally been crucial to the pursuits of technological innovation.

Third, the strategies and determination of the firms to embark upon the long and risky journey of R&D has made, not surprisingly, a significant difference in bringing about innovation. A comparison of the two groups of firms suggested that those innovative firms have allocated a portion of capital and personnel to R&D activities significantly higher than what was committed by the non-innovative firms (Table 4.9). Moreover, innovative firms devoted a larger share of workers to marketing purposes and managed to occupy a larger share of the top tier of the national market for their core products. For instance, over 35 percent of the innovative firms were able to occupy the top five positions in the national market for their core products, whereas only 16 percent of the innovative firms were able to do the same thing. This pattern suggests that corporate strategies and managerial skills of the firms have obviously played a role no less important, if not more important, than such external forces as production linkages or knowledge spillover in the process of technological innovation.

Finally, state-firm strategic coordination has exerted a significant influence on the innovative performance of firms. Because of the lack of data and information on project-based and award-based state-firm strategic coordination, this chapter only examines product-based state-firm strategic coordination at the firm's level. As shown in Table 4.9, for innovative firms, the share of government purchase in their total sales (13 percent) has been significantly higher than that for the non-innovative firms (4 percent). As has been illustrated above, the ability to mobilize capital for innovation is an important pre-condition for firms to be innovative. In the case of China, capital mobilization of the firms has remained highly dependent upon the support of the central and local governments who controlled the banking sector. Given the risk-averse characteristics of firms, coupled with the financial constraints and other obstacles in the process of innovation, motivation of the firms for innovation may be depressed and their corporate strategies may not cover the innovation-related investment. The significant role that product-based strategic coordination plays lies not only in alleviating the pressure from financial constraints on the firms, but also in inspiring the motivation of innovation-related investment of firms through the process of strategic coordination with the state. It is therefore not surprising to see that those firms with a better product-based coordination with the central or local governments have done a better job in technological innovation.

4.5. Summary

China's ICT industry has experienced dramatic expansion in the recent decade as the country widened and deepened its integration into the global theatre. The accession of China to the World Trade Organization in 2001 has simply accelerated the insertion of the Chinese economy not just in the regional array of the "flying geese" but more broadly in the "global shift" of manufacturing activities in which the ICT industry has been a major part. Production capacity of the Chinese ICT industrial sector has rapidly augmented to occupy a leading position in the global economy. This chapter gives an overall assessment of China's ICT industry with special attention paid to the spatial agglomeration, clustering and inter-firm linkages as well as technological innovation. The growth of a high-tech industry like ICT has to a large extent been affected by national S&T policies and the evolution of China's innovation system. Through mobilizing the necessary resources for significant technological projects, China achieved some technological breakthroughs that set a solid foundation for the late technological development. However, because of a lack of a reasonable system to commercialize the valuable research results, the ICT industry did not develop during that period. It was not until the 1990s that the industry started to expand. The period from 2000 to 2004 witnessed a sharp increase in the start-ups of both ICT manufacturing and software enterprises. An analysis of the large- and medium-sized enterprises of the ICT manufacturing sector displays an increasing innovative performance during the period 1990–2006. However, the ratio of innovation input to total sales revenue presents a downtrend from 1990 to 2006, which is believed to be related to the declining proportion of S&T funds from government as part of the total S&T funds raised by enterprises and the increasing number of small- and medium-sized enterprises that are confronted with the difficulty of raising enough capital for R&D activities.

A close examination of the structural composition reveals an increasing sophistication of China's ICT manufacturing with dominant products from household audio and video equipment at the end of 1990s to the electronic computer at present. However, China's ICT industry is still stuck at the low-end of the global value chain and relies on foreign technology and investment. Foreign-funded enterprises accounted for the lion's share of ICT manufacturing output value, exports and total profits, but they obtained their technology mainly through import rather than from localized R&D activities. The leading position in sales revenue and total profits of domestic software enterprises owes a lot to the determination and efforts of the central government to develop an indigenous capability in the software industry.

In the meantime, the recent rapid growth of the ICT industry did not occur evenly across different regions of China. An analysis of the geographical distribution of the industry reveals that both the ICT manufacturing and software sectors have presented a strong tendency to concentrate along the eastern coast. A county-level spatial analysis further confirms the uneven geographical distribution showing that the ICT manufacturing sector is concentrated in a few cities or county-level units on the eastern coast, which have contributed a great deal of output value and exports to the whole country. Systematic analysis of the statistical data gathered at the national level has found no significant association between spatial agglomeration of ICT manufacturing activities and either a better economic performance in productivity or profitability or a better innovative performance. A further comparison of firms with different levels of innovation revealed no significant contribution made by localized production linkages and knowledge exchange to technological innovation. This is the result of both the special nature of the Chinese ICT industry at this historical moment and its position in the "global pipeline" of production and technological innovation. For an industry preoccupied by labor-intensive manufacturing and dominated by the processing of imported materials, a high concentration in the coastal region can hardly generate any high-value-added product that is knowledge-based and technology intensive. The low-end position held by China in the global as well as regional division of labor has also made it difficult for a spatial concentration of manufacturing activities to bring about any substantial improvement in labor productivity or capital profitability. The mismatch between spatial agglomeration of ICT manufacturing activities and better economic and innovative performance at the national level intrigued one to further explore the influential factors determining technological innovation by individual firms with data from a questionnaire survey. The attributes of the firms, such as their regional setting, ability to mobilize venture and floating capital and their management skills, and the motivation and strategies of the firms, as well as product-based state-firm strategic coordination, are found to be the significant factors that set apart innovative from non-innovative firms. It suggests that the attributes, motivation and strategies of active actors and agents, including not only the firms but also local states in a region as well as state-firm strategic coordination at both firm and regional levels are worth further exploration to understand the technological innovation.

The poor technological performance of the ICT firms in China suggests that most of the indigenous firms have remained "trapped" in the low-end position of the global value chain with a lack of interest to engage in the risky venture of technological innovation. For China to break the deadlock of technological dependency, stronger and more proactive initiatives will have to be made by both the central and local governments to stimulate, mobilize and coordinate individual firms to embark on the long, challenging and yet unavoidable journey of indigenous technological innovation. The next chapter will examine how the central and local governments can build a favorable institutional structure and market environment to stimulate and encourage firms' innovative activities and how a different degree of the state-firm strategic coordination can contribute to the divergent innovative performance of firms with a case study of Shanghai, one of the most innovative metropolises in China.

Chapter Five

STATE-FIRM STRATEGIC COORDINATION AND THE GROWTH OF THE INTEGRATED CIRCUIT DESIGN INDUSTRY IN SHANGHAI

5.1. Introduction

The analysis of the data at the national level in the last chapter has revealed that the dynamics of innovation is not so much embedded in the industrial cluster and inter-firm linkages but is closely related to the regional institutional environment, the motivation and strategies of firms that are determined by their attributes and resources, and state-firm strategic coordination. Innovation is full of uncertainty and is highly dependent upon long-term investment that can hardly be committed by a firm without necessary support from the state in current China. This chapter aims at investigating state-firm strategic coordination and uneven technological innovation in Shanghai, one of the most agglomerated and innovative city-regions of the ICT industry, with a special focus placed on the firm-level innovative performance of the integrated circuit (IC) design industry. The issues to be addressed essentially concern how various innovative performances of firms are related to the policies, strategies and selectivity of the central and municipal governments. How do the governments influence the growth, distribution and innovation of Shanghai's IC design sector? How does the Shanghai municipal government forge its S&T environment and boost the innovation-related activities of firms? How do individual firms respond to the local environment and national/local industrial policies and selectivity? What is the relationship between state-firm strategic coordination and uneven technological innovation?

Shanghai, one of the largest and most innovative city-regions in China, has played a strategic role in the growth of the national economy and technological innovation. With only 0.1 percent of land resources, the city-region contributed 4.9 percent of GDP and 14.2 percent of fiscal revenue to the national economy at the end of 2007 (CSSB, 2008). The R&D expenditure in Shanghai accounted for 8.4 percent of the total expenditure in the country (SSB, 2008). With one-third of China's IC design firms, Shanghai offered a significant theoretical and methodological lens to examine the growth and innovative capability of IC design firms in one of the largest and rapidly growing national economies in the globalizing world.

The chapter is organized in five sections. It begins with an examination of the growth, distribution and innovation of the IC design sector in Shanghai. This is then followed by a narrative documentation to shed light on the strategies and selectivity of the central and local governments to improve technological innovation in Shanghai. The third part focuses on the explanation of the different responses of firms to changing state policies and selectivity, the different motivations of firms to innovation-related investment, and the process of state-firm strategic coordination. A case study was undertaken to further understand how state-firm strategic coordination took place and how this coordination affected the motives of innovation-involved activities and the innovative performances of the firms. Important research findings are summarized and their theoretical and practical implications discussed in the last section.

5.2. Growth, Distribution and Innovation of the IC Design Industry in Shanghai

The IC design sector in China in general, and in Shanghai in particular, has experienced significant growth since 2000. There were only 24 IC design establishments in Shanghai in the year 2000 but it roared up to 100 within two years with a growth rate of 192 percent in 2001 and 43 percent in 2002. After 2003, the number of IC design firms maintained a stable growth with a growth rate of over 10 percent each year, much higher than the growth for China as a whole (Fig. 5.1). The sales revenue of the IC design industry also dramatically expanded during the period 2000–2007 in Shanghai. As shown in Fig. 5.2, the sales revenue in the year 2007 was 17 times larger than that in 2000. The growth rate for the year 2002 reached the highest level at 80 percent. After 2005, the growth rate still remained at a high level of 50 percent.

The rapid growth of Shanghai's IC design sector has not taken place evenly across different districts of Shanghai. There were 19 districts in Shanghai in 2007 and approximately 80 percent of IC design firms were

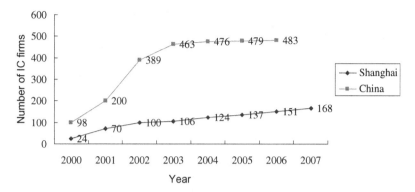

Figure 5.1.   Growth of the IC design industry in Shanghai and China, 2000–2007.
Source: SMIC and SICA (2008, p. 60); Zhao (2002a, p. 4; 2002b, p. 2; 2003, p. 21; 2004, p. 2; 2005, p. 49); Zhou (2007, p. 13).

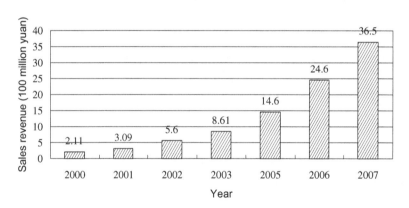

Figure 5.2.   Sales revenue of the IC design industry in Shanghai, 2000–2007.

Note: Data of the year 2000 and 2001 is the output value rather than the sales revenue.
Source: SICA (2006, p. 8); SMIC and SICA (2008, p. 56); Zhao (2002a, p. 4; 2003, p. 21; 2004, p. 4).

located in Pudong New Area and Xuhui District (Fig. 5.3). Pudong New Area hosting more than 50 percent of Shanghai's IC design firms had become the most clustered area. It was followed by Xuhui District which has attracted 26 percent of Shanghai's IC design firms. A close scrutiny has revealed that most of the IC design firms in Pudong and Xuhui were agglomerated in two important national level high-tech parks, namely Zhangjiang High-tech Park in Pudong and Caohejing High-tech Park in Xuhui.

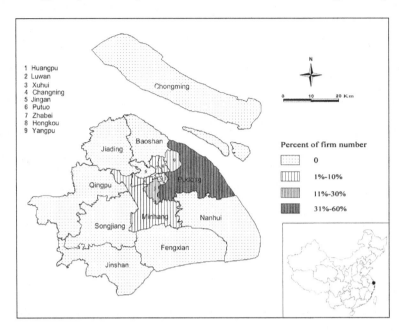

Figure 5.3.   Spatial distribution of the IC design firms in Shanghai, 2007.

Source: Organized and calculated from (SMIC and SICA, 2008), online database established by Shanghai Silicon Intellectual Property Exchange (SSIPEX) and websites of firms.[1]

Zhangjiang High-tech Park has committed itself to establishing an IC industrial center with the most intact value chain of the IC industry in China since the foundation of Hua Hong NEC Electronics Company Limited and Hua Hong Integrated Circuit Co. Ltd., two major products of the National Project 909.[2] The strategy to "focus on Zhangjiang", implemented

---

[1]There are 164 IC design firms in Shanghai with 131 of them focusing on the fabless (fabrication-less) business model, excluding three non-profit organizations and one fabless firm that had closed down in April 2008. However, this map was made on the basis of 100 firms who focus on the fabless business model. Information on 63 IC fabless firms was found in the report edited by SMIC and SICA (2008) while the information about the remaining 37 was obtained from the online database established by SSIPEX.
[2]The Project 909 is initiated by the central government with an intention to establish the national IC industry to narrow the gap between China and advanced countries in the IC field. It is documented that the Project 909 has obtained the largest-scale investment from governments in the history of the development of the electronics industry in China (Hu, 2006). This project gave birth to Hua Hong NEC Electronics Company Limited and Hua Hong Integrated Circuit Co. Ltd. at the end of the 1990s that were demonstrated to play a significant role in the growth of China's IC industry.

by the Shanghai municipal government in 1999, further accelerated the growth of Zhangjiang's IC industry. Attracted by the favorable industrial environment, Semiconductor Manufacturing International Corporation, now a well-known IC manufacturer in the world, chose Zhangjiang High-tech (Industrial) Park to establish its 8-inch wafer fab (wafer fabrication) in August 2000 with a total investment of 1.48 billion U.S. dollars (Hu, 2006, p. 115). Meanwhile, Grace Semiconductor Manufacturing Corporation invested 1.63 billion U.S. dollar to build up its wafer fab in Zhangjiang in November 2000 (Hu, 2006, p. 115). While the existence of the IC fabrication plants has attracted many IC design firms to locate nearby, the "incubator" center that was built up by the municipal government to a larger extent reduced the costs of the small start-ups through providing a series of public services and offering office space with extremely low rents. The IC industry as a whole in Zhangjiang High-tech Park produced 41.7 percent of output value and its IC design sector alone contributed 68.3 percent of output value to Shanghai in 2006 (Zhangjiang, 2007). By the end of 2007, the sales revenue of the IC industry in Zhangjiang accounted for 59 percent of that of Shanghai (Wang, 2008, p. 22).

In a similar manner, Caohejing High-tech Park in Xuhui District was initially established to bring together Shanghai's research and production capabilities to develop the semiconductor industry in response to the call of the central government to build China's Silicon Valley (Simon and Rehn, 1988). The investment in this project reached 100 million RMB with 80 percent of the investment coming from the Shanghai municipal government and the other 20 percent from the central government in 1984 (Simon and Rehn, 1988). The financial support from both the central and local governments as well as the clustering effect explained the fact that around 26 percent of Shanghai's IC design firms are located in Xuhui District.

A close scrutiny revealed that most of the IC design firms were founded after 2001 each with a payroll of less than 100 (Figs. 5.4 and 5.5). Nevertheless, the technological innovation of Shanghai's IC industry has reached a high level in recent years. Shanghai has accounted for approximately 20 percent of the total granted patents in China since 2004 and this percentage climbed to its peak in 2007 with a contribution of 22 percent (Fig. 5.6). It is well known that the invention patent is much more valuable than the utility model patent and design patent. Therefore, it is necessary to examine the internal structure of the types of granted patents in the IC industry. As shown in Table 5.1, IC firms in Shanghai held many more invention patents than utility model patents and the ratio of invention patents slightly

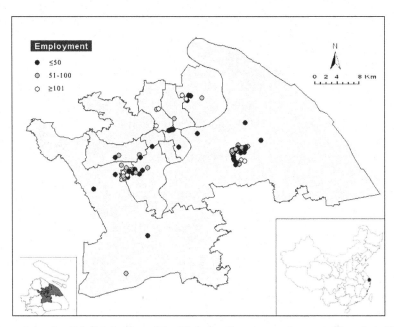

Figure 5.4.   Spatial distribution of the IC design firms by employment, Shanghai, 2007.

Note: Information on 13 IC design firms is not available. However, they are included in the group with a payroll smaller than 50, considering that IC design firms that do not have their own website tend to be very small (usually under 10 people).

Source: Authors' collection from the internal report, Internet and interviews.

increased in 2007 when the ratio for the whole nation dropped around 15 percent.

A comparison between fab-less firms in Shanghai and Shenzhen revealed a much better innovative performance in the former (Table 5.2).[3] Approximately 74 percent of IC design firms in Shenzhen were not interested in patent application, a much higher number compared to 55 percent in Shanghai at the end of 2007. As such, around 91 percent of firms in Shenzhen failed to achieve any granted invention patents compared to 80 percent in Shanghai. A T-test analysis further revealed a significantly better innovative performance in Shanghai than in Shenzhen measured by both the invention patent application ($t = 1.993$, $p = 0.047$) and the granted invention patents ($t = 1.669$, $p = 0.096$).

---

[3]Fab generally refers to the fabrication plant where IC is manufactured, while fabless refers to the firm which solely researches and designs the IC but outsources its production to a third-party.

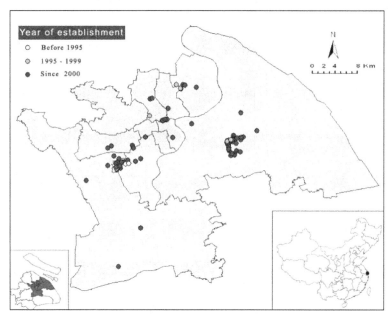

Figure 5.5.   Spatial distribution of IC design firms by foundation year, Shanghai, 2007.

Note: There are eight IC design firms missing in the figure because the information concerning the year of their establishment is not available.

Source: Authors' collection from the internal report, Internet and interviews.

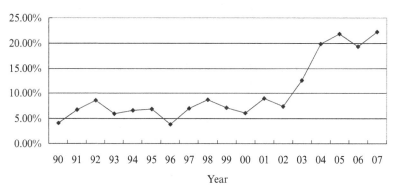

Figure 5.6.   Shanghai's share of granted patents in the IC industry in China, 1990–2007.

Source: SMIC and SICA (2008, p. 130).

Table 5.1.   Comparison of different types of granted patents in Shanghai and China.

	2006		2007	
Year	China	Shanghai	China	Shanghai
Invention	1903	435	1226	434
Utility model	1003	126	1191	105
Ratio of invention to total patents	65.49%	77.54%	50.72%	80.52%

Note: This table only compares the invention patents to utility model patents because the IC industry seldom or never is involved in the design patent.
Source: Organized and calculated from (SMIC and SICA, 2008, p. 132).

Table 5.2.   Difference in firm-level technological innovation measured by invention patent application and certification in Shanghai and Shenzhen, 2007.

	Percentage of firms with patent applications		Percentage of firms with patent certifications	
No. of invention patents	Shenzhen	Shanghai	Shenzhen	Shanghai
0	73.5	55	90.6	80
1–10	20.6	28	7.7	16
11–20	3.6	9	0	2
21–30	0.9	3	1.7	2
31–40	0	2	0	0
41–50	0.9	1	0	0
50–100	0.9	1	0	0
100–200	0	1	0	0
Total	100	100	100	100

Source: Organized and calculated from the data of online database established by Shanghai Silicon Intellectual Property Exchange (SSIPEX).

Although IC design firms in Shanghai as a whole have achieved a great innovative performance, there exists a significant difference in the degree of technological innovation at the firm level. Among the surveyed 100 IC fabless firms in Shanghai, there were 55 percent of firms who did not apply for any invention patent, while the most innovative firm had applied for 155 invention patents at the end of 2007 (Table 5.2). Around 25 percent of the firms that applied for the protection of their innovative results failed to obtain an official certification, which results in 80 percent of firms without any granted invention patents at all. The number of granted invention patents held by the firms varied from 1 to 25.

5.3. State-Firm Strategic Coordination and Uneven Technological Innovation in Shanghai

5.3.1. *Strategies and selectivity of the central government*

The rapid growth and better innovative capability of Shanghai's IC design sector owed a lot to the strategies and selectivity of the central government. Given the strategic role played by the IC industry in the national economy, the central government has since the 1970s taken initiatives to establish its own IC industry in order to reduce its reliance on Western countries. The central government has released general policies to stimulate the growth of the whole industry and at the same time selected certain potential firms and founded several firms to facilitate the process of technological innovation. A historical examination of the efforts made by the central government to improve the technological capability of China's IC industry is necessary to understand the strategies and selectivity of the state.

China imported 24 wafer semiconductor lines from the U.S. at the end of the 1970s. However, this move failed to achieve its goal of establishing an indigenous IC industry due to inadequate capital investment and a limited technological capability to absorb the imported technologies (Hu, 2006). An important effort made by the central government in the mid-1980s was to launch the national 908 Project. In its Eighth Five-Year Plan, China decided to invest a great deal of capital to build up a 6-inch wafer fabrication with 0.8–1 μm node technology and a monthly capacity of 10 thousands wafers of integrated circuits in order to keep pace with the world's IC industry (Hu, 2006, p. 5). Unfortunately, the low level of technology and inefficient management, as well as bureaucracy, together led to a huge deficit and failure (Pecht, 2006). Despite the establishment of four semiconductor companies, namely Huajing, Shougang-NEC, Shanghai Belling and Shanghai Philips, China's IC industry remained lagging behind advanced countries and the national IC output was far from meeting domestic demands (Hu, 2006). Around 85 percent of integrated circuits had to be imported. It was estimated that there was a technology gap of at least three generations between China and advanced countries in the IC industry at the end of the Eighth Five-Year Plan in 1995 (Hu, 2006, p. 4; Pecht, 2006, p. 94). China generated a mere 0.3 percent of the IC output of the world, took 0.2 percent of the world market and occupied less than 15 percent of the domestic market in 1994 (Hu, 2006, p. 10). The IC manufacturing capacity of the whole of mainland China was one-third that of a semiconductor company in Taiwan (Hu, 2006, p. 10).

The slow growth of the IC industry impeded the growth and technological development of the whole ICT industry. Although China became a world manufacturing center for TV sets with an annual capacity of 100 million *yuan*, the most valuable chip was imported, which led to a very thin profit margin and weak negotiating power for Chinese TV manufacturers in the world market. For years, Western countries blocked advanced technology from China and the technology level of semiconductor equipment that was permitted to be exported to China was at least two generations behind the internationally advanced level (Hu, 2006, p. 37). With the outbreak of the Gulf War, Chinese leaders increasingly recognized that China would be stuck at the lowest end of electronic assembly and processing for ever if China did not take serious actions to push the technological development of its IC industry (Hu, 2006, p. 10). In these circumstances, China decided to launch the national Project 909 aiming at building an 8-inch wafer fab with 0.5 μm node technology in December 1995. Project 909 was executed under the direct leadership of the CCP Central Committee and the State Council. The scale of capital investment in Project 909 was over 10 billion *yuan*, which is the largest in the history of China's investment in its electronics industry (Hu, 2006, p. 6). The amount of investment was also larger than the sum of all investments in microelectronics-related projects since 1949 (Hu, 2006, p. 6).

Shanghai has contributed to Project 909 which laid a good foundation for the growth of China's IC design sector. The Pudong New Area of Shanghai was identified as the preferred site of the 8-inch wafer fab by the then Vice-Premier Zhu Rongji (Hu, 2006, p. 5). One of the most important reasons for the central government to select Shanghai as the site of Project 909 was that Shanghai had become a center for the fabrication of semiconductors at that time. It was reported that Shanghai generated more than 50 percent of the output of integrated circuits in the whole country by the end of 1995 (Pecht, 2006, p. 94). It was also revealed that Shanghai started its R&D efforts in IC technology in 1964, even earlier than that of the central government (Simon and Rehn, 1988, p. 91). The Shanghai municipal government contributed 40 percent of the registered capital of Project 909 with a capital investment of 4 billion RMB (Hu, 2006). The national Project 909 has exerted a significant influence on the IC design sector. It gave birth to several firms who have remained in a long-term relationship with the central government and have shown an interest in technological innovation.

5.3.2. Institutional environment as well as strategies and selectivity of local governments

The innovative performance of Shanghai's IC design sector cannot be explained in a regional institutional vacuum. Decentralized decision-making in recent years has given local governments greater freedom and resulted in fiercer competition among regions (Lin, 2002). One of the strategies that the Shanghai municipal government has adopted to sustain its competitive advantages is to improve the local S&T environment. A regional comparison revealed that Shanghai built up a favorable S&T environment for its enterprises. According to *China's Statistical Yearbook on Science and Technology* (CSSB and MOST, 2007), there were 137 independent research institutes and 60 institutes of higher education as well as 234 R&D institutions that were affiliated to these higher-education institutes in Shanghai in 2006. These institutes not only nurtured a large number of talents but also significantly improved the local technological capability. The S&T personnel in these institutions have accounted for 2.5 percent of the total personnel in Shanghai. This ratio is much higher than that of other regions in China (Table 5.3). Meanwhile, the technology transaction in Shanghai has been active. There were 28,102 technology contract agreements that were signed in Shanghai in 2006 and the contracted value reached 310 million RMB, much higher than in other regions and next only to Beijing (Table 5.3).

Moreover, the Shanghai municipal government invested large capital to develop its science and technology. As shown in Fig. 5.7, the ratio of local government expenditure on science and technology to total government expenditure in Shanghai was increasing during the period 2001–2006. Although this ratio was lower than that of China prior to 2005, the growth rate of government expenditure on science and technology in Shanghai has been above the national level from 2001 to 2006. Shanghai has, since 2005, exceeded China as a whole in the ratio of government expenditure on science and technology to total government expenditure and this ratio in Shanghai further climbed to over 5 percent in 2006.

Innovation funds, established mainly by the municipal governments to encourage local innovation-related activities of firms, have a significantly

Table 5.3.   Major indicators of S&T environment in China by provinces, 2006.

Region	Ratio of personnel engaged in S&T activities in research institutes/universities to total employment (percent)	Value of technology contract agreements (100 million *yuan*)
Beijing	3.44	697.33
Tianjin	1.16	58.86
Hebei	0.49	15.61
Shanxi	0.69	5.92
Inner Mongolia	0.44	10.71
Liaoning	1.00	80.65
Jilin	1.22	15.37
Heilongjiang	0.68	15.69
Shanghai	**2.46**	**309.51**
Jiangsu	1.00	68.83
Zhejiang	0.59	39.96
Anhui	0.73	18.49
Fujian	0.35	11.32
Jiangxi	0.73	9.31
Shandong	0.48	23.20
Henan	0.40	23.73
Hubei	0.95	44.44
Hunan	0.66	45.53
Guangdong	0.45	107.03
Guangxi	0.88	0.94
Hainan	0.40	0.85
Chongqing	0.88	55.35
Sichuan	1.17	25.93
Guizhou	0.42	0.54
Yunnan	0.74	8.27
Tibet	1.14	—
Shaanxi	1.70	17.95
Gansu	0.72	21.45
Qinghai	0.61	2.47
Ningxia	0.54	0.53
Xinjiang	0.37	7.61
National average	0.89	58.11

Source: Calculated from data obtained from CSSB (2007); CSSB and MOST (2007).

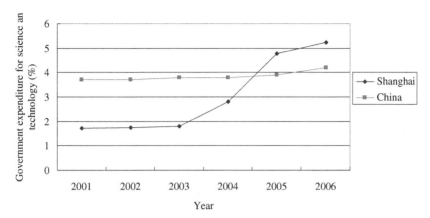

Figure 5.7. Government expenditure on science and technology in total in Shanghai and China, 2001–2006.

Source: CSSB (2007); CSSB and MOST (2007).

positive influence on the innovative performance of firms.[4] Table 5.4 shows significant correlations between innovation funds and the innovative performances of industrial firms measured by both the ratio of output value of new products to total industrial output and the average output value of new products per industrial firms created. In view of the importance of capital in innovation-related activities of firms, the Shanghai municipal government has laid much emphasis on the establishment of innovation funds since the 1980s. The ratio of innovation funds to total government expenditure in Shanghai had remained over 15 percent during the 1980s and it surpassed 27 percent in 1988. In spite of the slight decline of this ratio in recent years, it has been much higher than that of China as whole from 1995 to 2006. As shown in Fig. 5.8, this ratio in Shanghai has remained above 10 percent during the period 1995–2000 and it ascended to 14 percent after 2000. In contrast, the ratio for China has been decreasing during the period 1995–2006 and it has been lower than

---

[4]Innovation funds of the enterprises are one of the items of government expenditure. Innovation funds of the enterprises refer to "the funds appropriated from the government budget for the enterprises to tap latent power, upgrade the technology and carry out innovation, including the innovation fund of the departments, loans for enterprises for innovation, subsidies for the innovation of a small fertilizer plant, small cement plant, small coal mines, small machinery plants and small steel plants, the expenditure of interest on the loan for innovation" (CSSB, 2006, p. 304).

Table 5.4.   Pearson correlation results between innovation funds and innovative performance of large- and medium-sized industrial enterprises, 2006.

		Ratio of output value of new products to total industrial output value	Output value of new products per firms created
Ratio of innovation funds to total government expenditure	Pearson correlation	0.441*	0.563**
	Sig. (2-tailed)	0.015	0.001
	No. of observations	30#	30#

*Correlation is significant at the 0.05 level (2-tailed).
**Correlation is significant at the 0.01 level (2-tailed).
#Data on Tibet is not available in this table.
Note: Large- and medium-sized industrial enterprises refer to industrial firms whose employment is equal to or larger than 300 persons, annual sales revenue is equal to or larger than five million *yuan* and total capital assets are equal to or larger than 40 million *yuan*. Available at: http://www.stats-sh.gov.cn/2004shtj/tjzd/tjbz/gjbz/gjbz2.htm, accessed 10 August 2008.
Source: Calculated from data obtained from CSSB (2007); CSSB and MOST (2007).

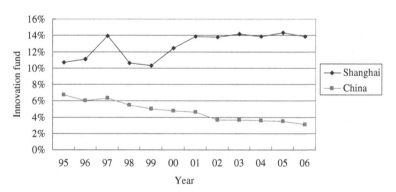

Figure 5.8.   Ratio of innovation funds to total government financial expenditure in Shanghai and China, 1995–2006.
Source: Calculated from CSSB (1991–2008); SSB (2007).

4 percent since the year 2002. Also, the ratio of innovation funds to local government expenditure in Shanghai was 14 percent in 2006, 3.5 times higher than that of Beijing and much higher than the rest of the country (Fig. 5.9).

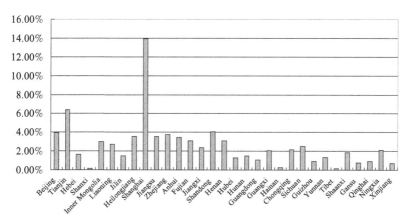

Figure 5.9. Ratio of innovation funds to total government financial expenditure by province, 2006.

Source: Calculated from data obtained from CSSB (2007).

However, the great capital support from the Shanghai municipal government did not go evenly to every firm in Shanghai. The municipal government appeared to have a strong inclination to give the priority and preference to certain sectors. Much of the government funds were directed to the industrial sectors of Manufacture of Communication Equipment, Computers and Other Electronic Equipment, within which each above-scale enterprise obtained an average 281,700 *yuan* from the government for its S&T activities.[5] Firms in this sector showed a higher interest in R&D activities and a better innovative performance than those in other sectors, indicating that the capital support of the municipal government for the S&T activities of firms is beneficial to stimulating R&D investment and improving the innovative performance of industrial firms (Table 5.5).

5.3.3. *Industrial policies and IC design developments in Shanghai*

The historical foundation established by the central government and the Shanghai municipal government have provided a favorable external environment for the firms in Shanghai while the rapid growth of Shanghai's

---

[5] "Above-scale" includes all state-owned enterprises and non-state-owned enterprises with annual product sales revenue equal to or larger than five million *yuan*. Available at: http://www.stats.gov.cn/was40/gjtjj_detail.jsp?searchword=%B9%E6%C4%A3%D2% D4%C9%CF&channelid=18938&record=70, accessed 10 August 2007.

Table 5.5.   Government financial support, R&D expenditure and innovation of enterprises in Shanghai by sectors, 2006 (10,000 *yuan*).

Sector	Government funds for S&T activities per industrial enterprise	R&D expenditure per enterprise	Output value of new products per enterprise
Processing of Food from Agricultural Products	1.22	9.59	117.12
Manufacture of Foods	0.22	17.68	352.45
Manufacture of Beverages	—	30.29	213.93
Manufacture of Tobacco	—	3142.15	114017.45
Manufacture of Textiles	0.44	8.42	171.18
Manufacture of Textile Wearing Apparel, Footwear and Caps	—	0.61	57.65
Manufacture of Leather, Fur, Feather and Related Products	—	—	—
Processing of Timber, Manufacture of Wood, Bamboo, Rattan, Palm and Straw Products	0.12	1.66	35.45
Manufacture of Furniture	—	59.40	1822.07
Manufacture of Paper and Paper Products	—	1.69	84.12
Printing, Reproduction of Recording Media	0.17	9.66	396.55
Manufacture of Articles for Culture, Education and Sport Activities	—	6.07	88.13
Processing of Petroleum, Coking, Processing of Nuclear Fuel	11.35	204.00	26601.21
Manufacture of Raw Chemical Materials and Chemical Products	2.08	54.01	1210.73
Manufacture of Medicines	12.45	452.65	2178.60
Manufacture of Chemical Fibers	0.27	5.55	51.71
Manufacture of Rubber	0.40	80.89	927.26
Manufacture of Plastics	0.39	8.00	186.46
Manufacture of Non-Metallic Mineral Products	0.81	15.19	273.77
Smelting and Pressing of Ferrous Metals	14.08	706.69	18991.48
Smelting and Pressing of Non-Ferrous Metals	0.37	5.10	620.66
Manufacture of Metal Products	0.04	4.64	185.06
Manufacture of General Purpose Machinery	5.32	133.27	2674.75
Manufacture of Special Purpose Machinery	3.03	58.55	877.68
Manufacture of Transport Equipment	58.77	578.15	15165.88

(*Continued*)

Table 5.5. (*Continued*)

Sector	Government funds for S&T activities per industrial enterprise	R&D expenditure per enterprise	Output value of new products per enterprise
Manufacture of Electrical Machinery and Equipment	3.10	63.38	1720.73
Manufacture of Communication Equipment, Computers and other Electronic Equipment	**28.17**	456.00	21720.91
Manufacture of Measuring Instruments and Machinery for Cultural Activities and Office Work	7.19	74.37	1845.08
Manufacture of Artwork and other Manufacturing	—	2.69	49.69
Recycling and Disposal of Waste	—	—	—

Note: — data not available
Source: Calculated from data obtained from SSB (2007).

IC design sector has been triggered, to a large extent, by two new state policies. The 18th Document of Policies about Encouraging the Development of Software and Integrated Circuit Industries (*guli ruanjian chanye he jicheng dianlu chanye fazhan ruogan zhengce*) represented an important effort made by the State Council in the middle of 2000 to facilitate the development of China's IC design sector. In this document, the central government encouraged IC firms through the provision of direct and indirect capital support. The state allocated significant budgeted capital construction funds to infrastructure and industrialization projects in the IC industry and established venture capital (VC) mechanisms to encourage investment in the IC industry in the period of the Tenth Five-Year Plan (FYP). Moreover, newly established IC design firms were exempted from income tax in the first and second years and allowed a 50 percent reduction in the third to fifth years. The value-added tax for IC design firms was 3 percent and redundant value-added tax (the legal value-added tax was 17 percent) would be refunded before the year 2010. IC design firms may list the entire amount of their actual personnel remuneration and training expenses as a before-tax expense for enterprise income tax purposes. In addition to raising funds and giving preferential tax exemption for the IC design sector, the rest of the document also released a series of policies with regard to industry technology, exports, income distribution, attraction and cultivation of human talents and government procurement to comprehensively improve the IC design industry.[6] Since 2000, the IC industry has continued to be a top priority for the national Tenth FYP (2001–2005) and the Eleventh FYP (2006–2010). The IC industrial park in Shanghai has received special attention from the state since the Eleventh Five-Year Special Planning of the Integrated Circuit Industry.[7]

The Shanghai municipal government released the Document of Regulation for Encouraging the Development of Software and Integrated Circuit Industries in Shanghai (*guanyu benshi guli ruanjian chanye he jicheng dianlu chanye fazhan ruogan zhengce guiding*) at the end of 2000, right after the release of the national 18th Document.[8] Following the spirit of the 18th Document of the State Council, this document allocated 500 million RMB as special funds to develop the infrastructure, initiate key projects as well as facilitate the industrialization of S&T achievements for the IC design industry in Shanghai. At the same time, the Science and

---

[6]See the 18th Document of the State Council "*guli ruanjian chanye he jicheng dianlu chanye fazhan ruogan zhengce*". Available at: http://www.miit.gov.cn/art/2008/05/24/art_4182_45493.html, accessed on 9 October 2008.

[7]Major projects to strengthen China's IC design and fabrication capabilities in the Tenth FYP included: (1) establishing national IC R&D centers to develop high-volume IC production technology and system-level integrated circuits under joint investment by the governments and firms; (2) selecting 5–10 complete-system enterprises to establish computer-aided design companies with annual revenue over 100 million RMB; (3) establishing two to three 6-inch IC production lines, three to five 8-inch IC production lines with 0.18–0.35 technology, and one to two 12-inch lines with 0.18–0.13 μm technology. The key tasks to develop the IC industry in the Eleventh FYP included: (1) establishing the platform of IC public service to offer a better environment for developing and testing IC products of small–medium IC design firms; (2) developing the wide-application ICs and facilitating the cooperation between IC design firms and the complete-system vendors; (3) upgrading the technology level of Project 909; (4) establishing more than five 12-inch fabrication lines with 90 nm node technology and ten 8-inch production lines with 0.13–0.11 μm node technology; (5) strongly supporting the national IC industrial parks in Beijing, Tianjin, Shanghai, Suzhou, Ningbo and so on. The Tenth Five-Year Special Planning of the Integrated Circuit Industry can be retrieved from http://www.chinawenni.com/3ne/news01.htm, accessed on 5 October 2008. See also (Pecht, 2006, p. 94). The Eleventh Five-Year Special Planning of the Integrated Circuit Industry is available at http://www.miit.gov.cn/art/2008/01/08/art_4199_48819.html, accessed 5 October 2008.

[8]The Document released by the Shanghai municipal government is available at http://www.shanghaiit.gov.cn/shxxw/zcfg/xxcy/userobject1ai32209.html, accessed 5 October 2008.

Technology Commission of the Shanghai Municipality allocated special funds to establish an IP database and an IC design platform so as to provide a series of services for IC design firms, including EDA software and testing services, etc. In order to encourage technological innovation of IC design firms, the document stated that technical staff would be exempted from individual income tax if they could develop the product with their own intellectual property. A special organization, the Shanghai Integrated Circuit Design Industrial Center, was established in 2000 by the former Ministry of Science and Technology and the Shanghai municipal government to nurture the IC design industry in China. The Shanghai municipal government initially invested 12 million RMB in the construction of the Shanghai Integrated Circuit Design Industrial Center and offered over 215,000 square feet of office space with low rents to IC design firms (Liu, 2000). The center also provided public services to reduce the layout and foundry costs for the prototype and low-volume products developed by local designers (Liu, 2000).

Recently, the Shanghai municipal government announced that it would commit more than 25 percent of S&T development funds every year and meanwhile set up "funds for the technological innovation of small and medium S&T firms" to support the R&D activities of the IC design firms (Zhou, 2007, p. 58). Shanghai's Development and Reform Commission, Informalization Commission, Science and Technology Commission and Economic Commission have launched a series of programs to facilitate the technological innovation of the IC industry, such as the major program of "revitalizing the city by science and education" (*kejiao xingshi zhongda xiangmu*), the program of "cooperation between complete-system vendors and IC design firms" (*zhengji yu xinpian sheji liandong xiangmu*) and "S&T key programs" (*keji gongguan xiangmu*) and so on. IC design firms in Shanghai applied for more than 100 programs and obtained 115 million RMB from local governments in 2007 (SMIC and SICA, 2008, p. 70).

5.3.4. State-firm strategic coordination and innovation-related strategies of IC design firms in Shanghai

Despite significant efforts made by both the central and local governments to promote Shanghai's IC design sector, to create a better institutional environment and to encourage and support the innovation-related activities of local firms, the strategies and responses of firms to the policies and selectivity of the government to technological innovation are variable from firm to firm. In the case of the IC design industry in Shanghai, project-based coordination includes the project of Shanghai high-tech achievements transformation, the project of special funds for the software and IC industry, the project of national funds for innovation, the project of national technological innovation funds for scientific SMEs, the project of Shanghai special funds for IC design firms and so on. Product-based coordination involves the products of a national second generation identity card and the transit smart card for Shanghai. Comparatively, product-based coordination is much weaker than project-based or award-based coordination, not only because the firms are less likely to claim it publicly but also because the IC design industry seldom involved government procurement. Award-based coordination includes the award for high-tech enterprise in Shanghai, the award for innovation in S&T enterprises in Shanghai, the award for Shanghai science and technology progress, the award of a National Golden Card and Golden Ant, the award for best market performance of Chinese chips and so on. In general, among the 98 surveyed IC design firms in Shanghai, 25 percent of them achieved project-based state-firm strategic coordination, 5 percent achieved product-based state-firm strategic coordination and 42 percent of them achieved award-based state-firm strategic coordination (Table 5.6).

A first glance at Shanghai's IC design firms easily identified the fact that those IC design firms selected by the central government or the Shanghai municipal government for promotion appear to be more innovative than others. As shown in Table 5.7, Shanghai Hua Hong Integrated Circuit

Table 5.6.   State-firm strategic coordination in Shanghai.

	Project-based	Product-based	Award-based
Number of firms with strategic coordination with government	24	5	41
Number of firms without strategic coordination with government	74	93	57
The degree of the state-firm strategic coordination	25%	5%	42%

Source: SSIPEX; the website of each firm and face-to-face interview with selected firms.

Table 5.7. Top five patent-held firms and their strategic coordination with governments in Shanghai, 2007.

Name of firm	Number of granted invention patents	Strategic coordination
Spreadtrum	25	Project-based, product-based and award-based
Shanghai Huahong	21	Project-based, product-based and award-based
Huaya Microelectronics	14	Award-based
Magima Inc.	13	Project-based
Fudan Microelectronics	7	Project-based, product-based and award-based

Source: SSIPEX; the website of each firm and face-to-face interview with selected firms.

Table 5.8. Correlations between innovative performance and state-firm strategic coordination.

		Strategic coordination	Project-based coordination	Product-based coordination	Award-based coordination
Granted invention patents	Pearson Correlation	0.754**	0.626**	0.710**	0.649**
	Sig. (2-tailed)	0.000	0.000	0.000	0.000
	N	98	98	98	98

**Correlation is significant at the 0.01 level (2-tailed).
Source: SSIPEX; the website of each firm and face-to-face interview with selected firms.

Co. Ltd., established as a part of the national Project 909, is ranked number two according to granted invention patents. It has undertaken a series of innovation-related projects and achieved many awards. It is also one of the providers of the national second generation ID card. Another provider of the ID card is Fudan Microelectronics that has had great coordination with government based on not only products but also projects and awards. Fudan Microelectronics is invested by Shanghai Commercial Investment Co. Ltd., that is under the direct supervision of Shanghai's Commerce Commission. Spreadtrum Telecommunication Inc. has participated in the national Project 863 and other national special projects and has recently been on the list for government procurement. The rest of the firms presented in Table 5.7 also reached a different degree of coordination with the Shanghai municipal government. Magima had project-based cooperation with the Shanghai municipal government and Huaya Microelectronics has received more than six kinds of awards from the Shanghai municipal government. An analysis of the Pearson correlation further confirms that there exists a significant and strong correlation between the innovative performance and state-firm strategic coordination. All of the coefficients are high and significant at a 0.01 level (Table 5.8).

In order to further understand the relationship between innovative performance of individual firms and state-firm strategic coordination, the 98 firms sampled were divided into innovative and non-innovative groups. Of the total, 18 of the surveyed firms were identified as innovative firms and all of them had established some kind of state-firm strategic coordination based on projects, products or awards. As a group, the innovative firms on average conducted nearly three research projects and achieved more than two awards, considerably more than those of non-innovative firms (Table 5.9). Although innovative firms provided only a few product types for government, the non-innovative firms failed to have a chance to provide any product for government at all. However, there were a few anomalous firms that were strategically coordinated with government based on projects and awards but their innovative performance was poor. Meanwhile, there are several innovative firms that have not strategically reached any type of coordination with local governments at all (Table 5.9).

Table 5.9. Descriptive statistics of innovative and non-innovative IC design groups in Shanghai.

	Number of projects		Number of types of products		Number of awards	
	Inno-vative	Non-innovative	Inno-vative	Non-innovative	Inno-vative	Non-innovative
Minimum	0	0	0	0	0	0
Maximum	16	4	2	0	6	3
Mean	2.83	0.29	0.39	0	2.39	0.30
Std. Deviation	4.68	0.77	0.68	0	2.15	0.58
No. of firms	18	80	18	80	18	80

Source: SSIPEX; the website of each firm and face-to-face interview with selected firms.

This implies that while state-firm strategic coordination reflects a common interest in innovation-related activities of both the state and the firms as well as removing certain general obstacles facing firms in the process of technological innovation, state-firm strategic coordination is not a panacea for successful technological innovation but is also contingent upon the internal resources held by firms and the external opportunities presented. In the case where certain firms with a vision for long-term competitiveness were able to mobilize adequate resources to support their innovation-related activities, they could be innovative without actual coordination with the state. On the contrary, if those firms who obtained assistance from the state were still not able to overcome the barriers to innovation, they might have given up on innovation-related investment. Moreover, under the transitional economic system governed by the immature market environment and state intervention in China, state-firm strategic coordination played a significant role in the innovation of firms. This does not mean that this coordination will be equally significant forever. As the Chinese economy continues to "grow out of the plan" with the maturity of the market environment and the emerging high-tech firms becoming stronger than they used to be, it is foreseeable that the market mechanism and competition will play a growing part in IC industrial production and innovative activities.

Furthermore, the positive relationship between state-firm strategic coordination and firm-level innovative performance can be further illustrated by the information obtained from in-depth face-to-face interviews. We are informed that there still exist many situations in which firms are reluctant to invest in R&D activities in spite of the fact that Shanghai has built up a more innovation-supportive environment than other regions. First of all, the motivation for innovation-related investment by some firms was depressed because a satisfactory profit can be made without any investment in innovation. It is pointed out that innovation is not the terminal goal of firms. What a firm pursues is increasing profits while innovation is only a tool for them to achieve a satisfactory profit margin. A deputy CEO emphasized that

> No matter the technology-oriented or market-oriented corporate strategy that the firm adopts, the terminal goal of the firms is to make profits, while innovation is the instrument to realize this goal. We focus on low-end chip design for consumer electronics, such as electronic toys which do not need much investment in R&D activities... So far we have made a satisfactory profit. (Interview notes, 16 July 2008.)

This shows a clear-cut attitude of some IC design firms to innovation that is a mere tool to seek profits. It is evident that if firms could achieve a satisfactory profit without innovation, they would not invest in R&D activities. Also, it became evident that some indigenous firms were easily satisfied by a very thin profit margin.

> Our indigenous firms can achieve a satisfactory profit without too much investment in innovation-related activities because of the existence of the huge low-end market demands in China. In particular, most of the indigenous firms would be satisfied by a 5 percent or less profit margin while MNCs pursued at least 50 percent profit margin or even more. (Interview notes, 16 July 2008.)

Second, financial difficulty has hampered certain firms' motivation for innovation. Apart from the input of capital and talents in innovative activities, each tape-out per IC costs from 0.2 to 1 million RMB. Sometimes it costs more because it typically takes two or three times longer for the design firm to successfully fabricate a chip. Most of China's IC design firms are small startups and they generally cannot afford the expensive costs. The large amount of capital required for innovative activities further intimidated many firms. A manager confessed that they pursed a low-cost strategy with little or no innovation investment because of financial difficulties.

> Abundant capital is an essential precondition for innovative activities. We do not have enough money to invest in innovation. And I think increasing or reducing R&D input should be mainly dependent on the performance and profit that the firm made. For us, we do not currently have the ability to invest in high-risk innovative activities. (Interview notes, 7 July 2008.)

To make things worse, it is very difficult for small firms to finance their R&D activities from bank loans, it has been revealed.

> We financed our R&D activities all by ourselves. In China, it is extremely difficult for privately-owned enterprises to get a loan from a bank. I tried once but they only loaned me 1 or 2 million with a request for my house as mortgage. So I gave up. (Interview notes, 5 July 2008.)

In the meantime, the venture capitalists that proved to be an important capital source for the IC industry in advanced countries tend to be more and more reluctant to invest in the high-risk sectors such as IC design in China because this kind of investment could easily fail, while investing in other traditional sectors could produce profits in a short time without big risk.

> In China, those who previously invested in the IC industry have currently turned to shoes or food chain stores, such as Bally (*baili*), Ajisen Ramen (*weiqian lamian*), and Chamate (*yicha yizuo*), etc. that could bring them a quick return on their investment. When investing in the IC industry, it takes a long time to know whether this kind of investment can make a profit. People in venture capital work on commission. They do not care in which industrial sectors they invest as long as they can make profits as soon as possible and by as much as possible. (Interview notes, 22 July 2008.)

The experience of these managers reflects that for small firms the financing system in China is poorly established and inapproachable. Venture capital in advanced countries prefers to invest in high-tech firms whose success could bring huge profits. Nevertheless, the only way to finance small IC firms in China was for them to borrow money from their personal network. Therefore, it is not surprising that many small IC firms chose a conservative strategy to develop their business instead of taking the risk of investing in innovation.

Third, the lack of a risk-taking spirit and an insufficient ability to conduct innovative activities by some firms hampered the process of state-firm strategic coordination and hence led to an unsatisfactory innovative performance.

> Blindly investing in innovative activities could easily lead to a failure, you know. You have to take a big risk... Our design does not involve complicated or high-level technology and hence we can totally handle it by ourselves. Our firm was founded only two years ago. To be honest, we are small, young, short of capital and highly-qualified talent. At present, there is no way for us to afford ambitious investment in state of the art technology. We have to imitate others and learn how to survive in the market before we can commit to long-term investment in innovation. (Interview notes, 7 July 2008.)

These comments show that firms established their business model and decided whether or not to invest in innovative activities and how much they should put in these kinds of activities according to their internal resources and the self-evaluation of their capability. It also indicates that there exists a group of firms that selected a low-end technology route and only involved simple technology in their design. Although the Shanghai municipal government has made great efforts to stimulate the innovative activities of its firms, the internal capabilities of firms determined their various interests in involving innovative activities. Most small IC design firms are used to make profits by reducing their costs and promptly occupy the market at a rather low price at the expense of product quality. They are quite well qualified to handle less complicated technology and satisfied with a low profit margin. The experience of the aforementioned firm that adopted a conservative strategy and only involved low-end technology suggests that a low technology capability has impaired its risk-taking spirit. Meanwhile, this strategy further weakened their innovative capability and hence led to a vicious circle and left no chance for such firms to reach a better coordination with government.

Fourth, pessimistic self-estimation and negative anticipation by firms of the government selection process reduced the possibility of a higher degree of state-firm strategic coordination. A firm told us that

> Great support from the Shanghai municipal government merely goes to a few of firms. It tends to select some special industries and give substantial support to potential firms within these industries. Although we are engaged in the electronics industry that has been promoted by government, we know we are not included in the list of firms who are going to be selected by government. (Interview notes, 6 August 2008.)

This comment suggests that the firm is not self-confident regarding its capability and resources and takes a negative attitude toward the selectivity of the state, which could have been the result of its actual insufficient ability and resources for innovation. This firm does realize that the government acts with a strong selectivity and has high expectations for its selected firms, which further confirms that the relations between firms and the Shanghai municipal government significantly varied from firm to firm.

It is disclosed that a firm which strategically coordinated with the government turned out to be more innovation-involved than it used to be because of the enlarged internal resources and external support.

> As a matter of fact, with the support of both the central and local governments, we indeed have invested a lot in R&D activities and have achieved a great innovative performance in recent years. (Interview notes, 7 August 2008.)

Also, the innovative performance will be improved through the process of state-firm strategic coordination. Both the central and local governments have taken many steps to support certain firms, for instance national standard-setting firms and high-end technology-oriented firms, especially those who developed the complicated technology that China was not able to achieve before, to cultivate their innovative capability. Firms have realized that governmental support has exerted a significant influence on innovation. A manager expressed her opinion as follows:

> As far as I am concerned, state-firm strategic coordination indeed has a very significant influence on the technological innovation of a firm. If this firm has the potential to achieve a high-end technology breakthrough and commits itself to innovation-related activities while at the same time receiving great support from government, it would be more innovative than others; at least, it would get more chance to be innovative than others. Spreadtrum is a good example in this case. (Interview notes, 8 July 2008.)

Her opinion suggests that although state-firm coordination will promote the innovative performance of firms, state-firm coordination is far from a simple process but sensitive to many variable factors. An important precondition is that the strategies of firms are accordant with the innovation-related strategies of the state and their resources allow for innovation-related investments. Both the resources of the firm and the strategies of the state tended to change over time and space. As a result, state-firm coordination also varied according to different contexts and regions.

With the increase in overseas returnees, the technology level of China's manufacturing has been greatly improved in recent years. More and more entrepreneurs started to devote themselves to Chinese indigenous innovation and were involved in Chinese technology standards. As an example, Spreadtrum is a representative of self-dependent innovation. This company was founded by several overseas returnees from the U.S. and focuses on a Chinese technology standard for wireless telecommunication named TD-SCDMA. It has drawn the attention of the Shanghai municipal government since its foundation and received great support from not only the Shanghai municipal government but also the central government. Spreadtrum provided an interesting case for understanding how the process of state-firm coordination has affected the technological innovation of a firm.

5.3.5. *Spreadtrum Shanghai: A case study*

Spreadtrum Communications Shanghai Inc. (thereafter Spreadtrum), one of the most innovative and successful firms in China that listed on the

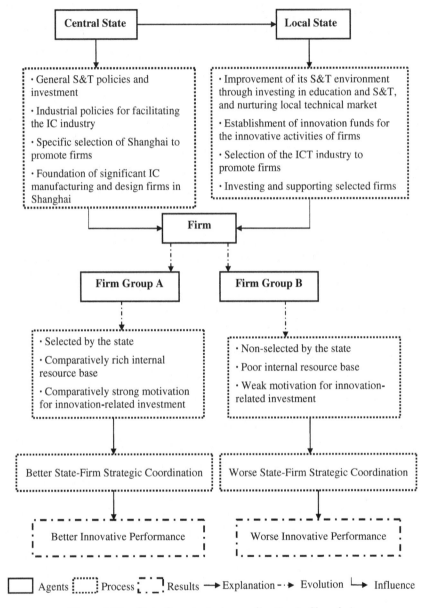

Figure 5.10.   State-firm strategic coordination in Shanghai.

NASDAQ in 2007, was founded in 2001 by several overseas returnees with over 20 years of IT experience. Spreadtrum has experienced significant growth since 2003. Its revenue was $12.9 million in 2004 and it increased to $38.3 million in 2005 with a growth rate of 196 percent (Spreadtrum, 2008, p. 8). The sales revenue reached $107.1 million in 2006 with a growth rate of 180 percent and $145.5 million at the end of 2007 (Spreadtrum, 2008, p. 8). In accordance with the rapid growth in the sales revenue, its research team grew from 20 at the beginning to 768 employees at the end of 2007, 546 of whom were engineers and over half of them hold a Master's Degree or PhD (Spreadtrum, 2008, p. 65).

Obtaining its start-up capital of eight million USD from Silicon Valley, Spreadtrum devoted itself to technological innovation since its foundation (Jiang, 2006). With a team of 37 experienced engineers from Silicon Valley, Spreadtrum Shanghai successfully developed its first GSM/GPRS (2.5G) baseband chip in April 2003. This series of chip was rewarded with the first award of "Shanghai S&T Progress" in 2005 and the first award of "National S&T Progress" in 2006. In July 2003, it became involved with the Chinese technology standard TD-SCDMA and announced the first TD-SCDMA/GSM dual mode baseband chip in the world in April 2004.

In 2001, high-tech firms like Spreadtrum in Shanghai were not as numerous as those in Beijing. It was told by its department manager that if Spreadtrum selected Zhongguancun for its location, it would not be taken seriously by the Beijing municipal government. Instead, its development would receive more attention from the Shanghai municipal government because the municipality committed itself to promoting local innovation through attracting potential high-tech firms to catch up with Beijing. Therefore, Spreadtrum has established a formidable relationship with the local government since its foundation. The great support from the Shanghai municipal government was one of the most important reasons for Spreadtrum to locate in Shanghai. Its deputy general manager said:

> Our CEO once told me that he had investigated several locations before he selected Shanghai to open his business. Of course, Beijing was one of the most significant considerations for him. However, the Shanghai municipal government offered him the most favorable policies and greatest support. Selecting Shanghai is actually a win–win for both the Shanghai municipal government and us. The Shanghai municipal

government needs us to promote its indigenous innovation while we need its support for better development. (Interview notes, 23 July 2008.)

After developing a baseband chip based on the Chinese homegrown technical standard, Spreadtrum Shanghai received even more support from both the central and local governments. It is told that

> Spreadtrum has received great support from both local and central governments since its foundation in Shanghai, not only in terms of preferential tax policies, but also many other favorable policies, such as freely-used land authorized by the local government. Our company held a press conference in the Great Hall of the People when we firstly developed a baseband chip adopting the Chinese homegrown technical standard, namely TD-SCDMA. Many state leaders visited our company, including Premier Wen Jiabao and the Vice-Chairman Xi Jinping. (Interview notes, 23 July 2008.)

The high-profile support from both the central and local governments led to the fact that Spreadtrum achieved a technology breakthrough in its field and, more importantly, made a great contribution to develop Chinese homegrown technical standards. In its annual report, Spreadtrum openly expressed its support for Chinese homegrown technical standards: "we have invested substantial time and resources in developing products that support TD-SCDMA" (Spreadtrum, 2008, p. 11). Other than the technical standard of TD-SCDMA, Spreadtrum started to research its products based on another Chinese homegrown technical standard named AVS (audio video coding standard) in 2007.

Its strong technological background and supportive attitude to Chinese homegrown technical standards totally matched the national innovation strategies of the state, which made it one of the favorite enterprises of both the central and local governments and further strengthened the strategic coordination between Spreadtrum and the state. Spreadtrum in its annual report admitted that "we have received government incentives in the forms of reduced tax rates, exemption from certain taxes, favorable lending policies, research grants and other measures. Our research and development expenses have been partially offset by subsidies, including grants we have received from PRC government authorities. The aggregate cash amounts of the subsidies we received were RMB13.5 million (approximately US$1.6 million), RMB10.3 million (approximately US$1.3 million) and RMB4.3 million (approximately US$587,000) in 2005, 2006 and 2007, respectively. For the years ended December 31, 2005, 2006 and 2007, US$1.2 million, US$950,000 and US$859,000 were recorded as offsetting the research and development expenses incurred, respectively" (Spreadtrum, 2008, pp. 21–22).

As a matter of the fact, Spreadtrum obtained far more support from government than it reported in its official document. One of the informants revealed that Spreadtrum built its own five-star hotel in Zhangjiang High-tech Park with not only a sanction for land-use but also with the capital support of 50 million RMB from the Shanghai municipal government. Profits from the hotel to some extent alleviated the pressure on the uncertainty of innovation-related investment (interview notes, 22 July 2008). At the same time, an expert in industrial research imparted:

> Spreadtrum is a successful case of a venture established by overseas returnees, not only because it has a great technological foundation but also because it knows very well how to play the business game in China. I know many failures of firms founded by overseas returnees. They also came back with advanced technologies and years of experience but they are not familiar with Chinese culture and have no idea how to establish a good relationship with government, which Spreadtrum handled very well. (Interview notes, 8 August 2008.)

His comments suggest that it is critical for a firm to be embedded in the local political, cultural and institutional environment, while strategically coordinating with governments is a key to paving the way to success. It is hard to say that Spreadtrum would have been so innovative and successful if its founders had selected to open their business elsewhere. However, it is not the state-firm coordination that directly led to the success of Spreadtrum, but it is the state-firm coordination that stimulated its motivation for innovation-investment and pushed this firm to get through its hard times and achieve success.

5.4. Summary

Recent theoretical attempts to understanding the dynamics of technological innovation have been based predominantly on the concepts of industrial clusters and knowledge spillover which see the innovation of a region as the result of the self-sustained accumulation of knowledge within a cluster. Important efforts have been made to apply this popular theory to cases of regional development and technological innovation in contemporary China. While the paradigm of knowledge spillover has significantly facilitated theoretical advancement in the understanding of the complex process of innovation and growth, its power to explain the variation in technological innovation among individual firms in the same cluster is noticeably limited because of its inherent tendency to emphasize knowledge spillover at the expense of some broader issues that may be hampering the process of innovation, such as capital mobilization, the regional institutional environment, motivation and strategies of firms to invest in innovative activities and strategies, as well as the selectivity of the state in improving the innovative capacity of the regional economy.

This chapter examines the diverse innovative performance of individual firms in Shanghai through an analysis of both the innovation-related strategies and actions of the state and firms, as well as the process of strategic coordination between them. At the core of the ICT sector, the growth in the IC design sector of Shanghai owes a great deal to the actions recently taken by both the central and local governments. The national Project 909 implemented in Pudong New Area laid a good foundation for shaping an intact value chain in the IC industry while two significant policies released in 2000 triggered an expansion of its IC design sector. The locational preference of the government has further led to a geographical concentration of the IC design industry in Zhangjiang High-tech Park of Pudong New Area and Caohejing High-tech Park of Xuhui District. The IC industry in Shanghai has achieved an overall impressive innovative performance, significantly better than that of Shenzhen and China as a whole. However, close scrutiny has revealed an interesting variation in the degree of technological innovation among individual IC design firms in Shanghai.

Shanghai has built up a favorable S&T environment for its firms. In order to facilitate economic growth and innovation, Shanghai municipal government not only selected certain firms to support their innovative activities but also invested in its S&T facilities to improve the overall environment for innovation. In this process, the Shanghai municipal government directed its support toward certain high-tech industries. A direct innovation-involved fund established by the municipal government is found to have significantly boosted the innovation of firms. An evaluation of the strategies of the central government has shown significant effort taken to improve China's technological capability and to move out of the technological control of Western countries through establishing and supporting certain firms that are perceived to be more innovative than others. A close examination of the most innovative firms in Shanghai's IC design sector has found that all of them have reached significant strategic coordination with the central or the Shanghai municipal government. A Pearson correlation analysis revealed that there exists a significant and strong correlation between state-firm strategic coordination and firm-level innovative performance in Shanghai. Among the 98 surveyed firms, 18 of them are identified as innovative firms and all of them have more or less reached a different degree of state-firm strategic coordination based on projects, products and/or awards. Furthermore, as a group, the innovative firms achieved on average much better state-firm strategic coordination than non-innovative ones.

Despite great support from the central and local governments to develop and promote Shanghai's IC design sector, firms have adopted different corporate strategies for innovation according to their own resources, business interests, capability and strength as well as external environment, leading to varying degrees of state-firm strategic coordination among individual firms within Shanghai. Interview notes have generated insightful information in understanding the diverse innovation-related strategies of firms. Some firms are not interested in innovation-related activities because a satisfactory profit can be made without any innovation investment, because of the large risk in innovation and financial difficulties due to such investment, and because of the low self-evaluation of their capabilities and a pessimistic attitude to the state's selectivity. State-firm strategic coordination therefore appears to be very crucial in inspiring the motivation to innovate and remove obstacles confronting firms during their process of innovation. This argument is backed up by a case study of one of the most innovative IC design firms in Shanghai and China.

The research results have important implications for further enquiries into the dynamics and geography of technological innovation. Theoretically, there exists a long-standing debate over the relationship between a firm's size and innovation (Acs and Audretsch, 1988, pp. 31–33; Rogers, 2004; Vaona and Pianta, 2008; Wright, 1997). Saxenian's research (1994) on Silicon Valley and Route 128 illustrated that the stifled organization model and retarded decision-making of big firms in the flexible market led to failure on Route 128 while a network-based system of agile small- and medium-sized enterprises (SMEs) contributed to the success of Silicon Valley. However, in the case of China, the high-end chip market is monopolized by the big MNCs while most of the small indigenous firms are stuck at the low-end of the value chain in the global market. In the case of Shanghai, larger IC design firms appeared to be more innovative than the smaller ones because it is easier for them to reach a better strategic coordination with the government. Small firms have to struggle for survival through squeezing the profit margin on the one hand and dealing with the difficulties in raising funds for R&D activities and recruiting highly-qualified talents on the other. By contrast, bigger firms hold more abundant resources to conduct their innovation-related activities and have a better chance to receive support from the government. It has been pointed out that the innovation model of Shanghai is similar to that of Japan and Korea and rather different to northern California because decision-makers in Shanghai tended to see bigger firms as more competitive and innovative than smaller ones (Segal, 2003, p. 94).

This study has shown a case in which the determination and capability of governments to guide its industry and select those firms with better potential have been instrumental to technological innovation. Support from government is important for the technological innovation of firms since China's IC industry is still in its fledging stage. However, the role played by the state cannot be over-estimated and over-simplified. Indeed, there exists great ambivalence toward the "visible hand" of the state in the process of technological innovation. The Shanghai municipal government has been highly praised by some but heavily blamed by others for bringing about its peculiar trajectory of industrial development (Han, 2000; Huang, 2008; Zhang, 2003). For ICT firms, there are both costs and benefits in relying upon state support. State backup is neither a pre-requisite nor a sufficient condition for a firm to become innovative. What this study has demonstrated is the fact that, other things being equal, firms with a strategic coordination with the government tended to fare better in their navigation over the uncertain and risky terrain of technological innovation than others, including those located in the same cluster. However, since local governments are variable in their capability and determination to guide their industry and economy, coupled with the different regional characteristics shaped by the historical trajectory, the degree of state-firm strategic coordination varies in different regions and contexts, leading to a variable innovative performance across the country. The next chapter will examine how a different degree of state-firm strategic coordination has taken place in another ICT agglomerated city-region whose growth trajectory and institutional environment are quite different from Shanghai.

Chapter Six

STATE-FIRM STRATEGIC COORDINATION AND THE GROWTH OF THE ICT INDUSTRY IN SHENZHEN

6.1. Introduction

The case study of the IC design firms in Shanghai in the last chapter has revealed that innovative performance of firms is embedded in state-firm strategic coordination that is contingent upon the strategic selectivity of the central government, the vision and capability of the local government as well as the internal resources and strategic considerations of firms. This chapter is intended to investigate how different state-firm strategic coordination in another geographical and institutional context such as Shenzhen had led to a divergent trajectory of technological innovation. As an emerging metropolis, Shenzhen is a representative case of those regions that had suffered from insufficient resources and an underestimated role by the central government before 1978 and had recently been allowed to move one step ahead of the entire country in market-oriented reforms and opening up (Vogel, 1989). The relatively liberal economy in Shenzhen has shaped a quite different institutional environment in comparison to Shanghai. Being assigned by the central government as China's first and foremost Special Economic Zone, Shenzhen is rather a center of industrial assembly and processing than a hub for time-consuming R&D activities. This city's image further affects the strategies and behavior of both local governments and firms. In spite of this, Shenzhen has attracted a large number of ICT firms and showed a high concentration of both ICT manufacturing and software sectors in the country. It provides a good case for investigating the nature and dynamics of the ICT industrial cluster and for probing into the strategies and behavior of ICT firms to understand the process of state-firm strategic coordination in Southern China. What is the nature and dynamics of the ICT industry in Shenzhen? What is the status of the state-firm strategic coordination there? What is the selectivity and what are the considerations of the central government regarding the position of

Shenzhen in the entire economy? What is the vision and the capability of the local government in terms of encouraging S&T activities and promoting a better institutional and market environment? What are the incentives and constraints confronting Shenzhen's ICT firms that affect their strategies and motivation regarding technological innovation?

This chapter starts with an overall examination of the nature and dynamics of Shenzhen's ICT industry, including its history, structural characteristics, spatial distribution and innovative performance, with special attention given to the production linkages and knowledge exchange among firms. The emphasis is then shifted to interrogate the status of the state-firm strategic coordination through probing into the selectivity of both the central and local governments and the strategic consideration of firms that is sensitive to their external environment and internal resources. Major findings and implications are summarized in the last part.

6.2. General Status and Nature of Shenzhen's ICT Industry

6.2.1. *Growth, structure and spatial distribution of the ICT industry*

Located in the southern corner of China's mainland and bordering Hong Kong, Shenzhen was designated to establish the first and foremost special economic zone (SEZ) in China in December 1979 when the "open door policy" was introduced. This designation coincided with the ascendance of neoliberalism across the Atlantic and the deepening of the spatial division of labor in the Asia-Pacific region and hence made Shenzhen able to attract considerable foreign investment aiming at a cost-reduction strategy in China (Harvey, 2005; Naughton, 1997; Wu, 2008). The status of an SEZ has brought to Shenzhen special authority and flexibility to offer preferential treatment to foreign investors, provide tax concessions and reduced tariffs, allow for easy imports of foreign machinery, equipment and raw materials and facilitate currency exchange and outward transfer of the profits made in China. The idea was to capitalize on Shenzhen's geographical proximity to and pre-existing social connections with Hong Kong so that a Chinese version of the successful export processing zones in many newly industrializing Asian economies could be created. As such, it was more a bureaucratic creation than any outcome of natural and evolutionary industrial development with dense production networks or traded and untraded interdependence. Cheap land was available for sale and Shenzhen was the very first city in the country to initiate the commodification of China's state-owned land and the introduction of a land market into socialist territory (Lin, 2009a, p. 78). A large and low-cost labor force consisted of primarily migrant workers coming from all over the country (Fan, 2008; Lin, 1997; Wu, 1999). The city was developed from a tiny little border town without any established technological and social infrastructure into one of the largest metropolises in the country with a total population of 8.62 million in 2007. There were no pre-existing universities or research institutions. The industrial labor force was young, energetic, cheap and yet poorly educated. For instance, less than 7 percent of the total employees in Shenzhen's software industry had achieved an education at Master's Degree or above, which is below the national average of over 10 percent (SZSB, 2005a; CSSB, 2005a). It is within this environment, one that differs significantly from that found in Boston or Silicon Valley, that the development of export processing industries, including ICT manufacturing and software design, has taken place.

Given the strategic position held by China in "reshaping the economic geography" of the region and the world, there is an important role for Shenzhen to play not only in the "global shift" of investment and manufacturing but also in the growth and restructuring of the ICT industry in the "China Circle" which includes Taiwan and Hong Kong (Fan, 2003, 2006; Naughton, 1997). In retrospect, the growth of the ICT industry in Shenzhen has since its opening up in 1979 gone through three main stages, as illustrated in Fig. 6.1. Prior to the 1990s, the emphasis on industrial development was placed initially on export processing industries, many of which were low-tech, labor intensive, and dependent upon the capital attracted from Hong Kong. There were very few ICT firms engaged in either manufacturing or software designs. It was only after the 1990s that ICT manufacturing activities started to emerge as a new and growing industrial sector in Shenzhen, partly because of the deepening division of labor within "the China Circle" externally and partly because of a growing government awareness internally to go beyond the labor intensive export processing industry (China Electronics News, 7 November 2008; Naughton, 1997). The real momentum for growth in the ICT industry, both manufacturing and software design, has appeared only after the year 2000, when special policies were introduced by both the central and municipal governments to promote the high-tech industry, develop indigenous research capacity, and reduce dependency upon external technology (Shenzhen Municipal

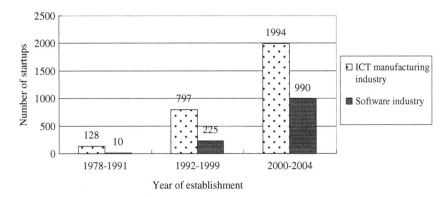

Figure 6.1.   Start-ups of Shenzhen's ICT industry at different stages.
Source: Calculated from SZSB (2005a).

Committee, 2004; Shenzhen Municipal Government, 2001; State Council, 1991, 1999). This special growth trajectory is shaped by both the special position of Shenzhen in the regional and global economies and the policies and approaches adopted by the central and municipal governments.

An analysis of the data obtained from the 2004 National Economic Census identified the structure of Shenzhen's ICT manufacturing typical to the national situation, as illustrated in Chapter 4. As shown in Table 6.1, the ICT manufacturing activities in Shenzhen were dominated by the processing of electronic computers which generated over 40 percent of output and over half of the exports. Although the processing of electronic computers has taken the lead in industrial production and exports, it was not the most profitable industrial sector. The manufacturing of telecommunication equipment contributed nearly half of the total profits for the ICT manufacturing industry although it generated only a quarter of output and about one-sixth of the ICT exports (Table 6.1). This pattern suggested that the role played by Shenzhen in the regional and global economies remained in the assembly and processing of electronic computers. There was a long way for Shenzhen to go to engage in more innovative and profitable ICT manufacturing and design.

By the end of 2004, Shenzhen had become one of the most developed and agglomerated ICT city-regions in China with a manufacturing employment location quotient of 6.67 and a software employment location quotient of 2.83. Within Shenzhen, both ICT manufacturing and software design activities have shown an uneven spatial distribution (Fig. 6.2).

Table 6.1.   Shenzhen's ICT manufacturing industry by sectors, 2004.

	Output value		Exports		Total profits	
	Billion yuan	**Percent**	**Billion yuan**	**Percent**	**Billion yuan**	**Percent**
Telecom equipment	112.15	25.25	44.53	15.03	8.93	**49.02**
Radar and related equipment	0.02	0.00	0.00	0.00	0.00	−0.01
Broadcasting and television equipment	3.98	0.90	2.51	0.85	0.12	0.64
Electronic computers	193.74	**43.62**	161.99	**54.67**	6.34	34.82
Electronic devices	39.16	8.82	31.29	10.56	1.09	6.00
Electronic components	37.36	8.41	29.45	9.94	1.39	7.65
Household audio and video equipment	56.28	12.67	25.84	8.72	0.32	1.76
Other electronic equipment	1.48	0.33	0.71	0.24	0.02	0.11
Total	444.17	100	296.32	100	18.21	100

Source: Calculated from SZSB (2005).

ICT manufacturing firms are highly concentrated in Bao'an District — a suburban region where land and labor costs are relatively lower than in the urban center of Futian and Luohu (Fig. 6.2(a)). In contrast, software design firms tend to cluster in the Nanshan District with more open space, easy access to educational and research institutions (although not many in Shenzhen), and a more pleasant physical environment (Fig. 6.2(b)).

Although there is a high concentration of ICT manufacturing and software design activities in Shenzhen, a critical evaluation of the economic and technological performance of these activities has revealed a pattern that leaves much to be desired. When the ICT firms (manufacturing and software designs) were grouped according to different ownerships, the performance of domestic firms appeared to be significantly behind that of foreign firms (Table 6.2). Although domestic firms accounted for 62 percent of ICT manufacturing and 81 percent of software design in Shenzhen, their average scale per firm was much lower than that of foreign firms. As shown in Table 6.2, the average year-end sales revenue per foreign firm was 11 times higher than that of domestic firms for ICT manufacturing and four times higher than domestic firms for software design. Moreover, both capital profitability and labor productivity of domestic ICT manufacturing firms were lower than those for foreign firms. For software design, capital profitability and labor productivity of the firms in Shenzhen (0.48 *yuan* and 225,566 *yuan*/person) were both lower than the national average (0.53 *yuan* and 244,628 *yuan*/person) (CSSB, 2005a; SZSB, 2005a). It is interesting to see that the ICT manufacturing and software design firms established by Hong Kong, Macao or Taiwan in Shenzhen showed the poorest capital profitability and labor productivity (Table 6.2).

6.2.2. *Clustering, network, knowledge exchange and technological innovation*

How does one make sense of the high concentration of ICT firms in Shenzhen without satisfactory technological performance? What is the strategic consideration for firms to locate in Shenzhen? What is the internal dynamics of industrial clustering in Shenzhen? How are they connected to each other? How do they obtain their core technology? The remainder of this section will report the findings of a questionnaire survey designed to answer these questions. The questionnaire included, among many other things, two main types of questions, namely the nature of production linkages with suppliers and customers within and outside the region, and the level and extent of technological innovation and interaction with firms within and outside the region. Answers to the first type of questions can be used to test whether or not the concentration of ICT firms in Shenzhen has amounted to an industrial cluster with interdependence. Responses to the second type of questions can help determine the nature and understand the dynamics of technological linkages and innovation.

Judging by a high location quotient in both employment and output, Shenzhen's ICT industry has shown a high degree of spatial concentration. Is this spatial concentration or agglomeration of ICT firms qualified to be an industrial cluster with frequent and extensive production linkages among the firms within the region? The results of the questionnaire survey have provided a positive response. Table 6.3 summarizes the responses of firms to the question concerning the reasons for choosing their location in Shenzhen. For the ICT manufacturing firms, the existence of clients in Shenzhen was most commonly identified as the reason and this is followed by the existence of an airport/seaport and technological talent. For software designs, the most popular reason was the existence of technology talent, clients and concentration of peers. Despite a slightly different ranking of

Table 6.2. Major economic indicators of the ICT industry in Shenzhen by ownership, 2004.

	ICT manufacturing sector			Software sector		
	Domestic	Hong Kong Taiwan, Macao	Foreign	Domestic	Hong Kong Taiwan, Macao	Foreign
Establishment	1868	747	377	1032	128	108
Average number of employees per firm (persons)	119	362	819	17	33	82
Total assets (100 million *yuan*)	1045.09	539.34	1040.41	96.81	18.94	30.48
Average assets per firm held (million *yuan*)	55.95	72.20	275.97	9.38	14.79	28.22
Year-end sales revenue (100 million *yuan*)	1032.05	1029.13	2392.89	42.39	6.80	20.51
Average year-end sales revenue per firm achieved (million *yuan*)	55.25	137.77	634.72	4.11	5.31	18.99
Capital profitability (*yuan*)	0.99	1.91	2.30	0.44	0.36	0.67
Labor productivity (10,000 *yuan*/person)	46.35	38.02	77.48	23.71	16.04	23.24

Source: Calculated from SZSB (2005a).

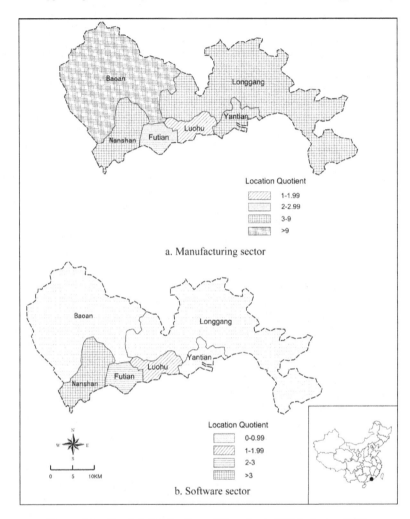

Figure 6.2.   Spatial distribution of Shenzhen's ICT industry, 2004.
Source: Calculated from SZSB (2005a).

the reasons, both ICT manufacturing firms and software designers have
made their locational decision on the basis of co-location with clients and
peers or what is conceptualized as the agglomeration economies. Indeed,
over 36 percent of ICT manufacturing firms and 40 percent of software
firms reported that concentration of peers, proximity to suppliers and co-
location with customers are the top reasons for them to be located in
Shenzhen. However, none of the software firms and less than 1 percent of

Table 6.3.   Top reason for locational selection of Shenzhen's ICT firms.

	ICT manufacturing firms		Software firms	
	Frequency	**Percent**	**Frequency**	**Percent**
Airport/Seaport	28	**18.5**	3	4.3
Concentration of peers	13	8.6	9	**12.9**
Close to suppliers	7	4.6	7	10.0
Technology talent	23	**15.2**	18	**25.7**
Low labor cost	6	3.8	3	4.3
Cooperation with local universities/R&D institutes	1	0.6	0	0
Location of clients	35	**23.2**	12	**17.1**
Local market potential	13	8.6	7	10.0
Industrial base	6	4.0	2	2.9
Preferential policies	11	7.3	2	2.9
Friendly government	0	0	3	4.3
Professional services	4	2.7	1	1.4
Amenities in the cities	1	0.7	0	0
Others	3	2.0	3	4.3
Total	151	100	70	100

Source: Questionnaire survey in Shenzhen in 2006.

the ICT manufacturing firms considered cooperation with local universities and R&D institutes to be an important reason.

Intensive forward and backward linkages did exist among the ICT firms located in Shenzhen and its vicinity. For ICT manufacturing, over 85 percent of the firms built their downstream linkages with firms in Shenzhen and the Pearl River Delta region and 94 percent has their upstream linkages with firms located within a 2-hour travel distance (Table 6.4). Almost 40 percent of the ICT manufacturing firms reported that over half of their customers are located in the PRD and 55 percent had their suppliers within a 2-hour travel distance. Nearly all of the surveyed firms had built, one way or another, upstream or downstream production linkages with other local firms in Shenzhen. For the software firms, they reported even closer linkages with the local firms that served as their customers. Over 91 percent of the software firms had served their customers in the PRD region (Table 6.5). It is interesting to note that very few software firms exported their products to Hong Kong, Macao, Taiwan or foreign countries. Over 80 percent of Shenzhen's software firms served the domestic market.

The existence of a sub-contracting relationship among local firms is also a significant indicator of the nature and extent of production linkages

Table 6.4.   Local linkages among ICT manufacturing firms in Shenzhen.

	Customers in PRD area		Suppliers within 2 h distance	
	Frequency	Percent	Frequency	Percent
0	20	**13.2**	9	**6.0**
1% < 25%	34	22.5	24	16.1
26%–50%	38	25.2	32	21.5
51%–75%	17	11.3	25	16.8
>75%	42	**27.8**	59	**39.6**
Total	151	100.0	149	100

Source: Questionnaire survey in Shenzhen in 2006.

Table 6.5.   Ratio of spatial distribution of customers for software firms in five major regions of China, 2006.

Ratio of customers	Beijing	Yangtze River Delta	Pearl River Delta	Hong Kong, Macao and Taiwan	Foreign countries
0	65.7	31.4	**8.6**	84.3	80
1%–25%	31.4	47.1	18.6	10.0	12.9
26%–50%	2.9	14.3	38.6	2.9	0
51%–75%	0	7.1	8.6	0	1.4
76%–100%	0	0	**25.7**	2.9	5.7
Total	100	100	100	100	100

Source: Questionnaire survey in Shenzhen in 2006.

among the firms. The results of the survey in this regard are listed in Table 6.6. Over 97 percent of the ICT manufacturing firms reported a subcontracting relationship with firms located within a two-hour travel distance and over 40 percent formed a subcontracting partnership entirely and only with firms located nearby (Table 6.6). In a similar manner, about 94 percent of the software firms had subcontracting relationships with local firms and over 45 percent found their subcontracting partners only within a two-hour travel limit. These responses suggested that the ICT firms highly concentrated in Shenzhen are not located here without production linkages. On the contrary, they have already developed a dense production network within the region to qualify themselves as the well-connected and interdependent elements of an industrial cluster.

The frequent and intensive production linkages existing among the ICT firms in Shenzhen may be taken as indicative of the growth of an industrial cluster in China with a leading role to play in terms of the contribution of output, employment and exports. Does this clustering of ICT firms lead

Table 6.6.   Subcontracting relations with local firms (2 h distance) in Shenzhen.

	ICT manufacturing firms		Software firms	
	Frequency	Percent	Frequency	Percent
0	2	**2.3**	2	**6.5**
1%–25%	17	19.7	8	25.8
26%–50%	16	18.6	4	12.9
51%–90%	16	18.6	3	9.7
100%	35	40.7	14	45.2
Total	86	100	31	100

Source: Questionnaire survey in Shenzhen in 2006.

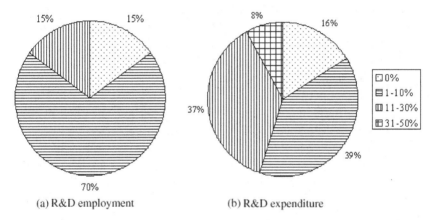

(a) R&D employment   (b) R&D expenditure

Figure 6.3.   Distribution of the ICT manufacturing firms by the share of R&D input.
Source: Questionnaire survey in Shenzhen in 2006.

to the formation of a "local buzz" with frequent interchange of ideas, information, knowledge and technological innovation? The results of the questionnaire survey have provided intriguing evidence that deviates from normal theoretical expectation. The majority of the ICT firms located in Shenzhen have not been actively involved in research and development (R&D). Among the ICT manufacturing firms that responded to the questionnaire, 70 percent indicated that their R&D employees accounted for less than one-tenth of the total labor force and 15 percent admitted that they hired no R&D employees at all (Fig. 6.3). As for the allocation of capital, 39 percent of the ICT manufacturing firms reported that they spent less than 10 percent of the capital on R&D activities and another 16 percent indicated that they did not invest any money in R&D activities. For software designs, most of the software firms in Shenzhen are small scale

Table 6.7.   Technological innovation of the ICT firms in Shenzhen.

Number of invention patents	ICT manufacturing firms		Software firms	
	Frequency	Percent	Frequency	Percent
0	124	82.12	52	75.4
1–10	22	14.60	16	23.2
11–30	4	2.65	1	1.4
40–50	1	0.66	0	0
Total	151	100	69	100

Source: Questionnaire survey in Shenzhen in 2006.

with a very limited labor force and capital. Over 70 percent of the surveyed software firms indicated that they hired less than 50 people. Theoretically, software design firms should devote their labor force and capital entirely or mostly to research and development. This theoretical expectation does not seem to be met in the case of Shenzhen, however. Among the software firms surveyed, 64 percent reported that less than half of their labor force was engaged in R&D and 82 percent indicated that less than half of their capital was devoted to support R&D activities.

With a limited input of capital and labor in R&D activities, it has come as no surprise that the level of technological innovation achieved by the ICT industrial cluster in Shenzhen has been rather low. Among the respondents to the questionnaire survey, 82 percent of the ICT manufacturing firms and 75 percent of the software firms reported that they had never been granted any invention patents (Table 6.7). Furthermore, only two of the 70 surveyed software firms indicated that they had managed to obtain the "Capability Maturity Model" certification which is an international standard to evaluate the innovative capability of a software firm.[1]

Where do the ICT firms in the Shenzhen industrial cluster obtain their core technology? Is there any interchange, cooperation, or transfer of technological innovation among the firms within the cluster? The survey has yielded some interesting insights into the nature and dynamics of technological innovation and transfer. The overwhelming majority of the ICT firms, 75 percent for manufacturing and 81 percent for software design, reported that the source of core technology originates from internal development (Table 6.8). This pattern of isolated technological development may be the result of the fact that firms within this cluster only used simple

---

[1]One of the two certificated firms is the branch of a foreign-owned enterprise.

Table 6.8.   Sources of core technology of the ICT firms in Shenzhen.

Source of core technology	ICT manufacturing firms	Software firms
Internal development	**75.3%**	**81.4%**
Imported technologies	14.7%	5.7%
Reverse engineering of imported technology	10.7%	**11.4%**
Domestic enterprises	10.0%	10.0%
Universities/Research Institutes	3.3%	1.4%

Source: Questionnaire survey in Shenzhen in 2006.

technology that does not require too much external knowledge, assistance, or cooperation. Nevertheless, necessary modification and adaptation of external technology were identified as an important source of innovation by some firms. About 11 percent of both the ICT manufacturing and software firms responded that reversed engineering was an important source of core technology. It is interesting to see that imported technologies were regarded by software firms as less important or less useful than domestic firms as a source to obtain core technology (Table 6.8). This could be the result of the fact that imported technology is usually more expensive than the domestic one and that the software firms here tended to engage in low-end technology that could be easily satisfied through purchasing specific models from domestic sources. For both ICT manufacturing and software designs, universities and research institutions were not considered to be the main source of core technology.

The ICT industrial cluster in Shenzhen was characterized by not only a lack of utilization of imports or local research institutions as the main source of core technology but also by a lack of technological cooperation with other domestic firms. Nearly 80 percent of the ICT manufacturing firms and 56 percent of the software firms surveyed had never had any technological cooperation with other domestic firms. Only 2 percent of the ICT manufacturing firms and 7 percent of the software firms considered technological cooperation with other firms to be very important. More intriguing is the lack of technology transfer and exchange of knowledge, information or personnel among the firms. Among the firms that responded to the survey, 87 percent of the ICT manufacturing firms and 74 percent of software firms indicated that they never had any technology transfer with other domestic firms (Table 6.9). Over 76 percent of the manufacturing firms and 58 percent of the software firms never took technological advice from other firms. In a similar manner, 81 percent of the ICT manufacturing firms and 67 percent of the software firms had no exchange of information with other domestic firms. The exchange of personnel among firms showed a similar pattern (Table 6.9). All of these responses have showed that the clustering of ICT firms did not cultivate technological cooperation, information exchange or knowledge spillover — a pattern that goes against the normal theoretical expectation. Although the ICT firms within the Shenzhen industrial cluster have built among themselves a dense and proximate production network, they are connected predominantly by regular supply and marketing relations and have seldom engaged in some knowledge-based technological transfer, interchange and cooperation. These firms have committed very limited input to research and development and generated no significant output of technological innovation.

All of the evidence presented above has consistently pointed to the fact that privileging industrial clustering, inter-firm linkages and networks over active agents and actors fails to provide a satisfactory explanation of the dynamics of technological innovation. The innovation-related strategies and motivation behind the ICT firms and government should be seriously taken into account. The next section will focus on the status of state-firm strategic coordination to understand the innovative performance of Shenzhen's ICT firms through scrutinizing the strategic selectivity of the central government regarding the position of Shenzhen in the whole country, the vision and capability of the Shenzhen municipal government in supporting local S&T activities and regulating the market environment as well as the motivation and strategic considerations with regard to technological innovation by local firms.

6.3. State-Firm Strategic Coordination in Shenzhen

6.3.1. *Industry strategies and regional deployment of the central government*

The rapid growth that Shenzhen's ICT industry has achieved in recent years cannot be understood without reference to the industrial strategies of the central government. The "oil crisis" of 1973 induced a basic restructuring of the global economy and paved the way for the "electronics and information revolution" which discarded the traditional production pattern that is characterized by the assumption of an abundance of energy, raw materials and natural resources and opened a new era of

Table 6.9.   Technology transfer and interaction of Shenzhen's ICT firms with other domestic firms.

	Technology transfer		Seeking advice		Exchange of technology information		Exchange of personnel	
	ICT manufacturing	Software	ICT manufacturing	Software	ICT manufacturing	Software	ICT manufacturing	Software
None	87.42%	74.3%	76.67%	58.6%	81.46%	67.1%	77.33%	55.7%
Seldom	8.61%	14.3%	6.0%	10.0%	2.65%	11.4%	2.67%	5.7%
Medium	2.65%	10.0%	12.67%	21.4%	11.92%	15.7%	12%	27.1%
Frequent	1.32%	0%	4.67%	4.3%	2.65%	5.7%	7.33%	7.1%
Very frequent	0%	1.4%	0%	5.7%	1.32%	0%	0.67%	4.3%
Total	100%	100%	100%	100%	100%	100%	100%	100%

Source: Questionnaire survey in Shenzhen in 2006.

production, storage and distribution of information as a center of economic and technological activities (Simon and Rehn, 1988, p. 48). The fact that many developed countries have committed themselves to carrying out research and development and technological innovation in the electronics industry with the expectation of keeping their lead in the global economy has not gone unnoticed in China. Under such circumstances, the Chinese government started to undertake substantial steps to develop its electronics industry and to try to close the technological gap between the industrialized countries and China, as has been elaborated in Chapter 4.

Other than the necessary investment initiated by the state in significant research projects, the central government also intended to attract more foreign capital and absorb imported technologies to build up the indigenous capability of the electronics industry. To achieve such objectives, certain places at the end of 1970s were selected as special economic zones within the socialist territory for the attraction of foreign investment, promotion of exports and adoption of modern technology, as well as advanced management know-how (Bruton *et al.*, 2005; Ng and Tang, 2004; Wong and Chu, 1985; Wu, 1999). Given that Shenzhen was only a border town without any industrial foundation or glorious history, there was no harm in using it as an experimental site to test the feasibility of the opening-up policy. To the central government, Shenzhen was more an import/export base than a technology center in the across-the-board deployment and plan for the development of the electronics industry and even the entire national economy.

Back in the mid-1980s, the central government selected several eastern coastal regions to build up high technology centers including Beijing, Shanghai, Jiangsu Province and Guangdong Province, with the intention of concentrating the limited national resources to promote the economic and technological performance of the electronics industry (Simon and Rehn, 1988). However, Shenzhen was not given such priority for two reasons. As the capital of Guangdong Province, Guangzhou was not only one of the most prosperous cities but also harbored a great amount of educational resources and large numbers of technical staff that made it a preferred site for the construction of a high-tech center for the electronics industry in southern China. Due to the complete lack of research institutes and universities, Shenzhen was totally unable to undertake responsibility for technological innovation and advancement at that time. When Shenzhen was selected by the central government to become the first and foremost special economic zone in China, it was positioned in a place where it could bring about an influx of foreign as well as domestic capital, massive internal migration of young and cheap workers from all over the country and create a rapidly growing urban economy with manufacturing and services as its two important pillars. However, it is impossible for Shenzhen to be a plateau of high-end technology in the eyes of the central government. Even Guangzhou was unable to undertake high-level R&D and production for the IC sector that involves the most high-end and complicated technology among the sub-sectors within the electronics industry. As shown in Table 6.10, there were 13 main facilities and eight major research institutes for IC manufacture and R&D in the 1980s, but none of them was located in Shenzhen or Guangzhou. In sharp contrast, Beijing and Shanghai had the capability to conduct IC manufacturing and R&D.

Table 6.10. Key IC R&D and production facilities in China, 1986.

Name	Location
Manufacturing	
Jiangnan Semiconductor Factory	Wuxi, Jiangsu Province
Tianguang Electronics Factory	Qinan, Gansu
Dongguang 878 Factory	Beijing
Changzhou Semiconductor Factory	Changzhou, Jiangsu Province
Bejing Semiconductor #2	Beijing
Bejing Semiconductor #3	Beijing
Shaoxing Electronics Factory	Shaoxing, Zhejiang Province
Shanghai #5 Components Factory	Shanghai
Shanghai #14 Radio Factory	Shanghai
Shanghai #19 Radio Factory	Shanghai
CAS Factory #109	Beijing
Lishan Microelectronics Corporation	Xian, Shanxi Province
Tianjin Semiconductor Factory	Tianjin
Research and Development	
Institute of Semiconductors, CAS	Beijing
Institute of Microelectronics, Qinghua University	Beijing
Institute of Metallurgy, CAS	Shanghai
Institute of Microelectronics, Fudan University	Shanghai
Solid state Research Institute, MEI (#24)	Sichuan Province
Nanjing Solid State Device Research Institute	Nanjing
Hebei Semiconductor Research Institute	Shijiazhuang, Hebei Province
Shenyang Liaohe Experimental Institute (#47)	Shenyang, Liaoning Province

Source: Simon and Rehn (1988, p. 67).

In addition, the strategically regional planning for the software industry designed by the central government did not cover Shenzhen either. The year 2001 witnessed the resolution of the central government to develop its software industry when it consolidated the original 40 software parks into 11 national software industry bases for better promotion. The location of these software industry bases included Beijing, Shanghai, Dalian, Chengdu, Xian, Jinan, Guangzhou, Changsha, Hangzhou, Nanjing and Zhuhai (Pecht, 2006, pp. 221–222). Shenzhen was not included in this group.

The next section will focus on the software industry, especially the IC design sub-sector to further understand the strategies, selectivity and capability of the Shenzhen municipal government and local state-firm strategic coordination, in order to avoid a discursive discussion of industrial strategies and policies and to eliminate the confusion arising from the different nature of firms, since the ICT industry broadly involves lots of sub-sectors. As one of the most innovative sectors with extremely high requirements for talent and finance-raising, the IC design sector mainly concentrated in three city-regions namely Beijing, Shanghai and Shenzhen, which together harbored around 80 percent of IC design firms in China at the end of 2006 (Zhou, 2007). Although Shenzhen attracted 25 percent of the IC design firms in the whole country, the sales revenue produced by Shenzhen's IC design sector was only 0.15 billion *yuan*, much lower than that of Shanghai (2.3 billion *yuan*) and Beijing (1.5 billion *yuan*) in 2006 (MII, 2007).

A brief analysis has identified the poor technology capability of Shenzhen's IC design firms, similar to the situation in the whole of the ICT industry in Shenzhen. The technology level of Shenzhen's IC design firms that can be measured by the line width adopted in the design was much lower than that of the national level. The finer the line width is, the higher the level of required technology. In general, it is rather simple to understand and reproduce the larger than 0.35 um technology of line width that has already been discarded by foreign IC design firms. Products designed on the basis of this technology level are easily duplicated, due to their less complicated design layout. As shown in Fig. 6.4, 41 percent of IC design firms in China adopted the smaller than 0.18 μm technology while only 4 percent of Shenzhen's IC design firms were able to use the same-level technology. Only 28 percent of IC design firms in China involved the larger than 0.35 um technology, while 44 percent of Shenzhen's firms were still stuck at this low technology level (Fig. 6.4).

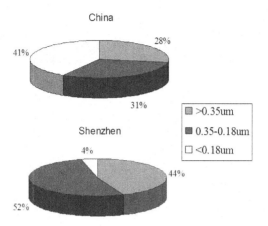

Figure 6.4.   Technology level of the IC design firms in China and Shenzhen.
Source: SMIC and SICA (2008, p. 34); Zhou (2007, p. 20).

6.3.2. *Selectivity and strategies of the Shenzhen municipal government*

Shenzhen municipal government appears to be uninterested in encouraging and supporting local S&T activities and disregards the problems facing local firms in their process of innovation, such as the shortage of highly-qualified talent and capital. During the period 2001–2005, the proportion of expenditure on science and technology by the Shenzhen municipal government to GDP had been much lower than that of the national level (Fig. 6.5).[2]

Meanwhile, there exists a long-standing problem in local policies concerning attracting and retaining highly qualified talent in Shenzhen. Local *hukou* policy is an important political tool for local governments to retain highly qualified talent. Residents with *hukou* not only have a sense of belonging but also enjoy a series of material benefits in education, medical care, insurance, etc. However, the current *hukou* policy of Shenzhen is detrimental to retaining talent because it is very difficult for migrants to obtain the certification of *hukou*. There were 312,600 residents with *hukou* and 1500 residents without *hukou* at the end of 1979 (SZSB, 2008). However,

---

[2]Expenditures on science and technology refer to the expenses appropriated from the government budget for the scientific and technological expenditure, including new products development expenditure, expenditure for intermediate trials and subsidies for important scientific research (CSSB and MOST, 2006, p. 304).

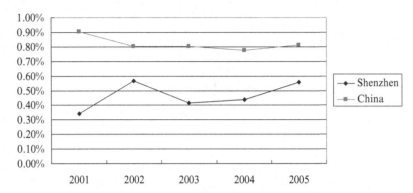

Figure 6.5.   Ratio of government expenditure on science and technology to GDP in Shenzhen and China, 2001–2005.

Source: CSSB (2006); CSSB and MOST (2006) and SZSB (2006).

the growth of residents without *hukou* has been much more rapid than that of residents with *hukou* during the period of 1980–2007. At the end of 2007, there were 2.12 million residents with *hukou*, far less than 6.49 million residents without *hukou* (SZSB, 2008). Furthermore, taking the year 1979 as an index, the gap in annual growth between residents with and without *hukou* appeared to be huge in the period 1980–2007 (Fig. 6.6). Residents with *hukou* in 2007 were seven times greater than those in 1979, while the number of residents without *hukou* had augmented 4303 times during the period 1980–2007 (Fig. 6.6). Furthermore, the relation of residents with *hukou* to residents without *hukou* was only 1:8 times in 1979, but a staggering 1:620 times in 2007. The average annual growth rate of residents with *hukou* was 7.8 percent in Shenzhen, significantly lower than 38 percent that for residents without *hukou* (SZSB, 2008). Compared to Shenzhen, Shanghai has a rather loose *hukou* policy to attract and retain its talent. There are 13.59 million residents with *hukou*, much larger than 4.99 million residents without *hukou* at the end of 2007 (SSB, 2008). The status of the overwhelmingly large numbers of residents without *hukou* made Shenzhen more like a hotel than a home for local people. The lack of a sense of belonging led to less enthusiasm and passion by local residents to make their contribution to Shenzhen.

Apart from the unreasonable *hukou* policy, the regulation for certifying the residence of external highly qualified talent released by the local government is also regarded as problematic for attracting and retaining talent (Laoheng *et al.*, 2004, p. 111). According to the "Regulations of Application

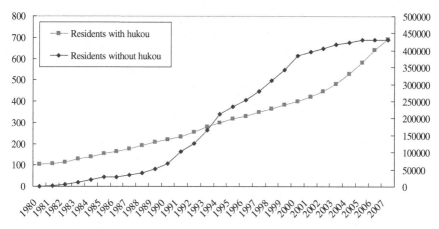

Figure 6.6. Comparison of population between residents with and without *hukou* in Shenzhen, 1980–2007 (population in 1979 = 100).
Source: SZSB (2008).

for Residence Certification of People with Ability in Shenzhen" released in 2002, people who have been hired to fill technology or management positions and held one of the following certificates: (1) senior specified technology; (2) senior technical engineer; (3) Master's Degree, are qualified to apply for the certification of residence in Shenzhen.[3] Once they were certificated, they were able to enjoy some treatment that only residents with *hukou* had been able to enjoy. This regulation was criticized by many people who thought that Shenzhen suffered from a loss of talent because of the inappropriate regulations released by the Shenzhen municipal government (Laoheng *et al.*, 2004). A resident in Shenzhen complained, "no one would like to work in the city which denies his contribution. My husband graduated from Shanghai Jiaotong University with a seven-year work experience in one of the biggest companies in his field. However, he could not obtain the *hukou* of Shenzhen. And one of my friends opened 4 companies and has contributed a lot to Shenzhen's economy, but he does not possess the *hukou* of Shenzhen either" (Laoheng *et al.*, 2004, pp. 111–112). Shenzhen is very different from China's other traditional cities in many ways while the Shenzhen municipal government seems unable to realize its uniqueness and make the best use of Shenzhen' advantages and bypass its disadvantages.

---

[3]Available at: http://www.szsti.net/law/stpy4/200607/P020060814535047223204.doc., accessed 10 January 2009.

In terms of industrial policy, the Shenzhen municipal government took less powerful action to develop its IC design sector. In order to carry out the national 18th Document released in 2000 by the State Council, the Shenzhen municipal government released its own 11th Document of "Policies about Encouraging the Development of the Software Industry" (*guli ruanjian chanye fazhan de ruogan zhengce*) and 14th Document of "Regulations about Facilitating Shenzhen's IC Manufacturing Industry" (*jiakuai fazhan shenzhenshi jicheng dianlu zhizaoye de ruogan guiding*) in 2001 to promote its software and IC manufacturing industries. Nevertheless, compared to the 18th document released by the State Council, there was no exclusive support for the IC design firms that appeared in Shenzhen's 11th and 14th documents. IC design firms did not enjoy a similar tax-reduction policy as their counterparts located in Beijing and Shanghai (Laoheng *et al.*, 2004, p. 225). Although the Shenzhen municipal government put forward a detailed proposal to develop its IC industry, the performance of Shenzhen's IC design firms was far behind its counterparts in Beijing and Shanghai due to the Shenzhen municipal government's lack of ability to estimate the risks and benefits that the investment in the IC industry would bring and the absence of great foresight and courage to invest in such a high-risk but pivotal industry (Laoheng *et al.*, 2004).

In addition to the failure to stimulate S&T activities as well as the inability to retain high-tech talent and develop the high-risk sector, the Shenzhen municipal government failed to regulate its market environment. It is very interesting to note that non-innovative software firms had achieved higher profit margins than innovative ones, and more innovative than non-innovative software firms in Shenzhen lost money during the period 2003–2005 (Fig. 6.7).[4] Around 14 percent of non-innovative firms, compared to 25 percent of innovative firms, lost money in 2005 when 44 percent of non-innovative firms obtained a profit margin larger than 10 percent, in contrast to 25 percent of innovative firms that achieved the same profit margin (Fig. 6.7(a)). More non-innovative firms made a higher profit margin and less non-innovative firms lost their money from 2003 to 2004. Around 29 percent of non-innovative firms lost money in 2003 and the number decreased to 14 percent in 2005. Meanwhile, 36 percent of non-innovative firms obtained a profit margin of more than 10 percent in 2003 and this number increased to 44 percent in 2005 (Fig. 6.7). This

---

[4]Innovative firms here refers to firms who at least hold one granted patent while non-innovative firms refer to those who do not obtain one patent certification.

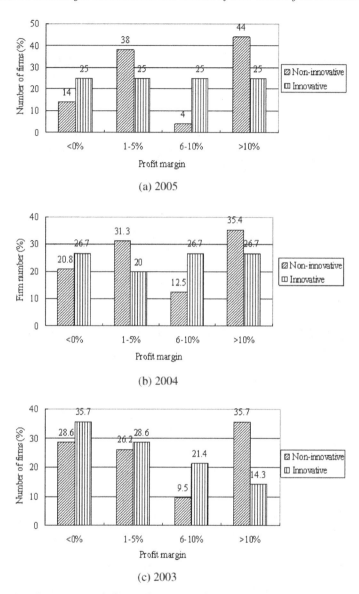

Figure 6.7.   Comparison of the profit margin of innovative and non-innovative firms, 2003–2005.

Source: Questionnaire survey in Shenzhen in 2006.

peculiar phenomenon suggests that those firms who did not invest in innovative activities were able to make more money while innovation-involved firms could easily fail in Shenzhen. In such an institutional and market environment, it is no wonder that most of the firms in Shenzhen showed no interest in innovation-involved activities.

6.3.3. State-firm strategic coordination in Shenzhen

In view of the *laissez-faire* attitude to S&T activities and insufficient ability to guide and regulate its economy and market environment by the Shenzhen municipal government, it comes as no surprise that state-firm strategic coordination in Shenzhen is rather weak. While the correlation analysis based on 110 IC design firms in Shenzhen has illustrated the significant and strong relationship between state-firm strategic coordination and firm-level innovative performance in Shenzhen ($r = 0.750$, $p = 0.000$), the degree of state-firm strategic coordination measured by project-based, product-based and award-based coordination has been disappointingly low in Shenzhen.[5] A close examination revealed that less than 15 percent of IC design firms participated at least once in research projects initiated by government or obtained financial support from government while only 2.7 percent of firms had opportunities to provide products for government in Shenzhen (Table 6.11).[6] Although 48 percent of IC design firms were awarded funding by government, most of them were awarded by the Shenzhen municipal government as "Shenzhen high-tech firms". It is revealed that the standard of examination for high-tech firms established by the Shenzhen municipal government is much lower than the national newly released examination standard, according to which more than 40 percent of Shenzhen's high-tech firms would be disqualified (Liu, 14 July 2008). Hence, the fact that a large number of firms were awarded funding by the Shenzhen municipal

---

[5]At the end of 2006, Shenzhen had hosted 120 IC design firms and industrial organizations. The innovative performance is measured by the granted intention patents that IC design firms hold, which is available on the online database established by Shanghai Silicon Intellectual Property Exchange (SSIPEX). The state-firm strategic coordination is measured by the sum of the project-based, product-based and award-based coordination, which can be collected from the website of each firm, in-depth face-to-face interviews and related newspapers.

[6]Again, the detailed information of the state-firm project-based, product-based and award-based coordination is obtained from the website of each firm, in-depth face-to-face interview and related newspapers, as well as an annual report by the IC industrial association (Zhou, 2007).

Table 6.11.   State-firm strategic coordination in Shenzhen.

	Project-based	Product-based	Award-based
Number of firms with strategic coordination with government	16	3	53
Number of firms without strategic coordination with government	95	107	57
The degree of state-firm strategic coordination	14.55%	2.73%	48.18%

Source: Zhou (2007); website of each IC design firm.

government does not point to a better award-based strategic coordination, but reflects the limited ability of the Shenzhen municipal government to distinguish the speculative firms from those who really invested in innovation-related activities.

The interview notes generated an insight into further understanding the innovation-related strategies and selectivity of Shenzhen's IC design firms. It is found that the barriers to innovation such as financial constraints and the lack of high-tech talent that have been highlighted by Shanghai's IC design firms appear to even more problematic for Shenzhen's IC design firms. An interviewee revealed that

> Shenzhen is a city that is well-known for its lack of highly-educated people. We come here not to conduct R&D activities but to open a sales office to better support our customers. Many of them are located in Shenzhen. (Interview notes, 18 August 2008.)

Another one disclosed that

> Innovation in Shenzhen is actually only the change in product appearance and simple functions based on market demands. Real technological innovation requires a great deal of capital which most of the firms like us cannot afford. I think that firms which intend to conduct innovation-related activities will not select Shenzhen because this city is not suitable for research and development but rather for marketing and sales. If we are lucky to survive and accumulate adequate capital in the future, we will move to Beijing and Shanghai to conduct R&D activities. But who knows what will happen tomorrow. (Interview notes, 21 August 2008.)

With inadequate capital, most of the firms in Shenzhen are small scale and are generally believed to be very reluctant to conduct innovation-involved activities, as an interviewee analyzed.

IC design firms are small-scale and employ less than 30 people, in most cases around 10 people in Shenzhen. Generally speaking, small IC design firms are more reluctant to invest in R&D activities than bigger ones for three reasons. First, small firms have far less resources for innovation, such as the shortage of highly-qualified engineers and inadequate money to invest in R&D activities but they are still able to easily make profits through quickly occupying the market at a much lower price. Second, it is more unbearable for small firms to confront the failure of their innovation-related activities, if they have any, while the capital strength of big firms enables them to stand the loss resulting from the failure of innovation and continue to invest in other innovation-involved activities. Finally, small firms do not need to worry about their brand and reputation but that is a significant restriction for bigger firms due to copying or imitation. For small firms, copying others' IC layouts did not engender any penalty and loss in the institutional environment characterized by poor protection of IP rights in Shenzhen. However, the bigger firms in Shenzhen might refer to the designs of others but will not totally copy or imitate without any modification in consideration of the reputation that it has taken them many years to build up. (Interview notes, 13 August 2008.)

Furthermore, the small-scale IC design firms without strong R&D background in Shenzhen have missed the opportunities to provide products for, or cooperate with, local large end product manufacturing firms, which in turn has impaired their capability to invest and conduct R&D activities.

The famous complete system vendors in many ICT fields such as Huawei, ZTE, Konka, TCL, Skyworth, etc. generated a great deal of demand for IC products, which is actually the most important reason for the location-selection of Shenzhen's IC design firms. However, these complete system vendors started to order products from IC design firms in Beijing and Shanghai besides foreign IC design firms, since the small-scale IC design firms in Shenzhen have been unable to meet the high requirements and demands. These complete system vendors even transfer their R&D departments to Beijing and Shanghai in pursuit of a better industrial environment and R&D resources. (Interview notes, 13 September 2008.)

A report edited by the Shenzhen Academy of Social Science asserted that Shenzhen currently is unable to take on high-level R&D tasks due to its lack of highly-qualified talent (Le and Wulan, 2008). It also warned that Shenzhen was confronted with the challenge of "hollowing out of research and development" as more and more of its high-tech firms relocated their R&D department to other places, because Shenzhen was not only short of highly-qualified talent but had also lost its intermediate technical staff (Le and Wulan, 2008, p. 40). Around 70 percent of invention patent applications were produced by only very few ICT giants such as Huawei, while most of the small- and medium-sized firms seldom invested in R&D activities and over 80 percent of S&T firms in Shenzhen failed to mobilize capital for innovation-involved activities (Le and Wulan, 2008, p. 35).

More strikingly, it has been disclosed that the motivation of Shenzhen's IC design firms for innovation-related investment has been depressed by the regional characteristics and market environment. Although the existence of large end product ICT firms attracted numerous IC design firms to locate nearby and made Shenzhen the largest consumer market for IC products in China, the active market environment failed to expedite competition and induce innovation. Instead, it leads to an eagerness by firms to accomplish quick success and instant benefits as well as an impatience regarding long-term investment in innovation. Producing nearly 20 percent of sales revenue and output value to China's ICT manufacturing industry, Shenzhen created an enormous consumer market for IC products at the end of 2004 (CSSB, 2005a; SZSB, 2005a). According to a report by Southern Metropolitan News, the market demand for IC products in the Pearl River Delta accounted for 70 percent of China's demand while Shenzhen approximately accounted for 80 percent of the demand in the Pearl River Delta.[7] This report also revealed that 80 percent of IC products in China were imported from Shenzhen and around 75 percent of them were used by Shenzhen's ICT manufacturing firms according to the statistics of the former Ministry of Information Industry. Along with the huge population and with the improvement in living standards of Chinese people, there is an increasing demand for low-end consumer electronics that do not require high-end technology. An IC design manager observed that

> As the electronic processing base in China, the PRD has produced a strong demand for IC products, which attracted a lot of IC design firms to locate in this region. Most of the IC design firms elsewhere had to establish their sales office in Shenzhen in order to grasp the market information as soon as possible and to better support their customers. Shenzhen's IC design firms enjoyed no preferential policies and no support from local governments, but the market opportunity is

---

[7] "Shenzhen touru 1.5yi wuchang fuchi Zhongxiao IC sheji qiye (Shenzhen invested 150 million to support small and medium size IC design firms)", 24 June 2003, *Nanfang dushi bao* (*Southern Metropolitan News*). Available at: http://tech.sina.com.cn/it/m/ 2003-06-24/1200201698.shtml. Accessed 18 December 2008.

the only resource of which IC design firms could take advantage because of the existence of main end product customers in Shenzhen (Laoheng *et al.*, 2004, p. 225).

In this sense, IC design firms in Shenzhen were quickly able to obtain market information and avoid the risks in marketing their products. However, the pattern of closeness to customers and prompt response to the market does not benefit innovation-related activities. A manager of an IC design firm summarized the characteristics of Shenzhen's IC design firms as follows:

> Shenzhen's IC design firms mainly focus on low-end chips that do not require complex technology and much capital investment. They occupy the market with extremely low prices and are satisfied with the narrow profit margin. They usually pursue the shortest design circle, lowest design cost and fastest speed to occupy the market. With this motto, they tend not to invest in R&D activities and hardly have a long-term orientation to innovation. Generally, they adopt a "replacement" (*tidai*) strategy, namely indigenous firms tend to develop the kinds of products that were introduced by leading foreign firms and accepted by the market in order to furthest reduce the risk. They try to lower the price as much as they can, which is not too difficult because of the transferred and mature technology involved in this kind of product as well as the cheap land and the existence of a large number of engineers in China. They do not need to worry about sales, not only because of the huge market demand in China but also because they have normally received design orders from their customers even before they started to design a product. Many of them even copy layouts in order to lower their costs and to more quickly occupy the market. (Interview notes, 13 August 2008.)

In a similar way, it has been revealed that

> Most of the end product manufacturers in China are located in the PRD. They indeed attracted a lot of IC design firms who pursue a prompt response to market demands with low-cost strategies. As you probably know, it normally takes us 1–2 years to develop a chip while the culture of "speed" in Shenzhen is against the slow process of research and development. Comparatively, the industrial environment is much better in Shanghai. Although Shanghai's IC design firms consider information from customers to be the most important source for developing a new product, they did not select Shenzhen as their location where most of their customers are located, in order to conduct R&D activities with great concentration and in a better institutional and market environment. (Interview notes, 6 August 2008.)

In view of the double difficulty (external environment and internal resources) involved in conducting innovation activities by Shenzhen's IC design firms, the local government should take effective actions to regulate the market, to cultivate or attract highly qualified talent and to stimulate and support the innovation-related activities of local firms. Again, it is emphasized by an IC design manager that the Shenzhen municipal government does not seem to be keen on taking such actions.

> I feel that the Shenzhen municipal government would not provide timely help to firms and I do not know whether it is because the municipal government is unable to do something to promote the institutional environment and encourage the innovation-related activities to improve the innovative performance of local firms or because it would not like to intervene in its economy and industry. To my knowledge, IC design firms such as ZTEIC, SMIT, Hisilicon, etc. who have achieved a better innovative and economic performance have a closer relationship with the central government than the local government. (Interview notes, 29 August 2008.)

Another person critically pointed out that the Shenzhen municipal government is reluctant to regulate its averse-innovation market environment because it cannot afford to damage the current prosperous economy that is mainly the result of low-end manufacturing, process and assembly, and is upheld by endless imitation, copying and disordered competition.

> We do not have any relations with local governments. Actually, most of Shenzhen's IC design firms do not have any strategic relationship with the local government. A benefit from locating in Shenzhen is to promptly get market information and feedback from our customers, rather than a better external innovative environment or well-regulated market. Shenzhen's IC firms are surely interested in and know the low-end market demand very well. We can "sense" the market information here, which you cannot achieve unless you open a sales office in Shenzhen. In fact, the energy and charm of Shenzhen lies in the disordered market competition and bad institutional environment as well as the *laissez-faire* attitude of local governments. I think without that Shenzhen could not have become the ICT manufacturing center in China and achieved a prosperous economy and urban growth. This is why the Shenzhen municipal government is reluctant to regulate its market and has to turn a blind eye to the unregulated market and institutional environment, so as to maintain high GDP growth as well as the prosperity and vitality of the city. (Interview notes, 20 August 2008.)

6.4. Summary

This chapter examined the process of state-firm strategic coordination in Shenzhen and its effect on the growth and technological innovation of the ICT industry. Detailed case studies revealed that although Shenzhen achieved a phenomenal growth in its ICT industry in recent years since it was selected by the central government in 1978 as the first special economic zone in China, the innovative performance of both ICT manufacturing and software sectors appeared to be rather poor. The successful story of Shenzhen (judging by its rapid growth in the ICT industry) was the result of a timely insertion designed by the central government into the restructured regional and global economy, along with the deepening of the spatial division of labor in the world. Exports and profits made by Shenzhen's industry were very much dependent upon low-end processing and the assembly of electronic products, with the core technology controlled by the advanced countries. Meanwhile, foreign-invested firms still took a lead in output value, exports and profits in this industry. Domestic firms will not be able to catch up within a short period of time. An analysis of the data and information obtained from a questionnaire survey disclosed that firms were persuaded to locate in Shenzhen by the agglomeration economies that owe a lot to the reform and opening-up policies. The ICT manufacturing and software design firms in Shenzhen developed among themselves frequent and extensive production linkages in supply and marketing, but little technological interaction and cooperation were found among firms within the ICT industrial cluster. This pattern is pre-determined by not only the pre-existing conditions and resources that Shenzhen held but also the design and planning of the central government who originally took Shenzhen as an experimental site for testing the validity of reform and opening-up policies and never built it up as a center of high-tech industry. Affected by this position that Shenzhen holds in the entire country, the local government showed no interest and limited capability in stimulating and encouraging local S&T activities and failed to promote a better institutional and market environment. In view of the disregard of both the central and local governments for technological innovation in Shenzhen, it is thus not surprising to observe that the degree of state-firm strategic coordination was very low. While the lack of highly qualified talent and mobilized capital has depressed the innovation-related motivation of Shenzhen's IC design firms, the huge and diversified market demand in China, especially the existence of many ICT manufacturing firms in Shenzhen, further resulted in the unpleasant fact that excess competition has forced Shenzhen's IC design firms to quickly occupy market segments with low prices at the expense of product quality. This process further contributed to the destruction of an innovative milieu, if there was any.

In recent decades, the nature and dynamics of uneven technological innovation in the globalizing world has attracted much scholarly attention. After a brief episode to proclaim the ascendance of a "flat" and "borderless world" over which nation-states seem to lose control and in which geography has lost its relevance, a "re-discovery" of "new economic geography" and "new regionalism" has placed back onto the research agenda issues concerning spatial agglomeration, industrial clusters, technological innovation and competitive advantages in "a regional world". However, endogenous growth and a regional perspective have been contested by others who stress the importance of external linkages along the production "pipelines" in the globalizing world. A central tenet brought up by the prolific literature of "new economic geography" or "new regionalism" is the perceived relationship between spatial agglomeration, industrial clustering and technological innovation, although the importance of internal and external linkages has been subjected to various interpretations. This tenet has been developed on the basis of theoretical and empirical research of cases in those regions that are economically advanced, technologically innovative and politically superior (Lin, 2009b). It remains uncertain whether or not the perceived notion concerning spatial agglomeration, industrial clustering and technological innovation can be applied to other regions and nations in the less developed world. Given the increasing and almost indispensable role played by China's ICT industry in the world economy, there are good reasons to believe that the production of knowledge in the "new economic geography" in the current era of intellectual globalization can no longer afford to miss the patterns, processes and practices found in the largest developing economy on earth, however irregular and abnormal they might be when benchmarked against Western norms. The intriguing patterns of spatial agglomeration, industrial clustering and technological innovation identified in Chapter 4 and this chapter seem to be contradictory to the normal theoretical expectation. However, they are not difficult to understand when the nature and strategies of key actors and agents involved is scrutinized and situated in an institutional and regional context. For the central government, its strategic support and selectivity in establishing several high-tech centers in China only reached few regions, while Shenzhen is too weak to be selected and promoted in terms of R&D and innovation. For the Shenzhen municipal government, its interests are not so much in building up a better innovative environment but maintaining the prosperous economy driven mainly by low-end production, processing and assembly. For the ICT firms in Shenzhen, their motivation and interests are not so much to explore any well-established research institutions or highly educated and innovative labor force, but rather to take advantage of the preferential treatments and concessional arrangements made by the local government as well as proximate linkages with suppliers and customers. The existence of cheap land and labor, coupled with a large and rapidly growing market domestically and internationally for ICT goods, has already presented to these firms an opportunity and potential lucrative enough for them to engage in mass assembly and processing of imported materials with a quick and substantial return. In contrast, knowledge-based and technology intensive activities usually require a long-term commitment without any secured and instant return. Few firms, if any, are interested in the risky venture of research and development while missing the opportunity to make quick money in Shenzhen and at this particular historical moment.

To further understand the uneven geography of technological innovation engendered by the different degree of state-firm strategic coordination in China, the next chapter will make a comparative study of Shanghai and Shenzhen with a focus on the software industry, since these two city-regions present a distinguished developmental trajectory, a distinct strategic position in the entire country, a different capability and determination of local governments to guide their industry and economy, and unique regional characteristics shaped by their history and pre-existing resources and conditions.

Chapter Seven

STATE-FIRM STRATEGIC COORDINATION AND TECHNOLOGICAL INNOVATION IN SHANGHAI AND SHENZHEN: A COMPARATIVE STUDY

7.1. Introduction

The study of the cases of Shanghai and Shenzhen in the previous two chapters has identified different patterns in the growth of the ICT industry and different degrees of state-firm strategic coordination. This chapter is intended to investigate and compare how the different degrees of state-firm strategic coordination taking place in different geographical and institutional contexts such as Shenzhen and Shanghai have led to their divergent innovation trajectories.

Shanghai and Shenzhen display a divergent historical trajectory that significantly shaped their strategic position which, in reverse, strengthened their path of growth. Shanghai has historically played a significant and irreplaceable role in the national economy. During the 1980s, one-sixth of the state revenues came from Shanghai. On the contrary, Shenzhen was only regarded as a small border town that was not harmful to be chosen as an experimental site to test the validity of the reform and open-door policies in China. The different strategic positions and historical trajectory interacted to exert a significant effect on the urban growth and the formation of different values, identity, culture and institutions between these two city-regions. Meanwhile, the Shanghai and Shenzhen municipal governments have adopted a different attitude and manner to involvment in their economy and industry. As identified in Chapters 5 and 6, the Shanghai municipal government was more powerful and more likely to guide its economy and had created a favorable environment for its enterprises, whereas the Shenzhen municipal government preferred a *laissez-faire* attitude to its economy and failed to build up an innovation-supportive environment. State-owned enterprises made a minor contribution to the growth of Shenzhen. However, they played a significant role in Shanghai's economy and historically dominated the growth of Shanghai. It is intriguing to see how these differences between Shanghai and Shenzhen have led to a divergent state-firm strategic coordination.

In explaining the regional difference in technological innovation, much attention has been paid to the inter-firm linkages in an industrial cluster and their effects on the production of knowledge and technology without taking into account other factors. As illustrated in previous chapters, the process of state-firm strategic coordination could stimulate and encourage innovation-involved activities, mitigate the risk of innovation and remove certain barriers to innovation in the case of China. Nevertheless, state-firm strategic coordination varies according to the different geographical and institutional contexts because local history and culture, local governments' capability and strategies, local firms nature and strategies and the central government's selectivity are vary across space. With the distinct characteristics of these two city-regions, Shanghai and Shenzhen can be greatly compared to understand how the different degree of state-firm strategic coordination has taken place to contribute to local innovative performance.

In order to make this point, this chapter is organized in five parts. It begins with a comparison of performance, industrial topology and capital structure of the software sector between Shanghai and Shenzhen. It is then followed by a historical review of the strategic role played by Shanghai and Shenzhen respectively in the entire country to understand the strategic consideration of the central government as well as the developmental trajectory of these two city-regions. Afterward, a detailed evaluation of the strategies and capability of local governments in building an innovation-supportive environment in Shanghai and Shenzhen will be conducted. Following this is an investigation of the difference in growth and innovation-related strategies of software firms between these two city-regions. Attention is then turned to a detailed comparison between Shanghai and Shenzhen in the process of state-firm strategic coordination to understand how this difference affected their innovative performance. The final part summarizes the major findings of this chapter.

7.2. Performance, Topology and Structure of the Software Sector in Shanghai and Shenzhen

The software sector in Shanghai and Shenzhen has presented very different characteristics in innovative and economic performance, topology of industrial clustering and capital structure. First of all, as illustrated in Chapter 5, Shanghai demonstrated a much better innovative performance than that of Shenzhen in the IC design sub-sector. A comparative analysis of the innovative performance in the whole software sector between Shenzhen and Shanghai revealed a similar pattern to the IC design sub-sector. As the national economic center, Shanghai attracted a large number of software firms with an employment location quotient of over three in 2004. As a representative of a successful economy during the period of economic transformation, Shenzhen was one of the most clustered city-regions in the software sector with an employment location quotient of nearly three in 2004. However, a close examination based on the data from a questionnaire survey on the software firms in Shanghai and Shenzhen has revealed a significant regional difference in innovative performance measured by both granted invention patents and new products. As shown in Table 7.1, on average the software firms in Shanghai held 0.9 granted invention patents, much higher than only 0.1 of Shenzhen's software firms. Over 21 percent of Shanghai's software firms achieved at least one granted invention patent, compared to less than 6 percent for the software firms in Shenzhen. Furthermore, the most innovative firm in Shanghai held 15 granted invention patents, three times higher than that of the most innovative firm in Shenzhen. As such, new products produced by Shanghai's software firms contributed 41 percent of sales revenue to the software sector, significantly higher than that of Shenzhen's software firms (25 percent).

Second, despite the high concentration of software firms in both Shanghai and Shenzhen, economic performance in Shanghai appears to be much better than that of Shenzhen. As shown in Table 7.2, the labor productivity of Shanghai was 0.37 million *yuan* per employee, much higher

Table 7.1. *T*-test results of innovative performance between software firms in Shanghai and Shenzhen, 2006.

Indicators	Mean		*T*-value	*P*-value
	Shanghai	Shenzhen		
Number of total granted invention patents (unit)	0.90	0.14	3.118**	0.002
Share of new products out of total sales revenue (percent)	41	25	2.255*	0.026

*The mean difference is at the 0.05 significance level.
**The mean difference is at the 0.01 significance level.
Source: Questionnaire survey in Shanghai and Shenzhen.

Table 7.2.   Major economic indicators of the software sector in Shanghai and Shenzhen, 2004.

	Shanghai	Shenzhen
Establishment	2863	1248
Employment (persons)	62,607	28,974
Ratio of employees with Master degree and above to total (percent)	13.30	6.86
Employment Location Quotient	3.19	2.83
Labor productivity (10,000 *yuan*/person)	37.49	24.05
Capital profitability (percent)	7.02	3.10
Average profits per firm achieved (10,000 *yuan*)	36.33	62.06

Source: SSB (2005a) and SZSB (2005a).

than 0.24 million *yuan* per employee of Shenzhen. As such, the capital profitability of Shanghai was over 7 percent, more than three times higher than that of Shenzhen. In addition, Shanghai's software firms achieved much higher profits than those of Shenzhen's software firms. The average profit per firm made in Shenzhen was 0.36 million *yuan*, much lower than 0.62 million *yuan* made by Shanghai. The software sector in Shanghai also attracted more highly qualified talent than Shenzhen. Over 13 percent of employees hold a Master's or higher degree in Shanghai, compared to only less than 7 percent in Shenzhen.

Third, Shanghai and Shenzhen present a different structure of software industrial clustering. Taking the IC design sub-sector as example, Shenzhen is full of small-scale domestic firms and the branches of MNCs with limited high-tech talents and capital (Fig. 7.1). The high concentration of Shenzhen's IC design sector is due to the existence of several large electronics end product manufacturers. They are located nearby to seize market information as soon as possible and provide the after-sales service as best as they can. In contrast, the average size of the IC design firms in Shanghai is larger than that of Shenzhen's firms. Many of Shanghai's IC design firms were founded by overseas returnees with high-end technologies, professional research teams with years of experience and abundant venture capital.[1] This

---

[1]Firms founded by the overseas returnees are singled out because of their specific characteristics. In general, they are grouped into foreign-invested firms in Chinese statistics since the registered capital came from foreign countries. However, the operational model, philosophy and strategies of these kinds of firms are significantly different from those of the foreign-invested firms. Some scholar even suggested that these kinds of firms should be classified as domestic firms.

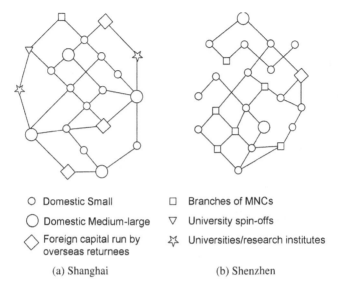

○ Domestic Small	☐ Branches of MNCs
◯ Domestic Medium-large	▽ University spin-offs
◇ Foreign capital run by overseas returnees	✠ Universities/research institutes

(a) Shanghai   (b) Shenzhen

Figure 7.1.   Typology of the spatial clustering in Shanghai and Shenzhen.
Source: Author's interview and observations.

type of IC design firm is claimed to be the most innovative group in China (Fuller, 2009). Several spin-offs from universities significantly benefited from easy access to technologies and talents. Given the different origin of clustering and regional milieu as well as the different types and attributes of local firms, Shanghai and Shenzhen surely presented interesting cases for comparison.

Finally, the software sector in Shanghai and Shenzhen shows a different structure of ownership. Although the privately-owned enterprises domi-nated in establishment and employment in both Shanghai and Shenzhen, the enterprises invested by Hong Kong, Macao and Taiwan capital played an important role in Shenzhen while the foreign-invested enterprises contributed a lot to the software sector of Shanghai. As shown in Table 7.3, privately-owned enterprises have accounted for 68 percent of establishments and 38 percent of employment in Shenzhen, much higher than those of other types of enterprises. Although 65 percent of establishments were invested with private capital in Shanghai, much higher than that of other types of enterprises, the privately-invested enterprises only accounted for 34 percent of total employment, lower than the 40 percent of the foreign-invested enterprises. Hong Kong, Macao and Taiwan invested enterprises accounted for 10 percent of establishments and 14 percent of employment in Shenzhen,

Table 7.3.   Ownership structure of the software sector in Shanghai and Shenzhen, 2004.

Types of enterprises	Establishment		Employment	
	Shanghai	Shenzhen	Shanghai	Shenzhen
State-owned enterprises	0.87%	0.55%	0.80%	1.15%
Privately owned enterprises	64.83%	68.22%	33.83%	38.14%
HK/Macao/Taiwan invested enterprises	5.03%	10.09%	8.60%	13.70%
Foreign-invested enterprises	19.39%	8.52%	39.78%	28.52%
Others	9.88%	12.62%	16.99%	18.50%

Source: SSB (2005a) and SZSB (2005b).

compared to only 5 percent and 7 percent, respectively in Shanghai. The foreign-invested enterprises accounted for 20 percent of establishments and 40 percent of employment in Shanghai, compared to only 9 percent and 29 percent, respectively, in Shenzhen.

7.3. Strategic Selectivity of the State

7.3.1. *Strategic position of Shanghai and Shenzhen assigned by the central government: A historical perspective*

(1) Shanghai: A National Economic Center with a Strong Industrial and S&T Foundation

Shanghai, the largest metropolis in China, has played a strategic role in modern China (Yeung and Sung, 1996). Located midway along the China coast, Shanghai enjoyed a convenient link with not only Chinese cities but also cities in Japan, Korea and other countries of the Asia-Pacific region, which laid a solid foundation for its strategic position in the whole nation (Yeung, 1996, p. 4). Shanghai has been evolving into a major metropolis since the 1860s and been recognized as "the greatest city and port in all Asia... and the fifth or sixth largest in the world by 1932" (Wei, 1987, p. 64). It once was one of the most innovative cities of the world hosting the world's first and largest textile mills and opening its cinema only five years later than the first large movie house in San Francisco (Howe, 1981, p. xv; quoted from Yeung, 1996, p. 8).

Shanghai continued to take the lead after the foundation of the People's Republic of China. In the first place, Shanghai has been one of the most developed city-regions in new China. It had contributed around 7 percent of GDP to the country during the period 1952–1978. This number even

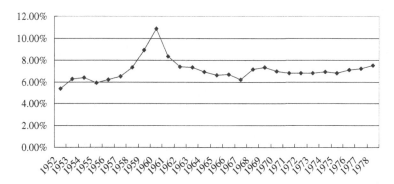

Figure 7.2.   Shanghai's share of GDP in China, 1952–1978.

Source: Calculated from CSSB (1999a, pp. 3 and 342).

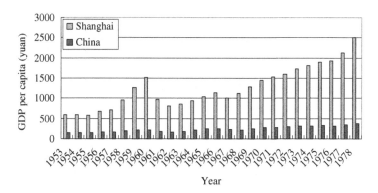

Year

Figure 7.3.   GDP per capita in Shanghai and China, 1953–1978.

Source: Calculated from CSSB (1999a, pp. 3 and 342).

reached 11 percent in 1960 (Fig. 7.2). Moreover, the GDP per capita of Shanghai had been much higher than that of the national level during the period 1953–1978. As shown in Fig. 7.3, Shanghai's GDP per capita was nearly 600 *yuan*, in sharp contrast to only 142 *yuan* of China as a whole in 1953. The gap further dramatically expanded at the end of 1978 when Shanghai had achieved a GDP per capita of 2738 *yuan*, six times higher than that of China as a whole.

Second, Shanghai was one of the most significant industrial centers in China since the founding of the PRC and made a great contribution to the state revenue during the period of reform and opening-up. Shanghai was the cradle of China's industry where the nation's first 10,000-ton hydraulic

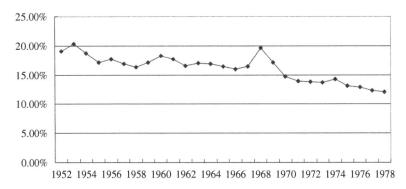

Figure 7.4.   Shanghai's share of gross industrial output value in China, 1952–1978.
Source: Calculated from CSSB (1999a, pp. 36 and 353).

compressor, first 10,000-ton ship, first man-made satellite, first roll of cable and first bag of laundry detergent were manufactured (Chen, 2007, p. 5). As shown in Fig. 7.4, Shanghai contributed 20 percent of gross industrial output value to the whole country in 1953 and this number remained at over 15 percent during the period 1952–1969. Although this number has descended since 1970, it had remained above 12 percent before 1978. Being a significant industrial center of China, Shanghai was flattered by the domestic consumers who were actually proud of using products labeled "made in Shanghai" because they generally believed that products manufactured by Shanghai symbolized a good quality and high taste. Furthermore, Shanghai was described as the "golden cash-cow" of the planned economy because around one-sixth of the state revenue had been derived from Shanghai (Chen, 2007; Yeung, 1996, p. 9). During the period 1949–1984, 84 percent of the local revenues of the Shanghai municipal government were remitted to the central government (White III, 1989, p. 9).

Finally, the earlier opening to foreigners made Shanghai an international metropolis attractive to talent and capital from the world. Back at the end of the Opium War (1839–1842), Shanghai became one of the treaty ports through which foreign ideas and practices flowed in and influenced its development in all aspects. From then on, Shanghai started to undertake international business and host a large number of foreign residents (Wei, 1987, p. 19). The foreign settlements had become an established society in Shanghai as early as the beginning of the twentieth century and the number of foreign residents doubled from 1915 to 1930 (Wei, 1987, pp. 104, 110). The value of foreign trade in Shanghai contributed approximately 56 percent to

China in 1936 (Sit, 1998, p. 86). At the end of 1989, Shanghai still received over 12 percent of the total foreign direct investment for the whole country (CSSB, 1999a, pp. 60 and 360). It is believed that international trade was the crucial factor affecting the formation of the huge metropolis as Shanghai is today (Rimmington, 1998).

(2) Shenzhen: An Experimental Zone with a Business Culture Advocating "Quick Response to the Market"

Shenzhen surely cannot compare with Shanghai in terms of Shanghai's glorious history. Nonetheless, Shenzhen has been an economic miracle over the past three decades. Shenzhen was a border village without any industrial foundation and any impressive history before the 1978 economic reform. Being a neighbor of Hong Kong, Shenzhen was assigned to be one of the SEZ to link the nation to the outside world. Shenzhen was originally labeled as the "window of the open-door policy" and in the 1980s to be an experimental base for testing the feasibility and efficiency of the reform and open-door policies in China (Liu, 2005, p. 9; Pan, 1996). It is revealed that the locational selection of SEZs made by the Chinese government was not based on whether the city-regions had a strong industrial foundation or a better innovative capability (Wu, 1999). On the contrary, the central government intended to avoid selecting places which had played a significant role in the national economy, such as Shanghai (Bathelt and Zeng, 2009). As an official in the Shanghai municipal government revealed, "Shanghai is so important to the national economy that the central government was less likely to allow experimentation that might threaten its revenues. Failure in Shanghai would affect the entire country" (Segal, 2003, p. 91).

Shenzhen has embarked on a path of rapid economic growth and urban expansion since the 1978 reform. "Shenzhen speed" was coined to characterize the amazing economic efficiency and rapid urban growth that Shenzhen has experienced in a short term (Liu, 2005, p. 107). At the outset of the economic reform, the GDP per capita in Shenzhen was only 600 *yuan*, much lower than the nearly 2600 *yuan* of Shanghai (SZSB, 2008; CSSB, 1999a). However, Shenzhen soon exceeded Shanghai at the end of 1984 with its per capita GDP of 3504 *yuan*, five times as high as it was in 1979 (SZSB, 2008). It was not until 1996 that Shanghai regained its lead in this competition. "Shenzhen speed" confirmed that the favorable policies could turn a laggard village into a wealthy urban region. It is noted that the phenomenal growth in Shenzhen could have not taken place without considerable foreign direct investment (FDI). The value of FDI that Shenzhen actually utilized

Table 7.4.   Actually utilized FDI in Shenzhen and Shanghai, 1979–1998.

Year	Shenzhen	Shanghai	China	Ratio of Shenzhen to China	Ratio of Shanghai to China
1979	0.05	—	—	—	—
1980	0.28	—	—	—	—
1981	0.86	0.03	—	—	—
1982	0.58	0.03	—	—	—
1983	1.13	0.11	6.36	17.77%	1.73%
1984	1.86	0.28	12.58	14.79%	2.23%
1985	1.80	0.62	16.61	10.84%	3.73%
1986	3.65	0.98	18.74	19.48%	5.23%
1987	2.74	2.12	23.14	11.84%	9.16%
1988	2.87	3.64	31.94	8.99%	11.40%
1989	2.93	4.22	33.92	8.64%	12.44%
1990	3.90	1.77	34.87	11.18%	5.08%
1991	3.99	1.75	43.66	9.14%	4.01%
1992	4.49	12.59	110.07	4.08%	11.44%
1993	9.89	23.18	275.15	3.59%	8.42%
1994	12.50	32.31	337.67	3.70%	9.57%
1995	13.10	32.5	375.21	3.49%	8.66%
1996	20.51	47.16	417.25	4.92%	11.30%
1997	16.61	48.08	452.57	3.67%	10.62%
1998	16.64	36.38	454.63	3.66%	8.00%

Note: — Data is not available.
Source: SZSB (2007) and CSSB (1999a).

accounted for over 10 percent of the total utilized FDI by China during the period 1979–1986. This number further climbed to nearly 20 percent in 1986 (Table 7.4). The value of FDI attracted by Shenzhen during this time had been much higher than that of Shanghai. The latter only started to play a pivotal role in attracting FDI at the beginning of the 1990s when the state was devoted to constructing Shanghai as a "dragon head" and an economic, financial and trading center to lead the Yangtze River Delta and even the whole country (Yeung, 1996, p. 16). FDI has increasingly favored Shanghai over Shenzhen in recent years (Zhao and Zhang, 2007).

Despite the outstanding performance of Shenzhen in attracting FDI, Shenzhen was considered as more of a manufacturing and processing base than a center of technological innovation in the eyes of foreign investors and the central government. In order to boost the growth of the electronics industry in an efficient and effective manner, the central state has mobilized limited resources to support four city-regions in recent years, namely Beijing, Shanghai, Jiangsu and Guangdong. All of them were assigned a pre-given role by the central government according to their regional characteristics. Shanghai was targeted to focus on the application and commercialization of electronic technologies while Guangdong Province only served the country as an electronics export area (Rehn, 1989, p. 149). The central government initiated a significant project in Shanghai to improve the technological capability of the IC industry, whereas Shenzhen, without any S&T resources, was not given similar priority (Rehn, 1989).

The strategic roles played by Shanghai and Shenzhen, coupled with their evolution of ownership structure in the last decades have shaped a distinct relationship between local governments and firms. FDI dominated Shenzhen's economic growth through producing 63 percent of total industrial output during the period 1979–1987 (Wu, 1990, p. 58). While the foreign-invested firms in Shenzhen contributed 30 percent of establishment, 39 percent of employment and 55 percent of industrial output to Guangdong Province, which made Shenzhen the leading city in China in terms of foreign-involved activities in 1986 (Yee, 1992, p. 180), the state-owned enterprises in Shanghai hosted 70 percent of employment, produced 90 percent of the gross value of industrial output and contributed nearly 92 percent of profits-tax at the end of the 1980s (Mok, 1996, p. 211). Despite the declining role played by the SOEs in Shanghai's economy during the 1980s, they still hosted over 60 percent of industrial workers, produced 74 percent of the gross value of industrial output and contributed 79 percent of profits-tax to Shanghai at the end of 1990 (Mok, 1996, p. 211). Furthermore, the SOEs remained as the engine of Shanghai's economic growth during the 1990s with the six largest state-owned enterprise groups, contributing 87 percent of total output value to Shanghai's information technology industry in 2000 (Segal, 2003, p. 88). As a result, when Shenzhen developed an industrial strategy that advocates a free economy without much state intervention, Shanghai adopted a strategy of "high input, high risk and a high level of reliance on government guidance" in their industrial growth (Segal, 2003, p. 92). The majority of high-tech industrial enterprises tend to be large state-owned enterprises that have a strong relationship with the municipal administration (Segal, 2003, p. 118). The Shanghai municipal government was powerful in guiding local industrial development: "In Shanghai, the local government dominates and it knows how to take advantage of the old planning system. Even branches of central state ministries must first answer to the local government" (Segal, 2003, p. 92).

The practices of open-door policies not only led to the rapid growth in Shenzhen but also brought about a local culture that advocates "speed" in production and market occupation and values immediate economic rewards instead of long-term R&D investment. One of the objectives in establishing the SEZs was to absorb the transferred technology and train local labor which, however, failed to be delivered by Shenzhen. The FDI, especially the capital investment from Hong Kong, Macao and Taiwan that dominated the industrial growth of Shenzhen, was mainly lured by the low cost of the labor force and land, with their operations merely confined to simple assembly and packaging at the outset of the economic reforms (Wong and Chu, 1985, p. 13). The foreign-invested firms tended to regard Shenzhen as one of their manufacturing and processing bases with a specific focus on reduced production costs and without paying attention to localized R&D activities, which failed to train well local labor and transfer valuable technologies to Shenzhen. A large number of local firms, founded to provide professional services to foreign-invested firms, developed an agile production and business model that promptly met customers' requirements and quickly responded to market demands (Diez *et al.*, 2008). The agile business model indeed brought considerable wealth to the investors in the short term and of course rapid growth to the city-region. However, the credo of "speed" at the expense of product quality depressed local innovation-related activities that require a great deal of time and capital investment and patience for a long-term return.

7.3.2. *Strategic selectivity of local governments*

Local institutional environment under which the firms operate has a crucial influence on the innovation-related motivation and strategies of the firms and consequently affects the innovative performance of a region. A local innovation-supportive institutional environment can be shaped by the state through nurturing local talent and attracting global talent, enriching local S&T resources, constructing an active technical market and establishing and maintaining a financial system in favor of fund-raising by firms. However, the efficiency of local governments in building such an institutional environment varies according to their capability and local pre-existing conditions as well as many other influential factors. There was a noticeable difference in the capability and power of local governments when comparing Shenzhen with Shanghai in three aspects.

First of all, Shenzhen failed to train and attract as many talents and forge as good a S&T environment as Shanghai. A strong educational and research system was non-existent in Shenzhen before the economic reform.

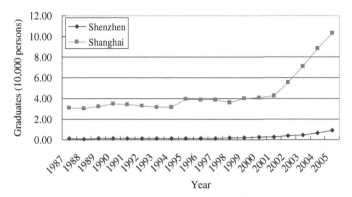

Year

Figure 7.5. Graduates of institutions of higher education in Shanghai and Shenzhen, 1987–2005.

Source: SSB (1990–2006) and SZSB (2007).

Not until 1983 did Shenzhen establish its first university, the Shenzhen University, to overcome the problem due to the lack of highly qualified talent. At that time, Shanghai had 43 institutions of higher education and trained over 29,000 graduates. As shown in Fig. 7.5, the number of graduates that Shanghai trained has been much higher than that of Shenzhen during the period 1987–2005. The first batch of 1028 students from Shenzhen University graduated in 1987 when Shanghai had trained over 30,000 graduates in its 51 institutes of higher education. Shenzhen constructed another eight institutes of higher education in the next two decades after 1983. The number of graduates in Shenzhen in 2005 reached 9000, still significantly lower than 100,000 graduates trained by Shanghai. In addition, Shanghai is one of the most clustered city-regions for institutes of higher education and research in China, including several with a domestic and even international reputation for excellence in research and teaching. Therefore, Shanghai had attracted a lot of domestic and overseas students, whereas universities in Shenzhen mainly served local students.

Meanwhile, Shenzhen suffered from the lack of S&T resources, such as research institutes to support and accelerate the process of technological innovation. In contrast, Shanghai hosted a large number of well-established R&D institutes to back up its technological capability. There were 140 independent R&D institutions with more than 30,000 employees in Shanghai in 2005, compared to only five independent R&D institutions with 104 employees in Shenzhen. Judging by the sources of S&T funds, Shenzhen's R&D institutes did not establish any relationship based on S&T

Table 7.5.   Sources of funds for S&T activities in the independent R&D institutions in Shenzhen and Shanghai, 2005.

Indicators	Shenzhen	Shanghai
Number of R&D institutes	5	140
Total funds for S&T activities (100 million *yuan*)	0.22	81.65
Government funds (100 million *yuan*)	0.22	63.18
Enterprise funds (100 million *yuan*)	0	6.97
Bank loans (100 million *yuan*)	0	0.30

Source: CSSB and MOST (2006) and GDSB and GDST (2006).

activities with local firms. As shown in Table 7.5, they raised no S&T funds from enterprises. The independent R&D institutes in Shanghai obtained 9 percent of total S&T funds from enterprises with a value of 697 million *yuan* in 2005. It suggests that the fruits of research achieved by Shanghai's R&D institutes are valuable and can be commercialized by local firms. Moreover, R&D institutes in Shenzhen merely spent 1.29 million *yuan* on R&D activities with an average 0.26 million *yuan* spent per institute in 2005. All of their money went to experimental development rather than basic or applied research. In sharp contrast, independent R&D institutes in Shanghai together expended 4490.81 million *yuan* on R&D activities with an average 32.08 million *yuan* spent by institution and 55 percent of the expenditure went to basic and applied research that is rarely conducted by firms but plays a significant role in the process of technological innovation (CSSB and MOST, 2006; GDSB and GDST, 2006). It is interesting to see that Shanghai's firms spent 20 percent of their R&D intramural expenditure on basic and applied research in which Shenzhen's firms were not interested (Table 7.6). This further demonstrates that firms in Shenzhen tend to focus on quick occupation of the market without paying any attention to the long-term R&D investment while Shanghai's firms laid much emphasis on creative activities rather than the simple modification of existing technology to cater to market demands.

Second, the financial environment in Shenzhen was worse than that in Shanghai. A bank loan is one of the most feasible and widely used ways to finance a firm in many countries. It is pointed out that around 15 percent of capital investment in firms is raised from bank borrowing (Sung, 1996, p. 194). The amount of total deposits reflects to some level the capability of local financial institutes to loan to firms. The greater the total deposits held by financial institutes, the greater the chance firms could get a loan and the greater the money they could borrow. Shanghai had committed

Table 7.6. Intramural expenditure on R&D of large- and medium-sized industrial enterprises in Shenzhen and Shanghai, 2005 (100 million *yuan*).

	Shenzhen	Shanghai
Total intramural expenditure on R&D	124.51	208.35
Expenditure on basic research	0.16	10.00*
Percent of total intramural expenditure on basic research	**0.13**	**4.80**
Expenditure on applied research	0.69	31.99*
Percent of total intramural expenditure on applied research	**0.55**	**15.36**
Expenditure on experimental development	123.11	—
Percent of total intramural expenditure on experimental development	**98.87**	—

*Intramural expenditure on basic and applied research in Shanghai only refers to the expenditure on activities that were conducted by independent R&D institutions and institutions of higher education, not including those conducted by enterprises.
Source: CSSB and MOST (2006) and GDSB and GDST (2006).

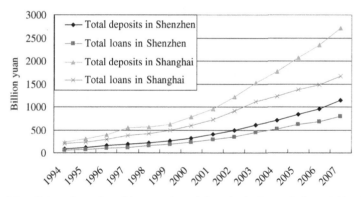

Figure 7.6. Comparison of total loans and total deposits in domestic financial institutes between Shanghai and Shenzhen, 1994–2007.

Source: SSB (2008) and SZSB (2008).

itself to building the financial center of the Yangtze River Delta and even the entire country in the 1990s. It became the center of foreign exchange transactions and attracted the largest number of foreign banks in China in 1995 (Sung, 1996, p. 194). Total deposits of domestic financial institutes in Shanghai were higher than those in Shenzhen and the gap between them widened during the period 1994–2007 (Fig. 7.6). Moreover, not only the total loans but also the total deposits in Shenzhen's financial institutes were much lower than the total loans in the financial institutes in Shanghai (Fig. 7.6).

Finally, compared to Shanghai, Shenzhen suffered from a much less active technology market. A local technology market is beneficial to local firms by offering them a great platform to achieve complementary knowledge and technology in a convenient and quick way. The frequency of technology transactions in a region reflects the regional technological foundations and the enthusiasm of local actors to pursue innovation. The activeness of the technology market can be measured by the value of technical contracts signed in a region. Shanghai established a quite active technology market. The value of technical contracts in Shanghai reached 7.39 billion *yuan*, almost seven times higher than that of Shenzhen in 2000. Though the technical contracts in both Shenzhen and Shanghai had been increasing during the period 2000–2005, the growth rate of Shenzhen was slower than that of Shanghai. At the end of 2005, the value of contract deals in Shanghai increased to 23.17 billion *yuan*, compared to only 3.59 billion *yuan* in Shenzhen (Fig. 7.7).

7.4. Growth and Strategic Selectivity of the Firms in Shanghai and Shenzhen

In order to enhance the technological capability and expedite the pace of modernization, the central government announced a series of preferential industrial policies in 2000 to develop the software industry in recognition of its importance to the national economy. Following the central

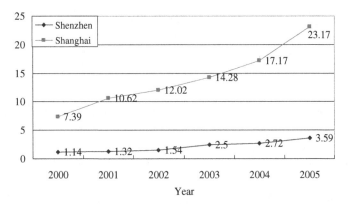

Figure 7.7.   Value of contract deals in local technical market in Shanghai and Shenzhen, 2000–2005 (billion *yuan*).

Source: CSSB and MOST (2006) and GDSB and GDST (2006).

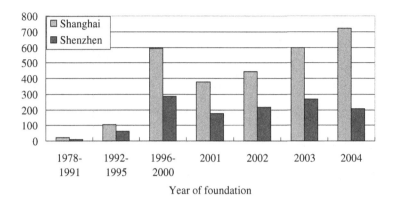

Figure 7.8. Start-ups of software firms in Shanghai and Shenzhen, 1978–2004.
Source: SSB (2005a) and SZSB (2005a).

government, Shanghai and Shenzhen proclaimed workable regulations to support local software firms in 2000 and 2001, respectively. The favorable policies facilitated the growth of the software industry in both Shanghai and Shenzhen. However, Shanghai hosted more software start-ups than Shenzhen. As shown in Fig. 7.8, there were few software firms in both Shenzhen and Shanghai at the first decade after the 1978 economic reform. During the period 1992–1995, the number of software start-ups in Shanghai was 107, compared to 63 in Shenzhen. This number in Shanghai increased to 592 in the period 1996–2000, compared to 282 in Shenzhen. After the year 2000, the gap in the number of software start-ups between Shenzhen and Shanghai further widened, with the number of start-ups in Shanghai three times more than that of Shenzhen. Shanghai hosted 2863 software firms and 62,607 employees, more than twice those of Shenzhen at the end of 2004 (SSB, 2005a; SZSB, 2005a).

In order to understand the innovation-related strategies of the software firms, the questionnaire survey that was conducted in Shenzhen and Shanghai in 2006–2007 was used to analyze the innovation-related activities in these two city-regions. The questionnaire survey covered 120 software firms in Shanghai and 70 in Shenzhen, with a sample rate of 4 percent in Shanghai and 5 percent in Shenzhen based on the statistics from the 2004 National Economic Census. Table 7.7 summarizes the responses of the firms to the question regarding their locational selection. For the software firms in both Shenzhen and Shanghai, the most popular reason was the existence of technology talent and clients. However, co-location with their

Table 7.7.   Three top reasons for location of software firms in Shanghai and Shenzhen.

	Top reason for location				Second reason for location				Third reason for location			
	Shenzhen		Shanghai		Shenzhen		Shanghai		Shenzhen		Shanghai	
	Frequency	Percent	Frequency	Percent	Frequency	Percent	Frequency	Percent	Frequency	Percent	Frequency	Percent
Location of clients	12	17.1	28	23.3	11	16.7	10	9.8	3	5.3	2	2.8
Concentration of peers	9	12.9	8	6.7	4	6.1	9	8.8	12	21.1	6	8.3
Close to suppliers	7	10.0	1	0.8	12	18.2	0	0	8	14.0	0	0
Airport/Sea Port	3	4.3	0	0	2	3.0	0	0	3	5.3	1	1.4
Technology talent	18	25.7	21	17.5	19	28.8	28	27.5	4	7.0	11	15.3
Low labor cost	3	4.3	1	0.8	1	1.5	1	1.0	2	3.5	0	0
Local market potential	7	10.0	28	23.3	8	12.1	12	11.8	6	10.5	10	13.9
Industrial base	2	2.9	6	5.0	2	3.0	10	9.8	10	17.5	6	8.3
Preferential policies	2	2.9	7	5.8	4	6.1	10	9.8	1	1.8	11	15.3
Friendly government	3	4.3	2	1.7	1	1.5	9	8.8	4	7.0	6	8.3

(Continued)

Table 7.7. (Continued)

	Top reason for location				Second reason for location				Third reason for location			
	Shenzhen		Shanghai		Shenzhen		Shanghai		Shenzhen		Shanghai	
	Fre-quency	Per cent	Fre-quency	Per cent	Fre-quency	Per cent	Fre-quency	Per cent	Fre-quency	Per cent	Fre-quency	Per cent
Professional services	1	1.4	1	0.8	0	0	2	2.0	3	5.3	7	9.7
Cooperation with local universities and R&D institutes	0	0	3	2.5	0	0	6	5.9	0	0	7	9.7
Amenities of the cities	0	0	5	4.2	1	1.5	2	2.0	1	1.8	2	2.8
Others	3	4.3	9	7.5	1	1.5	3	2.9	0	0	3	4.2
Total	70	100.0	120	100	66	100.0	102	100.0	57	100.0	72	100.0

Source: Questionnaire survey in Shenzhen and Shanghai in 2006.

peers was viewed as important by Shenzhen's firms while firms in Shanghai paid much attention to local market potential, which reveals a long-term developmental strategy rather than a short-term benefit orientation adopted by Shanghai's software firms. Firms in Shenzhen were mainly attracted by local agglomerated economies, such as co-location with clients, suppliers and peers. By contrast, local preferential policies are one of the important factors attracting software firms to Shanghai. This suggests that the Shanghai municipal government established a better industrial environment and the firms in Shanghai paid more attention to their external environment and governmental behavior than their counterparts in Shenzhen.

As illustrated in the beginning, Shanghai's software firms were more innovative than those in Shenzhen. A further examination revealed that the software firms in Shanghai adopted a more innovation-oriented strategy as they invested more capital and personnel in innovative activities than their counterparts in Shenzhen. As shown in Table 7.8, the R&D employees accounted for 52 percent of total employees in Shanghai, significantly higher than in Shenzhen. The R&D expenditure accounted for over one-third of the total expenditure in both Shenzhen and Shanghai. No significant difference had been found between them. However, a closer scrutiny revealed that many firms in Shenzhen did not expend any money on R&D activities in which, by contrast, all of Shanghai's firms invested something. The different attitudes and strategies to innovation by local software firms between Shanghai and Shenzhen were affected by their external environment, and at the same time shaped a divergent regional state-firm strategic coordination. The following section will compare the different degree of state-firm strategic coordination between Shanghai and Shenzhen to understand the different performance in technological innovation.

Table 7.8.   *T*-test results of innovation-related investment between software firms in Shanghai and Shenzhen, 2006.

Indicators	Mean		*T*-value	*P*-value
	Shanghai	Shenzhen		
R&D employees as percentage of total employees	52.42	43.10	2.264*	0.025
Percentage of R&D expenditure as share of total expenditure	36.10	35.43	0.153	0.878

*The mean difference is at the 0.05 significance level.
Source: Questionnaire survey in Shanghai and Shenzhen.

7.5. State-Firm Coordination in Shenzhen and Shanghai

State-firm strategic coordination can be further broken down into information-based, product-based and fund-based state-firm strategic coordination at the regional level. Information-based coordination is measured by the importance of the state in providing the innovation-related information evaluated by local software firms. It is believed that the firms who considered that the government played a very important role in providing innovation-related information would have a higher degree of information-based coordination with the government. As a result, a larger number of firms in a region viewed the government as "very important" or "important" in providing the innovation-related information, the higher degree of state-firm information-based strategic coordination in a region. Over 47 percent of Shenzhen's software firms considered that the information from the government did not help their innovation-related activities at all, whereas over 58 percent of firms in Shanghai viewed the information from the government as important or very important in their process of technological innovation (Table 7.9). The T-test result further illustrated that information-based state-firm coordination in Shanghai is significantly better than that in Shenzhen ($t = 2.968, p = 0.004$).

A manager in Shenzhen revealed the reason why Shenzhen's firms did not care about the information from the local government.

We located in Shenzhen to be close to our clients in order to understand their product demands and specific requirements as soon as and as best as possible. If we want to have a better relationship with government, we should have gone to Beijing or Shanghai. The advantage we can take in Shenzhen is its active market. We do not think that local governments could give us any valuable information to help us survive in the fierce market competition". (Interview note, 13 August 2008.)

Table 7.9. Importance of government in providing innovation-related information evaluated by the software firms in Shanghai and Shenzhen.

	Shanghai		Shenzhen	
	Frequency	Percent	Frequency	Percent
Unimportant	24	**20.0**	33	**47.1**
Medium	26	21.7	14	20.0
Important or very important	70	**58.3**	23	**32.9**
Total	120	100.0	70	100.0

Source: Questionnaire survey in Shenzhen and Shanghai in 2006.

In sharp contrast, a firm's manager in Shanghai expressed a very different opinion on the role played by the government in providing innovation-related information.

The industrial strategy of the government played a significant role for us. In order to catch up with the advanced economies, construct the technology foundation and improve the national technological capability, the state has started to establish its own technical standards in many fields. We are one of those firms that adopted the homegrown technical standards to develop products which, for us, is very risky because market demands for the homegrown standards-involved products are unknown. To what extent the government would like to support our own standards determined how much we should invest in the products that involved the national standards. Therefore, it is extremely important for us to obtain related information from the government. We should be very cautious in adopting the homegrown standards that are obviously less mature than the prevailing standards in the world. We surely could fight the international giants without any support from the government at the beginning of our development. (Interview notes, 22 July 2008.)

Second, product-based coordination between the government and firms in Shenzhen is found to be much worse than in Shanghai. Product-based coordination is measured by the share of government procurement in total sales revenue of the firms. On average, the government procurement only contributed 13 percent to the sales revenue of Shenzhen's software firms, significantly lower than the 21 percent of Shanghai ($t = 1.661$, $p = 0.099$). Furthermore, more firms in Shanghai than Shenzhen benefited from local government procurement. As shown in Table 7.10, 54 percent of Shanghai's firms had no product-based coordination with the government, compared to 64 percent in Shenzhen. In the meantime, almost 16 percent of firms in Shanghai sold over half of their products to the government while only 9 percent of Shenzhen's firms could achieve the same level.

Table 7.10.   Share of government procurement in Shenzhen and Shanghai.

	Shanghai		Shenzhen	
	Frequency	Percent	Frequency	Percent
0%	65	**54.17**	44	**63.77**
1–25%	24	20.00	12	17.39
26–50%	12	10.00	7	10.14
51–100%	19	**15.83**	6	**8.70**
Total	120	100.00	69	100.00

Source: Questionnaire survey in Shenzhen and Shanghai in 2006.

Finally, fund-based state-firm strategic coordination in Shenzhen was also much worse than that of Shanghai. Since the data regarding fund-based coordination in the software industry is not available, the analysis of fund-based coordination is extended to a wider industrial scale. Fund-based state-firm coordination is measured by the amount of innovation funds founded by the local government for encouraging and stimulating the innovation-related activities of local firms and by the ratio of the S&T funds from the government to total S&T funds of the firms. The Shanghai municipal government expended more money in supporting the innovative activities of local firms than the Shenzhen municipal government. As shown in Fig. 7.9, the innovation funds accounted for 14 percent of total government financial expenditure in Shanghai, compared to only 2 percent in Shenzhen during the period 2001–2005. The Shanghai municipal government had spent over 2 percent of its GDP in supporting the innovative activities of local firms since 2001 and this number increased during the period 2001–2005. By contrast, the Shenzhen municipal government merely expended around 0.2 percent of the GDP on the innovative activities of its firms in 2001 and 2002, and this number further decreased during the period 2002–2006 (Fig. 7.10). This number in Shenzhen had even been lower than that of China as a whole, with the latter reserving around 0.5 percent of the GDP as innovation funds during the period 2001–2006 (CSSB, 2007).

Furthermore, industrial firms in Shanghai obtained much more funds from the government to support their S&T activities than their counterparts in Shenzhen. Around 22 percent of the S&T funds obtained

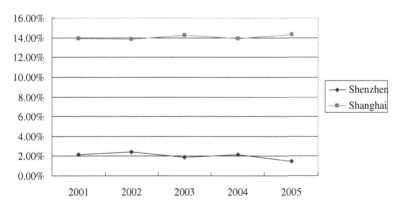

Figure 7.9.   Ratio of innovation funds to government financial expenditure in Shanghai and Shenzhen, 2001–2005.

Source: SSB (2006) and SZSB (2006).

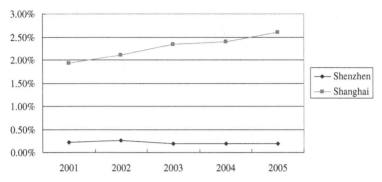

Figure 7.10.　Ratio of innovation funds to GDP in Shanghai and Shenzhen, 2001–2005.
Source: SSB (2006) and SZSB (2006).

Table 7.11.　Sources of funds for S&T activities of large and medium industrial enterprises in Shanghai and Shenzhen, 2005 (billion *yuan*).

	Shenzhen	**Shanghai**
Total funds	18.54	44.21
Government funds	0.74	9.91
Percentage of total funds	**3.97**	**22.41**
Enterprises funds	16.11	31.45
Percentage of total funds	86.88	71.14
Bank loans	1.29	0.64
Percentage of total funds	6.93	1.45

Source: CSSB and MOST (2006) and GDSB and GDST (2006).

by Shanghai's industrial firms came from government, much higher than less than 4 percent for Shenzhen's industrial firms (Table 7.11).

As an informant revealed, the Shenzhen municipal government has a passive attitude in guiding the local economy and industry, while the Shanghai municipal government has taken active steps to promote selected industries and firms. This leads to a different degree of product-based and fund-based state-firm strategic coordination between these two city-regions.

The growth of the high-tech industry in a region is to a larger extent affected by the local government. However, the Shenzhen municipal government paid much less attention to the local economy and industry. For example, the amount of innovation funds established by the Shenzhen municipal government for local IC design sector has been much lower than that of Shanghai. Since we are far behind the advanced countries in the IC industry, one of the most effective ways to develop the IC design sector is to attract capital investment from the international IC manufacturing giants to drive the growth of the small IC design firms, in which respect the Shanghai municipal government has done a great job. However, Shenzhen was unable to attract such investment until now because the local government hesitated to invest in such a huge project. This suggests a limited capability of the Shenzhen municipal government to guide and support the high-risk sector. Firms in Shenzhen also suffered from the shortage of office space which the Shenzhen municipal government is not about to deal with. (Interview notes, 13 September 2008.)

Another interviewee further pointed out the different capabilities in guiding the growth of the high-tech industry between the Shenzhen and Shanghai municipal governments to explain the spatial difference in the degree of state-firm strategic coordination,

> The governments should and must do something that firms are unable or reluctant to do in order to pave the way for high-tech industrial development. The Shanghai municipality is very wise in this respect, which is another advantage that we can take from Shanghai. By contrast, the Shenzhen municipality might be willing to do something to improve its IC industry but it has no idea how to do this, due to its limited capability. (Interview notes, 4 August 2008.)

In a word, with the better capability and more active attitude of the Shanghai municipal government to building a favorable institutional environment to encourage the innovative activities of local firms, it has come as no surprise that firms in Shanghai are more willing to engage in innovation-related activities and confront less obstacles in their process of technological innovation than their counterparts in Shenzhen. Therefore, there was a better state-firm strategic coordination based on information, products and funds in Shanghai than in Shenzhen (Table 7.12 and Fig. 7.11).

Table 7.12. State-firm strategic coordination between Shanghai and Shenzhen.

	Shanghai	Shenzhen
Selectivity of the central government	High	Low
Capability of the local government	Strong	Weak
State-firm strategic coordination	High	Low
Information-based	High	Low
Product-based	High	Low
Fund-based	High	Low

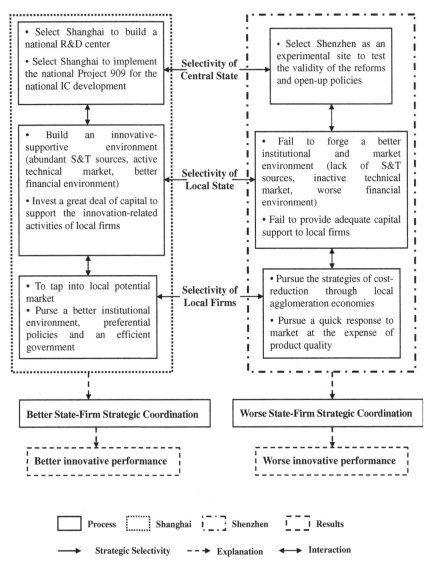

Figure 7.11.   State-firm strategic coordination and innovative performance in Shanghai and Shenzhen.

7.6. Summary

This chapter compares the degree of state-firm strategic coordination in Shenzhen and Shanghai through examining their role assigned by the central government in the national economy, the strategies and capability of local governments in building an innovation-supportive environment, local firms' responses to the external environment and their motivations for innovation-related investment, and information-based, product-based and fund-based state-firm strategic coordination between Shenzhen and Shanghai.

Shanghai has traditionally played a strategic role in China as the cradle of the national industry and as a significant source of state revenues, whereas Shenzhen was an unimportant small town that was selected to be an experimental base for testing the validity of China's reform and open-door policies. The different roles played by these two city-regions are both the cause and effect of the strategic consideration and arrangement of the central government for the overall development of the nation. The traditionally significant role played by Shanghai in the Chinese economy further paved the way for its late development and technological innovation. The Shanghai municipal government committed itself to establishing a better innovation-supportive institutional environment whereas the Shenzhen municipal government was not so interested in such efforts. It is revealed that Shanghai has trained more people, attracted more talent, hosted more S&T resources and established a better financial system and a more active technology market to support local innovative activities than Shenzhen. As a result, software firms selected Shanghai to open their business to a better platform constructed by the local government for them to be innovative and successful while the innovation-related motivation of Shenzhen's firms was depressed because of an immature institutional environment and a less supportive attitude of the Shenzhen municipal government to innovation. A close examination has illustrated that Shanghai shaped a better state-firm strategic coordination than that of Shenzhen.

This comparative study between Shanghai and Shenzhen has generated strong implications for research into technological innovation in a region. In the existing literature of innovation, for instance in industrial cluster and knowledge spillover, much emphasis has been placed on the capability of firms to acquire complementary technology and knowledge. A basic assumption is that firms are driven to invest in innovative activities without which they would have not been able to maintain survival and growth. Such an assumption may be self-evident in the Western economies characterized by a mature market environment and well-developed economic system, under which firms are regulated and forced to do so. However, it is untenable in the Chinese context, as the latter is undergoing a transition from the planned system to a market economy that leaves a big space for non-innovative firms to survive and even to make satisfactory profits. It is pointed out that innovation is a trade-off between routinization and change (Meeus and Oerlemans, 2000) and there are more reasons for not investing in innovation than the other way around in an underdeveloped institutional and market environment. In this sense, before jumping into the issue of how firms could achieve useful knowledge and technology so as to be more innovative, the regional institutional incentives, the innovation-related motivations behind firms, and local governments' strategies, selectivity and capability should be investigated and clarified. As it stands, the comparative analysis of Shenzhen and Shanghai suggests that what really matters for the latter's success is not simply the industrial clustering and localized knowledge spillover but more reasonably it is the outcome of the incentives and pressure from the regional institutional environment, the support and stimulus from local governments and the formation of state-firm strategic coordination in different geographical and institutional contexts. It is worth noting that this study has demonstrated that state-firm strategic coordination generated a significantly positive effect on the technological innovation of firms and state-firm strategic coordination is a crucial factor leading to the regional differences in innovative performance. It does not intend to totally deny the prevailing theoretical frameworks, but to offer a different angle to explain and understand the peculiar pattern of uneven technological innovation in China.

Chapter Eight

CONCLUSION

8.1. Major Findings

China's ICT industry has experienced so dramatic an expansion in recent years that it now has played a significant role in the national economy and the world's ICT landscape (Ning, 2009b; Pecht, 2006; Wang and Lin, 2008). Although the growth and innovation of China's ICT industry has been a subject attracting much scholarly attention in the world, its innovative capability has remained controversial as some argue that China's technological level has been high enough to establish its own technical standards while others insist that China has still been stuck at the lowest level of the global production network (Breidne, 2005; Fan, 2003, 2006; Lin and Wang, 2009; Suttmeier and Yao, 2004; Wang and Lin, 2008; Zhou et al., 2010). More systematic studies must be carried out to enhance the understanding of the nature and innovation dynamics of China's ICT industry.

While extensive documentation existed to explain the innovative performance of a region by making reference to localized production networks, innovative milieu and knowledge spillover, recent research has started to cast doubt over the perceived relationship between industrial cluster and technological innovation (Baptista and Swann, 1998; Oinas, 2000; Porter, 1990, 1998, 2000a; Simmie, 2004). The existing literature tends to exaggerate the benefit of innovation but underestimates the risk taken by the innovators. It also ignores the internal innovation-related strategies and motivation of firms. It therefore fails to explain why some firms are more innovative than others within an industrial cluster. Furthermore, the existing theoretical models place much emphasis on knowledge and technology in the process of technological innovation but overlook the influence of other factors that hold back the innovation-related activities such as financial constraints as well as the unfavorable institutional and market environment. While studies of China's high-tech industry pay much attention to foreign investment, international technology transfer, relations between MNCs and indigenous firms, and the role of the state in explaining the process of technological innovation, the Western-based theoretical models appear to be very questionable when applied to China's reality (Simon and Rehn, 1988; Zhou, 2006, 2008; Zhou and Tong, 2003). The inconsistency between the theoretical models and the Chinese reality has entailed the establishment of a more inclusive theorization to understand the innovation dynamics of the ICT industry in China's unique politico-economic circumstances.

This book examines the uneven technological innovation in China's ICT industry through probing into the motivation and strategies of the active agents and actors rather than only focusing on their linkages, connections and relations with others. Based on the critical review of existing theorizations of technological innovation, this study develops a new framework beyond industrial clustering to investigate state-firm strategic coordination that refers to the dynamic process in which firms' innovation-related strategies are coordinated to the "strategic selectivity" of the state. This new framework highlights the strategies and motivations of both the state and the firms considering the fact that the innovation-related motivation of firms is rather weak because a satisfactory profit can still be made without any innovation-related investment in China. Using this framework to interpret the uneven innovative performance of China's ICT firms has generated the following major findings:

(1) The rapid growth of China's ICT industry in recent years has been the result of the timely insertion into the restructuring of the global economy and the increasing priority given by the central government to the ICT industry. A historical examination revealed that although there had been many flaws in the innovation system before the economic reform and opening-up, China had indeed achieved significant technological breakthroughs through mobilizing the nation-wide resources to exclusively support important research projects. This suggests that the determination of a state could turn a poor country into a technology power in certain fields. Many valuable research results had been left unused during that period. These research fruits had been utilized by several domestic electronics enterprises, which laid a great foundation for their later success. The 1978 economic reform and opening-up allowed a great deal of foreign and private capital to participate in the construction of China's ICT industry. The output value of the ICT manufacturing industry had enlarged 64 times during the period 1990–2006. Along with the augmented capacity of ICT manufacturing, the innovation-related investment also increased during this time.

However, it is interesting to note that the ratio of ICT manufacturing firms with tech-activities to the total showed a significant decrease from 1990 to 2006, so did the expenditure on developing new products as a percentage of total sales revenue. Moreover, 34 percent of total sales revenue was completed by the development of new products in 1990, much higher than the 24 percent in 2006. It is believed that the declining interest in R&D activities and technological innovation is related to the increasing pressure on firms due to difficulties in financing innovation and the decreasing direct capital support from government.

(2) The rapid growth of China's ICT industry did not make China a self-dependent innovative country. Instead, China is still stuck at the low end of the global production network with a heavy reliance on foreign investment and technology. In recent years, China has made significant progress toward increasing the sophistication of its ICT manufacturing. A disaggregate examination of the sectoral composition revealed a significant structural difference among the eight sub-sectors of ICT manufacturing, with the sub-sector of manufacture of electronic computers taking the lead in every economic indicator, such as output value (by 33 percent), total profits (by 26 percent) and exports (by 41 percent). While China has been able to produce and export more sophisticated ICT goods than the simple consumer electronics products that had dominated its ICT manufacturing during the 1980s, China's ICT industry has been dominated by foreign-invested enterprises that have generated the lion's share of the output value (by 60 percent), total profits (by 55 percent), exports (by 72 percent) and new products (by 50 percent), and have achieved a much better economic performance than their counterparts invested with domestic capital. As the leading exporter of ICT products in the world, China completed 70 percent of total exports by using imported materials.

(3) Geographically, the spatial variations in growth and performance are very striking as most of the ICT activities are concentrated in a few eastern coastal city-regions and a better economic and innovative performance is only generated by a small number of city-regions. Statistical tests confirmed that there exists no positive correlation between industrial cluster and technological innovation. There is no significant correlation between spatial agglomeration and technological innovation measured by both granted invention patents ($p = 0.726$, $r = 0.086$) and new products ($p = 0.054$, $r = 0.390$) at the provincial level. Furthermore, a set of T-test analyses of the data from the questionnaire survey

illustrated that localized linkages and connections based on production and knowledge among firms did not lead to a better innovative performance either. The case study of Shenzhen revealed that although Shenzhen has been one of the most clustered city-regions in ICT manufacturing activities (6.67 by employment location quotient) and software design (2.83 by employment location quotient), and the localized linkages appear to be very intensive and frequent, the innovative performance in Shenzhen is rather poor. The technology level of the IC design firms in Shenzhen is even much lower than that of the national average. Statistical analyses further showed that the innovative performance of the firms is significantly affected by their attributes, interests and motivations and more importantly, state-firm strategic coordination.

(4) A significant and strong correlation has been found between state-firm strategic coordination and technological innovation in the case studies of Shanghai and Shenzhen. T-test analyses at the national level have identified state-firm strategic coordination as a significant factor differentiating innovative firms from non-innovative ones ($p = 0.000$, $t = -3.963$). Furthermore, correlation analyses in the cases of both Shanghai ($p = 0.000$, $r = 0.754$) and Shenzhen ($p = 0.000$, $r = 0.750$) have confirmed such a significant and strong relationship. Among the surveyed 98 IC design firms in Shanghai, 18 percent of them had been identified as innovative firms and all of them have shaped different extents of state-firm strategic coordination based on projects, products and awards. Only very few of the non-innovative firms have reached such strategic coordination. Meanwhile, the innovative firms as a group have on average achieved a much higher extent of state-firm strategic coordination than non-innovative firms. My interview notes further revealed that firms which are coordinated with the state based on the innovation-related strategies tend to be more innovative than others. Profit maximization is the only and terminal goal of the firms whereas innovation is only a tool for firms to realize this goal. Under an immature institutional and market environment, firms can still achieve a satisfactory profit without any innovation-related investments. The adequate resources of the indigenous firms and the inferior position that they hold in the global value chain further depressed their motivation for innovation-related investment. In recognition of this awkward situation facing the indigenous firms, the central state is eager to get rid of outside technology control has taken actions to encourage, support and assist its firms to be independently

innovative through the strategy of homegrown standards-setting and many other policies. A case study of one of the most innovative firms in Shanghai, Spreadturm, further proves that state-firm strategic coordination has led to the success of this firm. Nevertheless, it is noted that state-firm strategic coordination is not a panacea to guarantee the success of firms but a significant factor to inspire the innovation-related motivation of firms and to help them to get through their hard times in the process of technological innovation so as to achieve success.

(5) The different level of technological innovation of firms is related to the different degree of state-firm strategic coordination within a region. It is revealed that state-firm strategic coordination varied between individual firms within a region, mainly because the corporate strategies are impacted by their distinguishing combination of resources and because the strategic selection of the state does reach individual firms evenly. Although the central government selected Shanghai's IC sector and the Shanghai municipal government has showed an interest and capability in establishing the innovation-supportive institutional environment, supervising its economy and stimulating the innovative activities, there exists a variation in state-firm strategic innovation among firms in Shanghai. As such, there exist a few firms in Shenzhen with a better state-firm strategic coordination although Shenzhen is not selected by the central government to improve national technological capability and the Shenzhen municipal government presented a limited ability to forge an innovation-supportive institutional environment, a regulated local market and supervised local industry.

(6) The uneven geography of technological innovation in China is embedded in the different degree of state-firm strategic coordination in different regions. With a higher degree of state-firm strategic coordination, Shanghai has achieved a much better innovative performance than Shenzhen, which is characterized by a low degree of state-firm strategic coordination. The comparative analysis has illustrated that the different innovative performance between Shanghai and Shenzhen cannot be interpreted by the industrial clustering but instead is embedded in their locally specific process of state-firm strategic coordination.

(7) Different state-firm strategic coordination among the regions has been the result of the interactions of the strategic selectivity of the central government, the capability and selectivity of local governments as well as the response and selectivity of the firms. The strategic selectivity of the central state shapes and reshapes regional characteristics and

growth trajectory. The capability and selectivity of local states shape the local milieu and directly affect the strategies and behavior of local firms. The central government selected Shanghai as one of the technological centers and invested a lot in Shanghai's IC industry while Shenzhen was only an experimental site for testing the feasibility of the reform and opening-up policies in the eyes of the central state. In Shanghai, the municipal government invested a large amount of capital in its education and S&T activities as well as in the innovative activities of the firms. In sharp contrast, the Shenzhen municipal government failed to attract and retain highly qualified talent and to establish an innovation-supportive market environment. In the different regional contexts, it has come as no surprise that firms in Shanghai and Shenzhen adopted different attitudes to innovation-related investment since the innovation-related strategies and selectivity of the firms are affected by the regional institutional and market environment. Most of firms selected Shenzhen as their location for the purpose of cost-reduction rather than seeking the convenience of the R&D activities. They tended to struggle in cut-throat competition without any patience for innovation-related investment. Most of firms selected Shanghai for location because of the high efficiency of the Shanghai municipal government, the better regional institutional environment and the local market potential. With the non-innovative strategies of the firms and no interest by both the central and local governments in institutional growth and innovation, state-firm strategic coordination in Shenzhen based on information, products and funds was significantly worse than that in Shanghai.

8.2. Theoretical Implications

By developing a conceptual framework from the perspective of state-firm strategic coordination to an understanding of the uneven innovative performance of China's ICT firms, this book contributes to the theoretical developments in four ways.

First of all, this study has challenged the perceived relationship between industrial cluster and technological innovation. Analyses of China's ICT industry have found no correlation between spatial agglomeration and innovative performance. Localized linkages and exchange based on production and knowledge among the co-located firms failed to induce a better innovative performance either. It suggests that such a relationship may be more complicated than has been described in the existing literature, which is derived primarily from the experiences of advanced economies in the West. Although there is strong evidence to support the theoretical interpretation of a positive relationship between industrial clustering and technological innovation, the Chinese experience appears to deviate from the theoretical norm. While this anomaly does not mean that one can totally reject the well-established theoretical models, it does suggest that there exist significant irregularities for which conventional wisdom can offer no satisfactory explanation. This also suggests that the relationship between clustering and innovation is not independent of regional conditions. The positive relationship between clustering and innovation may work in some locations but not in others. It would be meaningless to discuss the relationship between industrial clustering and technological innovation outside a place-specific regional context. In view of the complicated regional variation identified in this study, a situational, place-specific and contextually sensitive understanding would be more appropriate in depicting the relationship between industrial clustering and technological innovation in different regions of a globalizing world. In addition, we are careful to apply this theoretical model to the developing countries since the innovation-related motivations and dynamics of the firms therein are very different from those in developed countries where the market economy is mature enough to force firms to conduct innovation-related activities.

Second, this study resonates with the recent appeal to re-evaluate how structure, agency and territory have actually reshaped the new economic geography of different world regions beyond the "loose and ubiquitous" network that "explains everything and nothing" (Sunley, 2008, p. 8). While the relational economic geography has placed too much emphasis on network embeddedness and learning processes as well as untraded assets, it actually exaggerates the "collaborative and cooperative nature of successful urban and regional economies" and ignores the conflicts of interest and different motivations among agents and actors (Sunley, 2008, p. 5). This study has revealed that firms vary in their business interests, strategies and motivation that determine how they build all kinds of networks, linkages and relations. Without the examination of innovation-related interests, strategies and motivation of the firms, indulging in the networks, linkages and relations is not helpful to understand the uneven technological innovation in China. China's ICT firms indeed are deeply embedded in localized production networks. However, the network embeddedness did not benefit technological innovation because the motivation and interests of many firms were not so much about exploring knowledge and the technologies but rather about pursuing preferential treatment and cost reduction. This study stresses that we should understand how and why these relations built by firms have been established and how they are going to change and evolve and why, through taking a serious look at the interests, strategies and behavior of the active actors and agents.

Third, this study contributes to studies on the geography of technological innovation. A plethora of literature on innovation builds the theoretical framework and empirical analyses on the basic assumption that all firms will be willing to invest in innovation-related activities and such investment will bring considerable rewards to them. While this assumption is self-evident in Western countries, it is untenable in the Chinese context. In an immature institutional and market environment, there are more reasons for not investing in innovation-related activities than the other way around. China's economy in transition is characterized by an immature market environment that has provided speculative firms with opportunities to make a big profit without any innovative activities. The innovation-related motivation of the firms in Shenzhen was badly depressed because the non-innovators could make more money than the innovators. As a consequence, it is misleading to probe into the innovative performance of firms through only focusing on knowledge and technology in the process of technological innovation without an examination of the incentives and pressures from the external environment and the constraints of internal resources confronting the firms.

Finally, this study has an important implication for state theory. There exist on-going debates over the role of the state in the economy and technological innovation (Chang, 2003). The discussions on the role of the state in the existing literature failed to place such a role in a time and context sensitive framework, which leads to prejudice and a partial understanding of this subject. The empirical evidence in this book has suggested that support and stimulus from government are significant for the technological innovation of ICT firms since China's ICT industry is still in its fledging stage. Nevertheless, the role played by the state cannot be over-estimated and oversimplified. For the emerging high-tech industries, the state should play an active role in stimulating growth as well as encouraging and supporting the innovation-related activities, since this industry is probably unable to grow without such assistance. In the case of the U.S., the federal spending in the military industry in the 1960s was instrumental in the growth of the risky high-tech sectors (Castells and Hall, 1994).

When China's ICT industry continues to develop to break free of outside technological control, the market economy will play a growing part in the innovative activities of firms. Meanwhile, in an explanation of the role of the state, the existing literature tends to focus on the central government but neglects the importance of the local state (Segal, 2003). While the central government releases a policy, whether or not this policy could exert a significant influence on the economy really depends on the capability and executive power of the local states (Segal, 2003). The role of the local state is not invariable across space. While the Shanghai municipal government has showed strong interest and a qualified capability to facilitate the innovative activities of local firms, the Shenzhen case revealed a limited capability of the local government as a vision provider and as a good supervisor for local innovation. Therefore, a time and place sensitive framework should be adopted to understand the role of the state.

8.3. Policy Implications

In addition to theoretical implications, this book also has important implications for policy making. First, this study challenges the validity of the government policy to establish national level and provincial level industrial parks or so-called high-tech parks in China. In recent years, it has become fashionable for local governments to establish high-tech parks as a means of fostering better economic performance and technological innovation. This study has found no convincing evidence to confirm the popular perception that industrial cluster necessarily leads to high productivity and technological innovation. What really matters is not the degree of concentration but rather the business interests and strategies of individual firms and the institutional environment within which production and innovation take place. It would be futile for local governments to mark out a designated zone and force related or competing firms to locate within it. A more effective approach would be for these local governments to provide a supportive institutional environment while at the same time encouraging, stimulating and supporting the innovation-related motivation of firms.

Second, this book suggests that local governments should improve their capability in providing visions for the future such as by guiding local industries and selecting potential firms to promote, since the local states played a significant role in regional growth and technological innovation. This study clearly indicated a lack of interest among ICT firms to engage in the risky venture of technological innovation. The poor economic and technological performance of the ICT firms in the leading industrial cluster in Shenzhen suggests that most of the indigenous firms have remained "trapped" in the low-end position of the global value chain. In view of this, how the central and local governments manage to stimulate, mobilize and coordinate individual firms to embark on the long, challenging and yet unavoidable journey of indigenous technological innovation becomes crucial. In doing so, the capability of local governments appears to be very important. While the Shanghai municipal government has successfully forged an innovation-supportive institutional environment as demonstrated in this study, it also has been criticized by other scholars (Zhang, 2003). In addition, the scandal of the "Hisyse" DSP (Digital Signal Processer) chip happened in 2006 and startled the world. A professor in Shanghai Jiaotong University claimed that he had developed China's first DSP chip, which was a significant technological breakthrough for China. This professor had therefore obtained around 100 million *yuan* capital support from both the central and local governments. As a matter of fact, his so-called self-dependant innovation in this chip was plagiarized from an MNC. It is not realistic to expect government to know detailed information about a technology, but this event does suggest that governments should improve their capability to evaluate a real innovation and distinguish the speculative firms from the real innovators.

Third, this book questions the developmental model adopted by some city-regions in China that blindly introduces and depends on foreign investment to create an illusive prosperity without taking into account the actual contribution and long-term influence of such investment on local growth and innovation. This study has demonstrated that the innovation-related strategies and interests of the indigenous firms are mainly determined by their internal resources and external environment. The growth pattern in Shenzhen illustrated that the large amount of foreign investment at the earlier stage of its growth failed to benefit local innovation. Most of the foreign-invested firms are not so interested in technological innovation in China. Instead, they seek a cost-reduction strategy rather than localized R&D activities. Their existence failed to bring about an innovation-supportive environment in the case of Shenzhen. This is not to say that the local government should not attract foreign investment, but to suggest that the state should evaluate whether or not this kind of investment will contribute to regional development and innovation and what influences it will exert on the regional milieu in the long term.

Finally, this book also suggests that it is imperative for the state to strengthen its executive power and eliminate the dispute between different government departments since the strategies and behavior of the central state play a significant role in technological innovation. While state-firm strategic coordination is significant for technological innovation, the coordination between different government departments should also be made to consistently support the innovation-related activities of firms. Technical standard settings were demonstrated to be effective in improving China's high-tech industry and in stimulating innovation-related activities. While the difficulty in completing the technical standards has been overcome and many firms started to adopt the homegrown standards, the struggle for benefits between different ministries stands out as a barrier to indigenous innovation and leads to market disorder. Although this book did not point out the problem of the inconsistency between different governmental departments, my interviews with the firms that are involved in Chinese homegrown technical standards have revealed that this problem has badly depressed innovation-related activities. A typical example was the dispute over China's own technical standard for the manufacture of mobile TV, with the former Ministry of Information Industry supporting the standard "T-MMB" (Terrestrial-Mobile Multimedia Broadcasting) and the State Administration of Radio Film and Television sticking to the standard "CMMB" (China Mobile Multimedia Broadcasting). The development of the indigenous IC firms had been consequently impeded by the pending national technical standard. Some firms had been waiting and adopting the "ride-the-fence" strategy while others were simultaneously preparing for two schemes to accord with both standards. Therefore, coordination among the different ministries and the internal self-management of the state are still issues calling for attention and solutions.

Appendix I

DATA COLLECTION

In recognition of the fact that "there is no fundamental clash between the purposes and capacities of qualitative and quantitative methods or data" (Glaser and Strauss, 1967, p. 17, cited from Yeung, 2003, p. 443), this book adopted a multi-method methodological framework to examine the nature and innovation of China's ICT industry as well as the strategies and performance of the ICT firms in different geographical contexts. Specifically, four sets of data were collected for detailed analysis and comparative study, including both quantitative and qualitative data.

1. Statistical Data

The first set of data is derived from the published statistical yearbooks, among which the most important is the *2004 Economic Census Yearbook* in China. This set of data is arguably one of the most comprehensive, comparable and consistent economic data sets that have ever been generated in the history of the People's Republic of China.[1] This data set

---

[1]The 2004 Economic Census is the first national economic census conducted in China. It combined the Second National Census on the Tertiary Industry (it was supposed to be conducted in 2003) with the Fourth National Census on Manufacturing (it was supposed to be conducted in 2005) and the Third National Census on Basic Units (it was supposed to be conducted in 2006), and brought on board the construction industry. The economic census classified all economic activities into 19 sectors and 875 classes according to the national economic and industrial classification standard. The data collected have been by far the most comprehensive in the history of China's statistics. The purpose of the economic census is to examine the actual situation of the scale, structure and efficiency of China's secondary and tertiary industry, compile a series of accurate and updated data for planning and policy making, and lay a solid statistical foundation for better management of economic development. Preparation work for the first economic census began at the end of 2003 and the beginning of 2004 when some districts or counties in Beijing, Sichuan, Zhejiang and Jilin were selected as the testing sites by the Directory Group of the First National Economic Census — a temporary establishment directly under the State Council. Based on the information gathered from these four testing sites

includes detailed information about each and every industrial sector. It also includes the information aggregated at the national level and disaggregated data for provinces and special municipalities. There are also data in digital form available at the county-city level for the coastal region where the population density and level of economic development are high. This data set is used to analyze the nature and characteristics of China's ICT industry, its structural composition, spatial distribution and the relationship between spatial agglomeration and economic performance.

Data from the *China Statistical Yearbook on Science and Technology* of selected years and the *Statistical Yearbook of Chinese Electronic Information Industry 2007* will be used complementarily to analyze the technological innovation and structural composition of China's ICT industry. The *Statistical Yearbook on Science and Technology* and the Statistical Yearbooks of selected years in Shanghai and Guangdong as well as *Comparative Statistical Data and Materials on 50 Years of New China* provided information on various economic indicators to compare the difference in state selectivity of both the central and local governments between Shanghai and Shenzhen.

---

and suggestions made by relevant departments, the Directory Group of the First National Economic Census submitted a proposal for a nationwide economic census to the State Council. The proposal was approved in September 2004 and the census work started in January 2005. The standard census time was set on 31 December 2004 to collect the data for the year 2004. The data and reports collected were then processed and evaluated during February to August 2005 and they were released in the end of 2005. It involved over ten million people and cost over ten billion *yuan*. The targets of the economic census included all corporate units (5.17 million), industrial establishments (6.82 million), and individual proprietors (39.22 million) engaged in the secondary or tertiary industry on China's mainland. Information collected included the basic attributes of all these units, employment, financial situation, the situation of production and sale, productive capability, consumption of raw materials and energies, science and technology activities and so on. Corporate units, establishments and individual proprietors were surveyed one by one. However, production and sale of individual proprietors were surveyed through random sampling because of their huge population and the difficulty to obtain this kind of information (see State Council, 2004; Legislative Affairs Office of the State Council, etc., 2004). All the statistical data were synthetically evaluated, checked and corrected by the National Bureau of Statistics in the end. The results of the economic census serve as not only an important reference for the formation of the Eleventh Five-Year Plan but also a benchmark for the statistical data collected in the previous regular surveys. In other words, if the data conducted in the previous surveys were contradictory to those in this economic census, the former would have to be revised in accordance with the latter. For a detailed discussion of the process and methodology of the 2004 National Economic Census, see Directory Office of the First National Economic Census of the State Council (2005).

2. Archived Data

The second set of data comes from internal reports edited by local governments on the IC industry in selected city-regions and the archive files and documents released by the central and local governments in different stages. The internal reports have not been made available to the public. They were obtained through contacting the persons in charge of growth and development of local IC design sectors in Shanghai and Shenzhen. Information on the state policies/documents regarding technological innovation and the ICT industry has also been obtained from Internet resources and newspapers. This set of data is used to understand the strategies, preferences and selectivity of the state and to identify the growth, distribution and innovation of the IC design sector in Shanghai and Shenzhen, to analyze the effects of industrial policies and state selectivity on the pattern of innovation in the IC design sector in Shanghai and Shenzhen.

3. Online Database and Internet Resources

This set of data is gathered from an online national patent-database of the IC industry and websites of each surveyed IC design firm in Shanghai and Shenzhen. This set of data was mainly collected to examine the statistical relationship between state-firm strategic coordination and firm-level innovative performance. To evaluate the technological innovation of service sectors is much harder than that of manufacturing sectors because there are almost no statistical data available for the former. This online database offered me such information to understand the innovative performance of individual IC design firms.

The national patent-database of the IC industry was established by Shanghai Silicon Intellectual Property Exchange (SSIPEX) in December 2004 under the authorization of the State Intellectual Property Office. The website of this online database can be retrieved from www.patentic.org without any charge. This database is established in order to offer a platform to China's IC firms to better know others' work before they start to design a product or apply for a protection of their own IP and hopefully enhance their awareness of IP right protection. It has collected over 150 million patent data that were registered in seven countries (China, U.S., Japan, Germany, France, Britain and Switzerland) and two organizations (The European Patent Office and World Intellectual Property

Organization) in 2006. This online database keeps updating with the patent database of the State Intellectual Property Office, which guarantees its authenticity and accuracy regarding patent data in the IC industry. Information offered by this online database includes the name of applicants, the affiliation of the applicants, the content of the patent and the date of application and certification. Therefore, the patent status of individual firms can be easily searched through typing the name of the firms or individuals into the online database. There are three sub-databases under the national patent-database of the IC industry. The first two sub-databases collect all the patents in the entire IC industry with the first one involving patents that were registered in China and the second one focusing on those registered in the other six countries and organizations mentioned above. The last sub-database is specially established for IC design firms. However, since the last sub-database only offers information related to IC layout design, the IC design firms applied for a legal protection of their layout design, rather than the patent information. This database is used in this study to identify and check the basic information of the surveyed IC design firms. Considering that almost all of the IC design firms in Shanghai and Shenzhen only applied for their IP protection in China, this study mainly uses the patent data obtained from the first sub-database.

The website of each IC design firm provided information about project-based, product-based and award-based state-firm strategic coordination, which will be further complemented by face-to-face interviews. Before starting to search for this kind of information, I required a list of the IC design firms in Shanghai and Shenzhen. The internal reports of the IC industry which I have obtained from the fieldtrip in Shanghai and Shenzhen provided the list of local IC design firms. According to the report edited by the Shanghai Municipal Informatization Commission (SMIC) and the Shanghai IC Industry Association (SICA) (SMIC and SICA, 2008), there were 165 IC design firms excluding three non-profit public organizations in Shanghai in 2007. Nevertheless, this report listed only 65 local IC design firms.[2] The other 36 IC design firms were found by a search in the last sub-database of the online national patent-database of the IC industry.[3] Based

---

[2]The book (SMIC and SICA, 2008) is an outcome of collective efforts made by SMIC and the SICA to present the recent progress of Shanghai's IC industry in 2007.

[3]There are three sub-databases in the national patent-database of the IC industry. The first two sub-databases contain patent information for the whole IC industry and the last one is related to the special information of IC design firms in China. Since the first sub-database covers a wide range of patent data that are registered by not only the IC

on the name list of 100 IC design firms, I have managed to establish my own database in Shanghai to identify the number of granted invention patents that each firm achieved and to understand their strategic coordination with government based on projects, products and awards.[4] In a similar manner, I also established a database of 110 IC design firms in Shenzhen. Since the government report of the IC design sector in Shenzhen has listed the basic information of all local IC design firms, I do not need to search for the name of IC design firms in the sub-database of the online national patent-database, as I did in the establishment of Shanghai's database. All in all, there were in total 120 IC design firms in Shenzhen according to Shenzhen's government report of the IC design sector. In the end I was able to obtain the information about 110 IC design firms that represent the general situation of the whole IC design sector in Shenzhen. It should be noted that the database in both Shanghai and Shenzhen was established in early October 2008.[5]

4. Structured Questionnaire Survey

The questionnaire survey on China's ICT manufacturing sector and software sector was conducted in 2006–2007 and completed under the joint efforts of the research team of Professor George C.S. Lin, Professor Yu Zhou, Professor Yifei Sun and Professor Dennis Y.H. Wei with a large

---

design firms but also other related firms and organizations within the IC industry in the whole country, it is almost impossible to obtain any basic information of IC design firms in Shanghai from this sub-database. However, the last sub-database of IC layout design gives me a chance to obtain the name list of Shanghai's IC design firms. Around 83 IC design firms in Shanghai are identified through this database. Combining them with the name list obtained from the SICA, a name list of 100 IC design firms in Shanghai is finally established.

[4] The information concerning project-based and award-based coordination is easily found in the websites of firms because they need to advertise themselves and to make their customers or partners trust them more. However, it is very difficult to find the information about product-based state-firm strategic coordination. A reasonable explanation is that the degree of product-based coordination is much lower than that of projects or award-based coordination. Also, it probably will not generate positive effects for the firms to put this kind of information on their website. However, the information of product-based state-firm strategic coordination can be complemented by in-depth interviews and related news.

[5] This database is ever-changing because both the number of patents that each firm has achieved and information of project-based, product-based and award-based state-firm strategic coordination are sensitive to time and contingent on the strategies of both the state and the firm.

amount of capital support from Hong Kong and the U.S. The purpose of this large-scale questionnaire survey is to investigate the inter-firm and extra-firm linkages and local and extra-local networks in the leading ICT industrial clusters in China and to understand how these linkages and networks affect the process of innovation of local firms.[6] The survey was

---

[6]The questionnaire included two parts, namely a set of questions consistent for all firms in the five city-regions (Beijing, Shanghai, Suzhou, Shenzhen and Dongguan which have generated the lion's share of output value, profits and exports of China's ICT industry) for the purpose of comparative study and a set of questions that are specific to the firms in a city-region. The administration of the questionnaire was carried out by a professional survey institution that was outgrown from China's State Statistical Bureau with its headquarters in Beijing and a number of branches in key Chinese cities including Shanghai and Guangzhou. The survey in Shenzhen and Shanghai was respectively conducted during 15 September to 31 October 2006 and in 2007. The targets of this survey included four sub-sectors of the ICT manufacturing industry, namely telecom equipment (industry code 401), electronic computers (404), electronic devices (405) and electronic components (406), and the service sub-sector of software (62) in Shenzhen and Shanghai. According to the data set established by the China State Statistical Bureau on the basis of the results from the first national economic census 2004, there were 2992 ICT manufacturing firms and 1248 software firms in Shenzhen and 1732 ICT manufacturing firms and 2863 software firms in Shanghai. The sample rate is both 5 percent in Shanghai and Shenzhen and the sample size was also proportionally based on sector and regional information provided by the Bureau of Statistics database. Adjustments were made to make sure that the sample size was larger than 30 in all except the semiconductor sub-category. The survey was unable to choose the firms out of the sample frame randomly due to the difficulty of conducting surveys in China. Instead, the agent chose to contact each individual firm in the database to ask for an interview. If rejected, the agent moved to the next case until the full size required was reached. This study analyzed the valid responses to the questionnaire survey by the 633 manufacturing enterprises and 390 software enterprises in these five city-regions. In particular, this study conducted a comparative study of Shanghai and Shenzhen based on this survey, including 151 manufacturing enterprises and 70 software enterprises in Shenzhen and 110 manufacturing enterprises and 120 software enterprises in Shanghai. The questionnaire was administered by making a telephone appointment first which was then followed by a face-to-face interview to explain and fill in the questionnaire. For those firms that rejected the request for a face-to-face interview, they were asked to respond to the questionnaire over the phone. All of the interviewers are trained and well-qualified to complete the interview. The survey started with a pilot to test the feasibility of the questionnaire. All of the problems found in the pilot survey had been immediately solved, which has guaranteed a successful undertaking of the subsequent large-scale survey. Around 70 percent of the returned questionnaires have been randomly chosen to double check their authenticity and accuracy after the large-scale survey was completed. For those questionnaires that were incomplete or questionable, the corresponding firms were re-interviewed to ensure the good quality of the survey. Although much effort has been made to ensure a satisfactory survey, there still exist several problems. The questionnaire involved many questions that can only be answered by the informants who really know the firm well, such as CEOs or senior managers. Unfortunately, not all of

undertaken at the firm-level and covered five city-regions, namely Beijing, Shanghai, Suzhou, Shenzhen and Dongguan, which have attracted the bulk of China's ICT firms and produced the lion's share of output value and exports of China's ICT industry. While this questionnaire survey has focused on the relationship between the growth and innovation as well as the networks and linkages in the ICT industry, it covered substantial information including the nature, attributes, motivation and innovative performance of the ICT firms as well as the relations between the state and the firms. This set of data is used to analyze the relationship between industrial clusters and technological innovation in China as a whole and in Shenzhen in particular. Also, it is used to compare the different degree of state-firm strategic coordination between Shanghai and Shenzhen.

5. In-Depth Interview

This set of data comes from the unstructured in-depth face-to-face interview with corporate managers, officials and related persons in the electronics industry and IC design sector. Interviews with corporate managers helped me to understand their basic information, business interests, innovation-related strategies and selectivity whereas interviews with relevant officials and persons who take charge in the local electronics industry and IC design sector provided me with the information regarding the preferences of both the central and local governments for certain firms and sectors as well as state policies, regulations and strategies that are important in understanding the state-firm relationship and ever-changing macro regulatory environment under which the firms develop.

The interviews in Shanghai were conducted through a snowballing method during the period 4 July to 8 August 2008. There were over 500 IC design firms and organizations in China among which Shanghai accounted for almost one-third (168 IC design firms and organizations) in 2007. There were 29 people who accepted the in-depth face-to-face

---

the questionnaires were answered by CEOs or senior manages as these are very busy people and reluctant to spend their time on the survey. Special efforts have been made to find the informants who are in charge of different departments in the firm to finish the questionnaire. There is also the problem of inconsistency between the responses instantly received and those obtained through a follow-up interview. Despite these problems, the results of the questionnaire survey appear to be consistent and reasonably accurate enough to provide insights into the interests, motivations and considerations of individual firms and yield valuable information that would not be able to be obtained through the aggregate analysis of statistical data.

interviews with one being interviewed by telephone. The informants include 14 managers/CEOs, three senior engineers and one marketing executive of IC design firms, five managers/CEOs and one senior engineer of related industries, both upstream and downstream sectors of the IC design sector, two principals of non-profit service organizations for the IC design houses (Shanghai IC Design Incubator and Shanghai Zizhu Venture Capital Co. Ltd.), one vice-secretary of Shanghai IC Industry Association (SICA) as well as two academic scholars who are experts in the ICT industry and innovation. Among all of the interviewed firms, 14 of them are located in Zhangjiang High-tech Park, seven in Caohejing High-tech Park and the other three firms in other districts. These interviews lasted from three minutes to three hours, depending on attitudes and responses of the informants. A micro-cassette recorder was used during the interviews. Only a few managers appeared to be very sensitive about recording the dialogue. Although the sample rate is not too high, the sample constitutes a series of representative firms. It included the byproducts of the national significant Project 909 — Shanghai Hua Hong NEC and Shanghai Hua Hong Integrated Circuit Co. Ltd., the promising star enterprises like Spreadtrum, the emerging innovation-involved indigenous firms, such as Natlinear and Maxscend, as well as some small unknown and non-innovative enterprises. Face-to-face interviews with firms generated a substantial load of information about firm-level strategies and behavior while those with non-profit service organizations helped me understand the state strategies, policies and selectivity with regard to technological innovation. The interviews with the industrial associations and academic scholars provided overall information about the innovative performance of IC design firms in Shanghai.

The in-depth face-to-face interviews conducted in Shenzhen can be divided into two stages. The first stage occurred during 2–13 July 2007 when I had a chance to join the research team led by Prof. Jici Wang in Peking University. This field-trip was intended to investigate the status and innovative performance of Shenzhen's ICT manufacturing industry, especially the cell-phone manufacturing sector, as Shenzhen has been called by the business circle the "center of cell phone manufacture and trade" (*shouji zhidu*). With the help of the then vice-Mayor Liu Yingli, we successfully interviewed thirteen firms, three industrial associations and one government-affiliated organization and the Shenzhen IP Bureau. Even though this field-trip did not provide me with information directly related to state-firm strategic coordination, I nevertheless obtained a basic understanding of the overall situation and innovation pattern of Shenzhen's ICT industry as well as the inter-firm linkages and intra-firm strategies among Shenzhen's ICT firms. With the basic knowledge from this experience, I conducted my own interview survey with the IC design firms and related organizations from 11 August to 6 September 2008 with an intention to understand the local market environment, the strategies and selectivity of the Shenzhen municipal government, and the strategies, interests and behavior of the IC design firms as well as state-firm strategic coordination and its influence on the innovative performance of individual firms in Shenzhen. Eventually, I was able to obtain information from 13 IC and handset design firms, including the design firms that are affiliated to the well-known domestic giants such as ZTE and BYD, and two related organizations, namely the Shenzhen IC Design Center and the Shenzhen IC Industrial Association with a total of 18 people being interviewed. More detailed information about the face-to-face interview survey in Shenzhen will be elaborated in the following section.

Appendix II
LIST OF QUESTIONS FOR THE INTERVIEW

I. Locational Consideration

1. Why did you select Shanghai/Shenzhen as the location of your enterprise? How do you evaluate the advantages of the city when compared with others? How do you appraise the local institutional and market environment?

2. Do you think co-locating with other establishments in the same industry a positive or negative locational attribute for innovative performance? Why?

3. How do you acquire production or innovation inputs? Are there any inputs that are "'stuck'" in the place?

II. Motivation and Performance of Innovation

4. Is the firm engaged in innovative activities? Why? If so, how does it finance R&D activities? What is the corporate strategy for innovation?

5. How many inventive patents have been certificated in the firm? And how many inventive patents did you apply for this year? Do you have any new products this year? Are the new products new to the nation or new to the world?

6. How does the firm acquire its core technology?

7. What do you think is the most important factor for the technological innovation of the enterprise? What kind of information is particularly important? What type of labor force is qualified to engage in technological innovation? How can you get this kind of labor force?

8. How can you overcome the constraints to innovation? What do you think is the most unsolvable problem for the firm that wants to be innovative?

III. Linkages with Other Firms

9. How do you acquire market information? In which ways can you find your suppliers and customers? How are the suppliers and customers distributed?

10. How frequently do you communicate with people from other establishments in your industry or with related officials? How do you view the importance of communications?

11. Under what conditions do you consider collaborative arrangements with other establishments? Do you fear that the collaboration may cause information/intellectual property about the firm to leak out?

12. How do you establish trust relations with the partner establishments? Do you think geographical proximity important in establishing and maintaining collaboration? Why?

13. How do you deal with the relations with your competitors?

14. Do you consider face-to-face contacts important in your technological innovation? Do you think geographical proximity facilitates the face-to-face contacts? Why?

IV. Relations with the State

15. Does the local government set up any standard before you set down, for example, any requirements for R&D activities or innovative inputs?

16. Do you know any of the policies for encouraging innovation? How do you react to them?

17. What do you think of the status of the protection of IP in China and in the place where the firm located? Do you think it has a negative or positive effect on industrial innovation?

18. How do you get important information for production and innovation? Is it important for you to build up linkages with related officials or bureau?

19. What do you think of the role of the state in establishing our own technical standard? Is state intervention good for the innovation of the whole industry? How do you react to the technical standard-setting of the state?

20. Has the firm participated in any research project sponsored by the central or local governments? Has the enterprise ever acquired financial support from government? Has the firm ever sold any products to the government? Has the firm ever received any awards from government?

21. What do you think of the TD-SCDMA industry alliance? Why do you participate/ not participate in this alliance? What do you think about the future of the TD standard in China, even in the world?

22. Haves the firm ever cooperated with a research institution under the State Council? How do you evaluate the role of the research institution in your technological innovation?

23. What is the relationship between the enterprise and local government as well as central government? What are the most influential policies and regulations for the growth and innovation of the ICT industry?

24. Does the government influence the location choice and the performance and innovation of the establishment? Why and how?

25. Does the enterprise benefit from the local institutional and cultural environment? How?

V. Others

26. What do you think of the role of the industrial giants in the field of mobile communication, such as Qualcomm and TI, since they grasp the most advanced technology in the world and guide the technological development of the world? Do they play a positive or negative role in China's technological innovation? How can China's firms overtake them or reduce the technological gap with them?

27. What do you think about Kaiming, the leading firm focusing on the TD standard, going bankrupt this April? What were the main reasons for its bankruptcy? How will its failure affect the development of the TD standard?

Appendix III

LIST OF INTERVIEWEES
AND INFORMANTS

Shanghai

1. Vice general manager, IC design firm, Shanghai Zhangjiang, 5 July 2008
2. R&D manager, IC design firm, Shanghai Yangpu, 7 July 2008
3. Vice CEO, IC Fab, Shanghai Zhangjiang, 7 July 2008
4. Vice Secretary-General, IC industrial association, Shanghai Zhangjiang, 8 July 2008
5. Former CEO, IC Foundry, Shanghai Zhangjiang, 8 July 2008
6. General Manager, IC design firm, Shanghai Zhangjiang, 10 July 2008
7. Marketing Manager, IC design firm, Shanghai Zhangjiang, 11 July 2008
8. Marketing Manager, IC design firm, Shanghai Xuhui, 15 July 2008
9. Vice Manager, handset design firm, Shanghai Xuhui, 16 July 2008
10. Senior Manager, software design firm, Shanghai, 16 July 2008
11. General Manager, handset design firm, Shanghai Xuhui, 18 July 2008
12. Product Director, handset design firm, Shanghai Xuhui, 21 July 2008
13. CEO, IC design firm, Shanghai Minhang, 22 July 2008
14. Vice General Manager of TD Products, IC design firm, Shanghai Zhangjiang, 23 July 2008
15. Marketing Executive, IC design firm, Shanghai Zhangjiang, 25 July 2008
16. Vice General Manager, IC design firm, Shanghai Yangpu, 31 July 2008
17. Vice CEO, IC design firm, Shanghai Zhangjiang, 4 August 2008
18. General Manager, IC design firm, Shanghai Zhangjiang, 4 August 2008
19. General Manager, IC design firm, Shanghai Xuhui, 5 August 2008
20. Senior Engineer, handset design, Shanghai Xuhui, 6 August 2008
21. Vice General Manager, investment company under the supervision of the government, Shanghai Minhang, 6 August 2008
22. Vice General Manager, IC design firm, Shanghai Xuhui, 6 August 2008
23. Director, Shanghai IC center, Shanghai Xuhui, 6 August 2008

24. Senior Manager, IC design firm, Shanghai Zhangjiang, 7 August 2008
25. Marketing Executive, handset design, Shanghai Zhangjiang, 7 August 2008
26. Vice General Manager, IC design firm, Shanghai Zhangjiang, 8 August 2008
27. Chairman and CEO, IC design firm, Shanghai Zhangjiang, 8 August 2008
28. Professor, Shanghai East China Normal University, Shanghai Putuo, 9 August 2008
29. Professor, Shanghai East China Normal University, Shanghai Putuo, 9 August 2008

Shenzhen

1. Department Manager, handset design and manufacture, Shenzhen Nanshan, 11 August 2008
2. Senior Engineer, handset design and manufacture, Shenzhen Nanshan, 13 August 2008
3. Vice General Manager, IC design firm, Shenzhen Nanshan, 13 August 2008
4. Marketing Manager, IC design firm, Shenzhen Nanshan, 14 August 2008
5. Secretary General, Shenzhen semiconductor association, Shenzhen Nanshan, 15 August 2008
6. Technical Director, handset design and manufacture, Shenzhen Nanshan, 18 August 2008
7. General Manager, IC design and other business, Shenzhen Longgang, 20 August 2008
8. Senior engineer, same firm as above, Shenzhen Longgang, 20 August 2008
9. Engineers, same firm as above, Shenzhen Longgang, 20 August 2008
10. Engineers, same firm as above, Shenzhen Longgang, 20 August 2008
11. Vice General Manager, handset design and manufacture, Shenzhen Futian, 21 August 2008
12. Deputy Director of R&D center, handset design and manufacture, Shenzhen Futian, 23 August 2008
13. Marketing Executive, branch of foreign-invested IC design firm, Shenzhen Futian, 25 August 2008
14. Engineer, IC design firm, Shenzhen Nanshan, 26 August 2008

15. Vice CEO, IC design firm, Shenzhen Futian, 26 August 2008
16. General Manager, IC service firm, Shenzhen Nanshan, 28 August 2008
17. General Manager of Technical Support Department, IC design firm, Shenzhen Nanshan, 29 August 2008
18. Director, Shenzhen IC Center, Shenzhen Nanshan, 13 September 2008

BIBLIOGRAPHY

Acs, Z. J. and Audretsch, D. B. (1988). Innovation in large and small firms: An empirical analysis. *The American Economic Review, 78*(4), 678–690.

Acs, Z. J. and Varga, A. (2002). Geography, endogenous growth, and innovation. *International Regional Science Review, 25*(1), 132–148.

Amin, A. (1999). An institutionalist perspective on regional economic development. *International Journal of Urban and Regional Research, 23*(2), 365–378.

Amighini, A. (2005). China in the international fragmentation of production: Evidence from the ICT industry. *The European Journal of Comparative Economics, 2*(2), 203–219.

Amin, A. and Thrift, N. (1999). Institutional issues for the European regions: From markets and plans to socioeconomics and powers of association. In Barnes, J. T. and Gertler, S. M. (Eds.), *The New Industrial Geography: Regions, Regulation and Institutions* (pp. 293–314). London: Routledge.

Anhui Statistical Bureau (AHSB) (2005). *Anhui Jingji Pucha Nianjian 2004 (Anhui Economic Census 2004)*. Beijing: China Statistics Press, Digital Version.

Archibugi, D. and Michie, J. (1997). Technological globalization and national systems of innovation: An introduction. In Archibugi, D. and Michie, J. (Eds.), *Technology, Globalization and Economic Performance* (pp. 1–23). Cambridge: Cambridge University Press.

Arrow, K. J. (1962). Economic welfare and allocation of resources for invention. In N. B. O. E. Research (Ed.), *The Rate and Direction of Inventive Activity*. Princeton: Princeton University Press.

Audretsch, D. B. (1998). Agglomeration and the location of innovative activity. *Oxford Review of Economic Policy, 14*(2), 18–29.

Audretsch, D. B. (2003). Globalization, innovation and the strategic management of places. In Bröcker, J., Dohse, D. and Soltwedel, R. (Eds.), *Innovation Clusters and Interregional Competition* (pp. 11–27). Berlin: Springer.

Audretsch, D. B. and Feldman, M. P. (1996). R&D spillovers and the geography of innovation and production. *The American Economic Review, 86*(3), 630–640.

Audretsch, D. B. and Feldman, M. P. (2003). Knowledge spillovers and the geography of innovation. *Prepared for the Handbook of Urban and Regional Economics, Volume 4*. Available at: http://www.core.ucl.ac.be/staff/thisseHandbook/audretsch:feldman.pdf, accessed 16 October 2008.

Bair, J. and Gereffi, G. (2001). Local clusters in global chains: The causes and consequences of export dynamism in Torreon's blue jeans industry. *World Development*, *29*(11), 1885–1903.

Baptista, R. (1998). Clusters, innovation and growth: A survey of the literature. In Swann, P., Prevezer M. and Stout, D. (Eds.), *The Dynamics of Industrial Clustering* (pp. 13–51). Oxford: Oxford University Press.

Baptista, R. and Swann, P. (1998). Do firms in clusters innovate more? *Research Policy*, *27*(5), 525–540.

Barnes, J. T. (1999). Industrial geography, institutional economics, and Innis. In Barnes, J. T. and Gertler, M. S. (Eds.), *The New Industrial Geography: Regions, Regulation and Institutions* (pp. 1–22). London: Routledge.

Barnes, J. T. (2001). Retheorizing economic geography: From the quantitative revolution to the culture turn. *Annals of the Association of American Geographers*, *91*(3), 546–565.

Bathelt, H. (2003). Geographies of production: Growth regimes in spatial perspective 1 — innovation, institutions and social systems. *Progress in Human Geography*, *27*(6), 763–778.

Bathelt, H. (2005a). Cluster relations in the media industry: Exploring the Distanced Neighbour paradox in Leipzig. *Regional Studies*, *39*(1), 105–127.

Bathelt, H. (2005b). Geographies of production: Growth regimes in spatial perspective 2 — knowledge creation and growth in clusters. *Progress in Human Geography*, *29*(2), 204–216.

Bathelt, H. (2006). Geographies of production: Growth regimes in spatial perspective 3—toward a relational view of economic action and policy. *Progress in Human Geography*, *30*(2), 223–236.

Bathelt, H. (2007). Buzz-and-pipeline dynamics: Towards a knowledge-based multiplier model of clusters. *Geography Compass*, *1*(6), 1282–1298.

Bathelt, H. and Glückler, J. (2003). Toward a relational economic geography. *Journal of Economic Geography*, *3*(2), 117–144.

Bathelt, H. and Glückler, J. (2005). Resources in economic geography: From substantive concepts towards a relational perspective. *Environment and Planning A*, *37*, 1545–1563.

Bathelt, H. and Gräf, A. (2008). Internal and external dynamics of the Munich film and TV industry cluster, and limitations to future growth. *Environment and Planning A*, *40*, 1944–1965.

Bathelt, H. and Kappes, K. (2009). Necessary restructuring or globalization failure? Shifts in regional supplier relations after the merger of the former German Hoechst and French Rhône-Poulenc groups. *Geoforum*, *40*(2), 158–170.

Bathelt, H., Malmberg, A. and Maskell, P. (2004). Clusters and knowledge: Local buzz, global pipelines and the process of knowledge creation. *Progress in Human Geography*, *28*(1), 31–56.

Bathelt, H. and Schuldt, N. (2008). Between luminaires and meat grinders: International trade fairs as temporary clusters. *Regional Studies*, *42*(6), 853–868.

Bathelt, H. and Zeng, G. (2009). Against the new economy? The changing social and spatial divisions of labor in the larger Shanghai chemical industry. *SPACES* [online], 7(3). Available at: www.spaces-online.com accessed on 20th June 2010.

Beaudry, C., Breschi, S. and Swann, P. (2000). *Cluster, Innovation and Growth: A Comparative Study of European Countries.* Working paper. Manchester Business School.

Beijing Statistical Bureau (BJSB) (2005). *Beijing Jingji Pucha Nianjian 2004 (Beijing Economic Census 2004).* Beijing: China Statistics Press, Digital Version.

Beugelsdijk, S. (2007). The regional environment and a firm's innovative performance: A plea for a multilevel interactionist approach. *Economic Geography,* 83(2), 181–199.

Block, F. (1994). The roles of the state in the economy. In Smelser, S. R. (Ed.), *The Handbook of Economic Sociology* (pp. 691–710). Princeton: Princeton University Press.

Boggs, J. S. and Rantisi, N. M. (2003). The "relational turn" in economic geography. *Journal of Economic Geography,* 3(2), 109–116.

Boschma, R. A. and Frenken, K. (2006). Why is economic geography not an evolutionary science? Towards an evolutionary economic geography. *Journal of Economic Geography,* 6, 273–302.

Bottazzi, L. and Peri, G. (2003). Innovation and spillovers in regions: Evidence from European patent data. *European Economic Review,* 47, 687–710.

Bröcker, J., Dohse, D. and Soltwedel, R. (Eds.) (2003). *Innovation Clusters and Interregional Competition.* Berlin: Springer.

Breidne, M. (2005). *Information and Communications Technology in China: A General Overview of the Current Chinese Initiatives and Trends in the Area of ICT.* Stockholm: VINNOVA.

Brenner, N. (2001). The limits to scale? Methodological reflections on scalar structuration. *Progress in Human Geography,* 25(4), 591–614.

Brenner, N. (2004). *New State Spaces: Urban Governance and the Rescaling of Statehood.* Oxford: Oxford University Press.

Breschi, S. and Lissoni, F. (2001a). Knowledge spillovers and local innovation systems: A critical survey. *Industrial and Corporate Change,* 10(4), 975–1005.

Breschi, S. and Lissoni, F. (2001b). Localised knowledge spillovers vs. innovative milieux: Knowledge tacitness reconsidered. *Papers in Regional Science,* 80(2), 255–273.

Breschi, S. and Malerba, F. (2001). The geography of innovation and economic clustering: Some introductory notes. *Industrial and Corporate Change,* 10(4), 817–833.

Brown, S. and Fai, F. (2006). Strategic resonance between technological and organisational capabilities in the innovation process within firms. *Technovation,* 26(1), 60–75.

Bruton, M. J., Bruton, S. G. and Li, Y. (2005). Shenzhen: Coping with uncertainties in planning. *Habitat International,* 29(2), 227–243.

Bunnell, G. T. and Coe, M. N. (2001). Spaces and scales of innovation. *Progress in Human Geography, 25*(4), 569–589.

Butters, J. K. and Lintner, J. (1945). *Effect of Federal Taxes on Growing Enterprises.* Boston: Harvard University.

Camagni, R. P. (1991a). Introduction: From the local milieu to innovation through cooperation networks. In Camagni, R. P. (Ed.), *Innovation Networks: Spatial Perspectives* (pp. 1–9). London: Belhaven Press.

Camagni, R. P. (1991b). Local "milieu", uncertainty and innovation networks: Towards a new dynamic theory of economic space. In Camagni, R. P. (Ed.), *Innovation Networks: Spatial Perspectives* (pp. 121–144). London: Belhaven Press.

Camagni, R. P. (Ed.) (1991c). *Innovation Networks: Spatial Perspectives.* London: Belhaven Press.

Camagni, R. P. (1995). The concept of innovative milieu and its relevance for public policies in European lagging regions. *Papers in Regional Science 74*(4), 317–340.

Canepa, A. and Stoneman, P. (2008). Financial constraints to innovation in the UK: Evidence from CIS2 and CIS3. *Oxford Economic Papers, 60*(4), 711–730.

Carpenter, R. E. and Petersen, B. C. (2002). Is the growth of small firms constrained by internal finance? *The Review of Economics and Statistics, 84*(2), 298–309.

Castells, S. M. and Hall, P. (1994). *Technopoles of the World.* London: Routledge.

Chang, H.-J. (2003). *Globalisation, Economic Development and the Role of the State.* London and New York: Zed Books Ltd.

Chen, M. (2007). Preface: Read about Shanghai from the one sixth. In Wu, C. (Ed.), *Old Industries in Shanghai.* Shanghai: Shanghai Culture Publishing House.

China Electronics News. (7 November 2008). Shenzhen: Dianzi xinxi chanye qiao-toubao he fengxiangbiao (Shenzhen: A bridgehead and direction indicator of China's ICT industry). *China Electronics News.*

Chongqing Statistical Bureau (CQSB) (2005). *Chongqing Jingji Pucha Nianjian 2004 (Chongqing Economic Census 2004).* Beijing: China Statistics Press, Digital Version.

Christensen, C. M. (1997). *The Innovator's Dilemma: When New Technologies Cause Great Firms to Fail.* Boston: Harvard Business School Press.

Clark, G. L. (1998). Stylized facts and close dialogue: Methodology in economic geography. *Annals of the Association of American Geographers, 88*(1), 73–87.

Cong, C. (2004). Zhongguancun and China's high-tech parks in transition: Growing pains or premature senility? *Asian Survey, 44*(5), 647–668.

Conroy, R. (1992). *Technological Change in China.* Paris: OECD.

Cooke, P. (2001). Regional innovation systems, clusters, and the knowledge economy. *Industrial and Corporate Change, 10*(4), 945–974.

Crang, M. (2003). Qualitative methods: Touchy, feely, look-see? *Progress in Human Geography, 27*(4), 495–504.

Crevoisier, O. and Maillat, D. (1991). Milieu, industrial organization and territorial production system: Towards a new theory of spatial development.

In Camagni, R. (Ed.), *Innovation Networks: Spatial Perspectives* (pp. 13–34). London: Belhaven Press.

China Statistical Bureau (CSSB) (1991). *Zhongguo Tongji Nianjian 1991* (*China Statistical Yearbook 1991*). Beijing: China Statistics Press.

China Statistical Bureau (CSSB) (1992). *Zhongguo Tongji Nianjian 1992* (*China Statistical Yearbook 1992*). Beijing: China Statistics Press.

China Statistical Bureau (CSSB) (1993). *Zhongguo Tongji Nianjian 1993* (*China Statistical Yearbook 1993*). Beijing: China Statistics Press.

China Statistical Bureau (CSSB) (1994). *Zhongguo Tongji Nianjian 1994* (*China Statistical Yearbook 1994*). Beijing: China Statistics Press.

China Statistical Bureau (CSSB) (1995). *Zhongguo Tongji Nianjian 1995* (*China Statistical Yearbook 1995*). Beijing: China Statistics Press.

China Statistical Bureau (CSSB) (1996). *Zhongguo Tongji Nianjian 1996* (*China Statistical Yearbook 1996*). Beijing: China Statistics Press.

China Statistical Bureau (CSSB) (1997). *Zhongguo Tongji Nianjian 1997* (*China Statistical Yearbook 1997*). Beijing: China Statistics Press.

China Statistical Bureau (CSSB) (1998). *Zhongguo Tongji Nianjian 1998* (*China Statistical Yearbook 1998*). Beijing: China Statistics Press.

China Statistical Bureau (CSSB) (1999a). *Xin Zhongguo Wushinian Tongji Ziliao Huibian* (*Comprehensive Statistical Data and Materials on 50 Years of New China*). Beijing: China Statistics Press.

China Statistical Bureau (CSSB) (1999b). *Zhongguo Tongji Nianjian 1999* (*China Statistical Yearbook 1999*). Beijing: China Statistics Press.

China Statistical Bureau (CSSB) (2000). *Zhongguo Tongji Nianjian 2000* (*China Statistical Yearbook 2000*). Beijing: China Statistics Press.

China Statistical Bureau (CSSB) (2001). *Zhongguo Tongji Nianjian 2001* (*China Statistical Yearbook 2001*). Beijing: China Statistics Press.

China Statistical Bureau (CSSB) (2002). *Zhongguo Tongji Nianjian 2002* (*China Statistical Yearbook 2002*). Beijing: China Statistics Press.

China Statistical Bureau (CSSB) (2003). *Zhongguo Tongji Nianjian 2003* (*China Statistical Yearbook 2003*). Beijing: China Statistics Press.

China Statistical Bureau (CSSB) (2004). *Zhongguo Tongji Nianjian 2004* (*China Statistical Yearbook 2004*). Beijing: China Statistics Press.

China Statistical Bureau (CSSB) (2005a). *Zhongguo Jingji Pucha 2004* (*China Economic Census 2004*). Beijing: China Statistics Press, Digital Version.

China Statistical Bureau (CSSB) (2005b). *Zhongguo Tongji Nianjian 2005* (*China Statistical Yearbook 2005*). Beijing: China Statistics Press.

China Statistical Bureau (CSSB) (2006). *Zhongguo Tongji Nianjian 2006* (*China Statistical Yearbook 2006*). Beijing: China Statistics Press.

China Statistical Bureau (CSSB) (2007). *Zhongguo Tongji Nianjian 2007* (*China Statistical Yearbook 2007*). Beijing: China Statistics Press.

China Statistical Bureau (CSSB) (2008). *Zhongguo Tongji Nianjian 2008* (*China Statistical Yearbook 2008*). Beijing: China Statistics Press.

China Statistical Bureau (CSSB) (2009). *Zhongguo Tongji Nianjian 2009* (*China Statistical Yearbook 2009*). Beijing: China Statistics Press.

China Statistical Bureau (CSSB), and Ministry of Science and Technology (MOST) (1991). *Zhongguo Keji Tongjian Nianjian 1991 (China Statistical Yearbook on Science and Technology 1991)*. Beijing: China Statistics Press.

China Statistical Bureau (CSSB), and Ministry of Science and Technology (MOST) (1996). *Zhongguo Keji Tongjian Nianjian 1996 (China Statistical Yearbook on Science and Technology 1996)*. Beijing: China Statistics Press.

China Statistical Bureau (CSSB), and Ministry of Science and Technology (MOST) (2001). *Zhongguo Keji Tongji Nianjian 2001 (China Statistical Yearbook on Science and Technology 2001)*. Beijing: China Statistics Press.

China Statistical Bureau (CSSB), and Ministry of Science and Technology (MOST) (2006). *Zhongguo Keji Tongji Nianjian 2006 (China Statistical Yearbook on Science and Technology 2006)*. Beijing: China Statistics Press.

China Statistical Bureau (CSSB), and Ministry of Science and Technology (MOST) (2007). *Zhongguo Keji Tongji Nianjian 2007 (China Statistical Yearbook on Science and Technology 2007)*. Beijing: China Statistics Press.

Döring, T. and Schnellenbach, J. (2006). What do we know about geographical knowledge spillovers and regional growth? A survey of the literature. *Regional Studies, 40*(3), 375–395.

Davelaar, J. E. and Nijkamp, P. (1997). Spatial dispersion of technological innovation: A review. In Bertuglia, C. S., Lombardo, S. and Nijkamp, P. (Eds.), *Innovative Behaviour in Space and Time* (pp. 17–40). Berlin: Springer.

David, P. A. (1997). Rethinking technology transfers: Incentives, institutions and knowledge-based industrial development. In Feinstein, C. and Howe, C. (Eds.), *Chinese Technology Transfer in the 1990s: Current Experience, Historical Problems and International Perspectives* (pp. 13–37). Lyme: Edward Elgar Pub.

De Groot, L. F. H., Nijkamp, P. and Acs, J. Z. (2001). Knowledge spillovers, innovation and regional development. *Papers in Regional Science, 80*, 249–253.

Dean, G. (1979). *Technology Policy and Industrialization in the People's Republic of China*. Ottava: International Development Research Center.

DeWoskin, K. J. (2001). The WTO and the telecommunications sector in China. *The China Quarterly, 167*, 630–654.

Dicken, P. and Malmberg, A. (2001). Firms in territories: A relational perspective. *Economic Geography, 77*(4), 345–363.

Diez, R. J., Schiller, D., Susanne, M., Soltwedel, R. and Liu, W. H. (2008). *The Agile Firm Model in Hong Kong and the Pearl River Delta*. Internal report published by Institution of Economic and Cultural Geography, Leibniz University of Hannover and The Kiel Institute for the World Economy, Germany.

Dodgson, M. and Rothwell, R. (Eds.). (1994). *The Handbook of Industrial Innovation*. Aldershot: Edward Elgar Publishing Limited.

Dorfman, N. (1987). *Innovation and Market Structure: Lessons from the Computer and Semiconductor Industries*. Cambridge, Mass: Ballinger.

Dosi, G. (1988). Sources, procedures and microeconomic effects of innovation. *Journal of Economic Literature, XXVI*, 1120–1171.

Ellison, G. and Glaeser, E. L. (1997). Geographic concentration in U.S. manufacturing industries: A dartboard approach. *The Journal of Political Economy, 105*(5), 889–927.

Evans, P. (1995). *Embedded Autonomy: States and Industrial Transformation*. Princeton: Princeton University Press.

Fagerberg, J. (2005). Innovation: A guide to the literature. In Fagerberg, J., Mowery, C. D. and Nelson, R. R. (Eds.), *The Oxford Handbook of Innovation* (pp. 1–26). New York: Oxford University Press.

Fagerberg, J., Mowery, C. D. and Nelson, R. R. (Eds.) (2005). *The Oxford Handbook of Innovation*. Oxford: Oxford University Press.

Fagerberg, J. and Verspagen, B. (2009). Innovation studies — The emerging structure of a new scientific field. *Research Policy, 38*(2), 218–233.

Fan, C. C. (2008). *China on the Move: Migration, the State and the Household*. London and New York: Routledge.

Fan, C. C. and Scott, A. J. (2003). Industrial agglomeration and development: A survey of spatial economic issues in East Asia and a statistical analysis of Chinese regions. *Economic Geography, 79*(3), 295–319.

Fan, P. (2003). Made in China: The Rise of the Chinese Domestic Firms in the Information Industry. PhD Thesis, Massachusetts Institute of Technology, Boston.

Fan, P. (2006). Catching up through developing innovation capability: Evidence from China's telecom-equipment industry. *Technovation, 26*, 359–368.

Feldman, M. P. (1994). *The Geography of Innovation*. Dordrecht: Kluwer Academic Publishers.

Feldman, M. P. (1999). The new economics of innovation, spillovers and agglomeration: A review of empirical studies. *Economics of Innovation and New Technology, 8*, 5–25.

Fingleton, B., Igliori, C. D. and Moore, B. (2004). Employment growth of small high-technology firms and the role of horizontal clustering: Evidence from computing services and R&D in Great Britain, 1991–2000. *Urban Studies, 41*(4), 773–799.

Fischer, M. M. (Ed.). (2006). *Innovation, Networks and Knowledge Spillovers*. Berlin: Springer.

Florida, R. (1995). Toward the learning region. *Futures, 27*(5), 527–536.

Friedman, T. L. (2005). *The World Is Flat: A Brief History of the Twenty-First Century*. New York: Farrar, Straus & Giroux.

Fujian Statistical Bureau (FJSB). (2005). *Fujian Jingji Pucha Nianjian 2004 (Fujian Economic Census 2004)*. Beijing: China Statistics Press, Digital Version.

Fuller, D. B. (2009). China's national system of innovation and uneven technological trajectory: The case of China's integrated circuit design industry. *Chinese Management Studies, 3*(1), 58–74.

Gai, W. (2002). *Chuangxin Wangluo: Quyu Jingji Fazhan Xin Siwei* (*Innovative Network: A New Perspective on Regional Development*). Beijing: Peking University Press.

Gerstenfeld, A. and Brainard, R. (Eds.) (1979). *Technological Innovation: Government/Industry Cooperation.* New York: John Wiley & Sons.

Gertler, M. S. (1995). "Being there": Proximity, organization and culture in the development and adoption of advanced manufacturing technologies. *Economic Geography, 71*(1), 1–26.

Giuliani, E. (2005). Cluster absorptive capacity: Why do some clusters forge ahead and others lag behind? *European Urban and Regional Studies, 12*(3), 269–288.

Giuliani, E. (2007). The selective nature of knowledge networks in clusters: Evidence from the wine industry. *Journal of Economic Geography, 7*(2), 139–168.

Glaeser, E. L., Kallal, H. D., Scheinkman, J. A. and Shleifer, A. (1992). Growth in cities. *The Journal of Political Economy, 100*(6), 1126–1152.

Glaser, B. G. and Strauss, A. L. (1967). *The Discovery of Grounded Theory: Strategies for Qualitative Research.* New York: Aldine.

Glasmeier, A. (2000a). Economic geography in practice: Local economic development policy. In Glark, G. L., Feldman, M. P. and Gertler, M. S. (Eds.), *Oxford Handbook of Economic Geography* (pp. 559–579). Oxford: Oxford University Press.

Glasmeier, A. (2000b). Economic geography in practice: Local economic development policy. In Clark, G. L., Gertler, M. S. and Feldman, M. P. (Eds.), *The Oxford Handbook of Economic Geography.* Oxford: Oxford University Press.

Gordon, I. R. and McCann, P. (2000). Industrial clusters: Complexes, agglomeration and/or social networks? *Urban Studies, 37*(3), 513–532.

Grabher, G. (1993a). Rediscovering the social in the economics of interfirm relations. In Grabher, G. (Ed.), *The Embedded Firm: On the Socioeconomics of Industrial Networks* (pp. 1–31). London and New York: Routledge.

Grabher, G. (1993b). The weakness of strong ties: The lock-in of regional development in the Ruhr area. In Grabher, G. (Ed.), *The Embedded Firm: On the Socioeconomics of Industrial Networks.* New York and London: Routledge.

Gu, S. (1999). *China's Industrial Technology: Market Reform and Organizational Change.* London and New York: Routledge.

Guan, J. C., Yam, R. C. M., Tang, E. P. Y. and Lau, A. K. W. (2009). Innovation strategy and performance during economic transition: Evidence in Beijing, China. *Research Policy, 38*(5), 802–812.

Guangdong Statistical Bureau (GDSB) (2005). *Guangdong Jingji Pucha Nianjian 2004* (*Guangdong Economic Census 2004*). Beijing: China Statistics Press, Digital Version.

Guangdong Statistical Bureau (GDSB), and Guangdong Provincial Department of Science and Technology (GDST) (2006). *Guangdong Keji Tongji Nianjian*

2006 (Guangdong Statistical Yearbook on Science and Technology 2006). China: China Statistics Press.

Guangxi Statistical Bureau (GXSB). (2005). *Guangxi Jingji Pucha Nianjian 2004 (Guangxi Economic Census 2004)*. Beijing: China Statistics Press, Digital Version.

Guangzhou Statistical Bureau (GZSB). (2005). *Guangzhou Jingji Pucha Nianjian 2004 (Guizhou Economic Census 2004)*. Beijing: China Statistics Press, Digital Version.

Guillain, R. and Gallo, L. J. (2006). Measuring agglomeration: An exploratory spatial analysis approach applied to the case of Paris and its surroundings. *REAL Working Paper*.

Hainan Statistical Bureau (HANSB) (2005). *Hainan Jingji Pucha Nianjian 2004 (Hainan Economic Census 2004)*. Beijing: China Statistics Press, Digital Version.

Hakanson, L. (2005). Epistemic communities and cluster dynamics: On the role of knowledge in industrial districts. *Industry and Innovation, 12*(4), 433–463.

Hall, B. H. (2002). The financing of research and development. *Oxford Review of Economic Policy, 18*(1), 35–51.

Han, S. S. (2000). Shanghai between state and market in urban transformation. *Urban Studies, 37*(11), 2091–2112.

Harrison, B., Kelley, M. R. and Gant, J. (1996). Innovative firm behavior and local milieu: Exploring the intersection of agglomeration, firm effects, and technological change. *Economic Geography, 72*(3), 233–258.

Harvey, D. (2005). *A Brief History of Neoliberalism*. New York: Oxford University Press.

Harwit, E. (2005). Telecommunications and the Internet in Shanghai: Political and economic factors shaping the network in a Chinese city. *Urban Studies, 42*(10), 1837–1858.

He, C. (2002). Information costs, agglomeration economies and the location of foreign direct investment in China. *Regional Studies, 36*(9), 1029–1036.

Hebei Statistical Bureau (HEBSB) (2005). *Hebei Jingji Pucha Nianjian 2004 (Hebei Economic Census 2004)*. Beijing: China Statistics Press, Digital Version.

Heilongjiang Statistical Bureau (HLJSB) (2005). *Heilongjiang Jingji Pucha Nianjian 2004 (Heilongjiang Economic Census 2004)*. Beijing: China Statistics Press, Digital Version.

Henan Statistical Bureau (HENSB) (2005). *Henan Jingji Pucha Nianjian 2004 (Henan Economic Census 2004)*. Beijing: China Statistics Press.

Hendry, C., Brown, J. and Defillippi, R. (2000). Regional clustering of high technology-based firms: Opto-electronics in three countries. *Regional Studies, 34*(2), 129–144.

Hennock, M. (2002). China: The world's factory floor. *BBC Online News*. Available at: http://news.bbc.co.uk/2/hi/business/2415241.stm, accessed on 13 May 2010.

Himmelberg, C. P. and Petersen, B. C. (1994). R&D and internal finance: A panel study of small firms in high-tech industries. *The Review of Economics and Statistics*, *76*(1), 38–51.

Hunan Statistical Bureau (HUNSB). (2005). *Hunan Jingji Pucha Nianjian 2004* (*Hunan Economic Census 2004*). Beijing: China Statistics Press.

Howe, C. (Ed.). (1981). *Shanghai: Revolution and Development in an Asian Metropolis*. Cambridge: Cambridge University Press.

Howells, J. R. L. (2002). Tacit knowledge, innovation and economic geography. *Urban Studies*, *39*(5/6), 871–884.

Hsu, J. Y. (2005). From transfer to hybridisation? In Alvstam, C. G. and Schamp, E. W. (Eds.), *Linking Industries Across the World: Process of Global Networking* (pp. 173–196). Aldershot: Ashgate.

Hu, Q. L. (2006). *Xinlu Licheng: 909 Chaoda Guimo Jicheng Dianlu Gongcheng Jishi* (*Building the Chip Industry: Record of Ultra Large Scale IC Project 909*). Beijing: Publishing House of Electronics Industry.

Hu, T. S., Lin, C. Y. and Chang, S. L. (2005). Role of interaction between technological communities and industrial clustering in innovative activity: The case of Hsinchu District, Taiwan. *Urban Studies*, *42*(7), 1139–1160.

Hu, Z. Y. (2006). Placing China's State-owned Enterprises: Firm, Region and the Geography of Production. PhD Thesis of the University of Hong Kong, Hong Kong.

Hubei Statistical Bureau (HUBSB) (2005). *Hubei Jingji Pucha Nianjian 2004* (*Hubei Economic Census 2004*). Beijing: China Statistics Press.

Huang, Y. S. (2008). *Capitalism with Chinese Characteristics: Entrepreneurship and the State*. Cambridge: Cambridge University Press.

Hyytinen, A. and Toivanen, O. (2005). Do financial constraints hold back innovation and growth? Evidence on the role of public policy. *Research Policy*, *34*(9), 1385–1403.

Inner Mongolia Statistical Bureau (IMSB) (2005). *Inner Mongolia Jingji Pucha Nianjian 2004* (*Inner Mongolia Economic Census 2004*). Beijing: China Statistics Press.

Jefferson, G. H., Huamao, B., Xiaojing, G. and Xiaoyun, Y. (2006). R&D performance in Chinese industry. *Economics of Innovation and New Technology*, *15*(4–5), 345–366.

Jessop, B. (1990). *State Theory: Putting the Capitalist State in Its Place*. Pennsylvania: The Pennsylvania State University Press.

Jessop, B. (1994). Post-Fordism and the state. In Amin, A. (Ed.), *Post-Fordism: A Reader* (pp. 251–279). Oxford: Blackwell.

Jessop, B. (2000). The crisis of the national spatio-temporal fix and the tendential ecological dominance of globalizing capitalism. *International Journal of Urban and Regional Research*, *24*(2), 323–360.

Jiang, H. (2006). Zhanxun zhanzai 3G menkanshang (Spreadtrum: Standing in the front yard of 3G). *Xinjingji Daokan* (*New Economic Weekly*), *115*, 44.

Jiangsu Statistical Bureau (JSSB) (2005). *Jiangsu Jingji Pucha Nianjian 2004* (*Jiangsu Economic Census 2004*). Beijing: China Statistics Press, Digital Version.

Jiangxi Statistical Bureau (JXSB) (2005). *Jiangxi Jingji Pucha Nianjian 2004* (*Jiangxi Economic Census 2004*). Beijing: China Statistics Press, Digital Version.

Jilin Statistical Bureau (JLSB) (2005). *Jilin Jingji Pucha Nianjian 2004* (*Jilin Economic Census 2004*). Beijing: China Statistics Press, Digital Version.

Katsuno, M. (2005). *Status and Overview of Official ICT Indicators for China OECD Working Papers*. Available at: http://oberon.sourceoecd.org/vl= 18652493/cl=11/nw=1/rpsv/cgi-bin/wppdf?file=5lgsjhvj74s6.pdf, accessed on 8 June 2008.

Kaufmann, A. and Tödtling, F. (2001). Science-industry interaction in the process of innovation: The importance of boundary-crossing between systems. *Research Policy, 30,* 791–804.

Keeble, D. and Wilkinson, F. (1999). Collective learning and knowledge development in the evolution of regional clusters of high technology SMEs in Europe. *Regional Studies, 33*(4), 295–303.

Kesidou, E. and Romijn, H. (2008). Do local knowledge spillovers matter for development? An empirical study of Uruguay's software cluster. *World Development, 36*(10), 2004–2028.

Khalil, M. A. and Hamid, J. (2005). The ICT Landscape in the PRC: Market Trends and Investment Opportunities. Available at: http://www.ifc.org/ifcext/eastasia.nsf/AttachmentsByTitle/IFCReport_Chinese/$FILE/Report+ V.2.0.pdf, accessed on 20 July 2007.

Kim, L. and Nelson, R. R. (Eds.) (2000). *Technology, Learning and Innovation: Experiences of Newly Industrializing Economies*. Cambridge: Cambridge University Press.

Krugman, P. (1991). *Geography and Trade*. Cambridge, MA: MIT Press.

Lagendijk, A. (2006). Learning from conceptual flow in regional studies: Framing present debates, unbracketing past debates. *Regional Studies, 40,* 385–399.

Lall, S. (1993). Promoting technology development: The role of technology transfer and indigenous effort. *Third World Quarterly, 14*(1), 95–108.

Lao, H., Jin, X. and Wowei yikuang. (2004). *Yintehu Shenzhen Baogao 2004: Shizi Lukou De Shenzhen* (*Yintehu Shenzhen Report 2004: Shenzhen at the Crossroad*). Beijing: China Modern Economic Publishing House.

Lazonick, W. (2005). The innovative firm. In Fagerberg, J., Mowery, C. D. and Nelson, R. R. (Eds.), *The Oxford Handbook of Innovation* (pp. 29–55). Oxford: Oxford University Press.

Le, Z. and Wulan, C. (Eds.) (2008). *Shenzhen Jingji Fazhan Baogao 2008* (*Annual Report on Economy of Shenzhen 2008*). Beijing: Social Sciences Academic Press.

Lee, C., Lee, K. and Pennings, M. J. (2001). Internal capabilities, external networks, and performances: A study on technology-based ventures. *Strategic Management Journal, 22,* 615–640.

Lerner, J. (1996). The government as venture capitalist: The long-run impact of the SBIR program. *NBER Working Paper Series.*

Liaoning Statistical Bureau (LNSB) (2005). *Liaoning Jingji Pucha Nianjian* (*Liaoning Economic Census 2004*). Beijing: China Statistics Press, Digital Version.

Lin, G. C. S. (1997). *Red Capitalism in South China: Growth and Development of the Pearl River Delta.* Vancouver: UBC Press.

Lin, G. C. S. (2002). The growth and structural change of Chinese cities: A contextual and geographic analysis. *Cities, 19*(5), 299–316.

Lin, G. C. S. (2009a). *Developing China: Land, Politics and Social Conditions.* London: Routledge.

Lin, G. C. S. (2009b). Scaling-up regional development in globalizing China: Local capital accumulation, land-centred politics and reproduction of space. *Regional Studies, 43*(3), 429–447.

Lin, G. C. S. and Wang, C. (2009). Technological innovation in China's high-tech sector: Insights from a 2008 survey of the integrated circuit design industry in Shanghai. *Eurasian Geography and Economics, 50*(4), 402–424.

Lin, G. C. S., Wang, C. C., Zhou, Y., Sun, Y. F. and Wei, Y. D. (2011). Placing technological innovation in globalizing China: Production linkage, knowledge exchange and innovative performance of the ICT industry in a developing economy. *Urban Studies, 48*(14), 2999–3018.

Liu, C. (2005). Meiguo guigu gaokeji chanye jiqun jiqi dui zhongguo de qishi (High-tech industrial cluster of Silicon Valley and its implications to China). *Gongye Jishu Jingji* (*Economy of Industrial Technology*), *24*(7), 35–39.

Liu, F. (2008). Shen gaoxin jishu rending, xuannian jiexiao (Standard for identification of high-tech firms announced by Shenzhen). *Nanfang Dushi Bao* (*Southern Metropolitan News*). Available at: http://tech.sina.com.cn/it/m/2003-06-24/1200201698.shtml, accessed on 27 December 2008.

Liu, H. (2005). China's Special Economic Zones: From Shenzhen to Shanghai — A New Path to Industrialization, Urbanization, Globalization and Modernization. PhD Thesis, The New School for Social Research, New York.

Liu, J., LIu, Y. and Xie, H. (2004). *Liangdan Yixing Gongcheng Yu Dakexue* (*The Project of Two Bombs, One Satellite: A Model of the Big Science*). Jinan: Shandong Education Press.

Liu, S. (2000). China to fund IC design complex. *EE Times,* 8 March. Available at: http://www.eetimes.com/showArticle.jhtml;jsessionid=NSD5MNMV2GSZUQSNDLPCKHSCJUNN2JVN?articleID=18303811, accessed on 31 October 2008.

Liu, W. D. (2000). Geography of China's Auto Industry: Globalization and Embeddedness. PhD Thesis, The University of Hong Kong, Hong Kong.

Liu, X. and Buck, T. (2007). Innovation performance and channels for international technology spillovers: Evidence from Chinese high-tech industries. *Research Policy, 36*(3), 355–366.

Lorenzen, M. (2005). Knowledge and geography. *Industry and Innovation, 12*(4), 399.

Lu, D. and Tang, Z. (1997). *State Intervention and Business in China: The Role of Preferential Policies.* Cheltenham: Edward Elgar.

Lu, Q. (1997). Innovation and Organization: The Rise of New Science and Technology Enterprises in China. PhD Thesis, Harvard University, Cambridge, Massachusetts.

Lu, Q. (2000). *China's Leap into the Information Age: Innovation and Organization in the Computer Industry*. Oxford: Oxford University Press.

Luo, Z. and Shi, Z. (2003). Cong meiguo guigu xiaoqiye jiqun kan Shanghai gaokeji yuanqu de fazhan (Development of high-tech science in Shanghai: Insights from SME cluster in Silicon Valley). *Dangdai Caijing (Contemporary Fianance & Economics)*, *3*, 70–73.

Macleod, G. and Goodwin, M. (1999). Space, scale and state strategy: Rethinking urban and regional governance. *Progress in Human Geography*, *23*(4), 503–527.

Maillat, D. (1995). Territorial dynamic, innovative milieu and regional policy. *Entrepreneurship and Regional Development*, *7*, 157–165.

Malecki, E. J. (1997). *Technology and Economic Development: The Dynamics of Local, Regional, and National Competitiveness*. Essex, England: Longman.

Malmberg, A. (1996). Industrial geography: Agglomeration and local milieu. *Progress in Human Geography*, *20*(3), 392–403.

Malmberg, A. and Power, D. (2005). (How) Do (firms in) clusters create knowledge? *Industry and Innovation*, *12*(4), 409–431.

Malmberg, A., Sölvell, Ö. and Zander, I. (1996). Spatial clustering, local accumulation of knowledge and firm competitiveness. *Geografiska Annaler. Series B, Human Geography*, *78*(2), 85–97.

Mann, M. (2003). The autonomous power of the state: Its origins, mechanisms and results. In Brenner, N., Jessop, B., Jones, M. and Macleod, G. (Eds.), *State/Space: A Reader* (pp. 53–64). Oxford: Blackwell Publishing.

Markusen, A. (1996). Sticky places in slippery space: A typology of industrial districts. *Economic Geography*, *72*(3), 293–313.

Markusen, A. (1999). Fuzzy concepts, scanty evidence, policy distance: The case for rigour and policy relevance in critical regional studies. *Regional Studies*, *33*(9), 869–884.

Marshall, A. (1920). *Principles of Economics: An Introductory Volume*. 8th edn. London: Macmillan.

Martin, R. (1999). The new "geographical turn" in economics: Some critical reflections. *Cambridge Journal of Economics*, *23*(1), 65–91.

Martin, R. (2000). Institutional approaches in economic geography. In Sheppard, E. and Barnes, T. J. (Eds.), *A Companion to Economic Geography* (pp. 77–94). Oxford: Blackwell Publishing.

Martin, R. and Sunley, P. (2003). Deconstructing clusters: Chaotic concept or policy panacea? *Journal of Economic Geography*, *3*, 5-35.

Maskell, P. (2001a). The firm in economic geography. *Economic Geography*, *77*(4), 329–344.

Maskell, P. (2001b). Towards a knowledge-based theory of the geographical cluster. *Industrial and Corporate Change*, *10*(4), 921–943.

262 *Upgrading China's Information and Communication Technology Industry*

Maskell, P., Bathelt, H., and Malmberg, A. (2006). Building global knowledge pipelines: The role of temporary clusters. *European Planning Studies, 14*(8), 997–1013.

Maskell, P. and Malmberg, A. (1999). The competitiveness of firms and regions: 'Ubiquitification' and the importance of localized learning. *European Urban and Regional Studies, 6*(1), 9-25.

Meeus, M. and Oerlemans, L. (2000). Firm behaviour and innovative performance: An empirical exploration of the selection-adaptation debate. *Research Policy, 29*(1), 41–58.

Meeus, M. and Oerlemans, L. (2005). Innovation strategies, interactive learning and innovation networks. In Casper, S. and van Waarden, F. (Eds.), *Innovation and Institutions* (pp. 152–189). Cheltenham: Edward Elgar.

Meng, Q. and Li, M. (2002). New economy and ICT development in China. *Information Economics and Policy, 14*, 275–295.

Miao, C. H., Wei, Y. H. D. and Ma, H. T. (2007). Technological learning and innovation in China in the context of globalization. *Eurasian Geography and Economics, 48*(6), 713–732.

Ministry of Information Industry (MII) (2004). *Zhongguo Dianzi Xinxi Chanye Tongji Nianjian 2003 (Statistical Yearbook of Chinese Electronic Information Industry 2003)*. Beijing: Publishing House of Electronics Industry, Digital Version.

Ministry of Information Industry (MII) (2005). *Zhongguo Dianzi Xinxi Chanye Tongji Nianjian 2004 (Statistical Yearbook of Chinese Electronic Information Industry 2004)*. Beijing: Publishing House of Electronics Industry, Digital Version.

Ministry of Information Industry (MII) (2006). *Zhongguo Dianzi Xinxi Chanye Tongji Nianjian 2005 (Statistical Yearbook of Chinese Electronic Information Industry 2005)*. Beijing: Publishing House of Electronics Industry, Digital Version.

Ministry of Information Industry (MII) (2007). *Zhongguo Dianzi Xinxi Chanye Tongji Nianjian 2006 (Statistical Yearbook of Chinese Electronic Information Industry 2006)*. Beijing: Publishing House of Electronics Industry, Digital Version.

Ministry of Information Industry (MII) (2008). *Zhongguo Dianzi Xinxi Chanye Tongji Nianjian 2007 (Statistical Yearbook of Chinese Electronic Information Industry 2007)*. Beijing: Publishing House of Electronics Industry, Digital Version.

Ministry of Information Industry (MII) (2009). *Zhongguo Dianzi Xinxi Chanye Tongji Nianjian 2008 (Statistical Yearbook of Chinese Electronic Information Industry 2008)*. Beijing: Publishing House of Electronics Industry, Digital Version.

Ministry of Science and Technology (MOST) (Ed.). (1999). *Tuqiang, Gaige, Chuangxin: Gongheguo Keji Shiye 50 nian (Rejuvenation, Reform, Innovation: The 50 Years of Science and Technology in China)*. Nanning: Guangxi Science and Technology Press.

Mok, V. (1996). Industrial development. In Yeung, Y. M. and Sung, Y. W. (Eds.), *Shanghai: Transformation and Modernization under China's Open Policy* (pp. 199–224). Hong Kong: The Chinese University Press.

Moulaert, F. and Sekia, F. (2003). Territorial innovation models: A critical survey. *Regional Studies, 37*(3), 289–302.

Naughton, B. (Ed.) (1997). *The China Circle: Economics and Electronics in the PRC, Taiwan and Hong Kong.* Washington, D.C.: Brookings Institution Press.

Naughton, B. and Segal, A. (2003). China in search of a workable model: Technology development in the new millennium. In Keller, W. W. and Samuels, J. R. (Eds.), *Crisis and Innovation in Asian Technology* (pp. 160–186). Cambridge: Cambridge University Press.

Nee, V. (1992). Organizational dynamics of market transition: Hybrid forms, property rights and mixed economy in China. *Administrative Science Quarterly, 37*(1), 1–27.

Nelson, R. R. and Winter, G. S. (1982). *An Evolutionary Theory of Economic Change.* Cambrige and London: Harvard University Press.

Ng, M. and Tang, W. S. (2004). The role of planning in the development of Shenzhen, China: Rhetoric and realities. *Eurasian Geography and Economics, 45*(3), 190–211.

Ning, L. (2009a). China's leadership in the world ICT industry: A successful story of its attracting-in and walking-out strategy for the development of high-tech industries? *Pacific Affairs, 82*(1), 67–91.

Ning, L. (Ed.) (2009b). *China's Rise in the World ICT Industry: Industrial Strategies and the Catch-Up Development Model.* New York: Routledge.

O'Donoghue, D. and Gleave, B. (2004). A note on methods for measuring industrial agglomeration. *Regional Studies, 38*(4), 419–427.

O'Neill, M. P. (1997). Bringing the qualitative state into economic geography. In Lee, R. and Wills, J. (Eds.), *Geographies of Economics.* London: Arnold.

O'Sullivan, M. (2005). Finance and innovation. In Fagerberg, J., Mowery, C. D. and Nelson, R. R. (Eds.), *The Oxford Handbook of Innovation* (pp. 240–265). Oxford: Oxford University Press.

OECD. (2005). OECD Finds That China is the Biggest Exporter of Information Technology Goods in 2004, Surpassing US and EU. Available at: http://www.oecd.org/document/8/0,3343,en_2649_33757_35833096_1_1_1_1,00.html, accessed on 28 May 2009.

OECD and Eurostat. (2005). Oslo Manual: Guidelines for Collecting and Interpreting Innovation Data. Available at: http://213.253.134.43/oecd/pdfs/browseit/9205111E.PDF, accessed on 23 April 2008.

Offe, C. (1984). Crises of crisis management: Elements of a political crisis theory. In Keane, J. (Ed.), *Contradictions of the Welfare State* (pp. 35–64). Cambridge: The MIT Press.

Oinas, P. (2000). Distance and learning: Does proximity matter? In Boekema, F., Morgan, K., Bakkers, S. and Rutt, R. (Eds.), *Knowledge, Innovation and Economic Growth: The Theory and Practice of Learning Regions* (pp. 57–69). Cheltenham, UK: Edward Elgar.

Paci, R. and Usai, S. (1999). Externalities, knowledge spillovers and the spatial distribution of innovation. *GeoJournal, 49*(4), 381–390.

Painter, J. (2002). State and governance. In Sheppard, E. and Barnes, T. J. (Eds.), *A Companion to Economic Geography*. London: Blackwell Publishing.

Pan, Z. (1996). The Uneven Development of Chinese Cities: A Comparison of Major Social and Economic Indicators among Shanghai, Shenzhen and Zhengzhou. MA Thesis, University of Louisville, Louisville.

Park, S. O. (1996). Network and embeddedness in the dynamic types of new industrial districts. *Progress in Human Geography, 20*(4), 476–493.

Pecht, M. (2006). *China's Electronics Industry: The Definitive Guide for Companies and Policy Makers with Interests in China*. New York: William Andrew Publishing.

Penrose, E. (1959). *The Theory of the Growth of the Firm*. New York: Sharpe.

Ponds, R., Oort, F. V. and Frenken, K. (2010). Innovation, spillovers and university-industry collaboration: An extended knowledge production function approach. *Journal of Economic Geography*, 10(2), 231–255.

Porter, M. E. (1990). *The Competitive Advantage of Nations*. New York: Free Press.

Porter, M. E. (1998). Clusters and the New Economics of Competition. *Harvard Business Review, 76*(6), 77–90.

Porter, M. E. (2000a). Location, competition, and economic development: Local cluster in a global economy. *Economic Development Quarterly, 14*(1), 15–34.

Porter, M. E. (2000b). Locations, clusters and company strategy. In Clark, G. L., Gertler, M. S. and Feldman, M. P. (Eds.), *The Oxford Handbook of Economic Geography* (pp. 253–289). Oxford: Oxford University Press.

Powell, W. W. and Grodal, S. (2005). Networks of innovators. In Fagerberg, J., Mowery, C. D. and Nelson, R. R. (Eds.), *The Oxford Handbook of Innovation* (pp. 56–114). New York: Oxford University Press.

Qin, S. (1992). High-tech industrialization in China: An analysis of the current status. *Asian Survey, 32*(12), 1124–1136.

Rehn, D. (1989). Organizational reforms and technology change in the electronics industry: The case of Shanghai. In Simon, F. D. (Ed.), *Science and Technology in Post-Mao China*. Cambridge: The Council on East Asian Studies/Harvard University.

Rimmington, D. (1998). History and culture. In Hook, B. (Ed.), *Shanghai and the Yangtze Delta: A City Reborn* (pp. 1–29). Hong Kong: Oxford Univeristy Press.

Rogers, E. M. (2003). *Diffusion of Innovations*, 5th edn. New York: Free Press.

Rogers, M. (2004). Networks, firm size and innovation. *Small Business Economics, 22*(2), 141–153.

Rumelt, R. P. (1998). Evaluating business strategy. In Mintzberg, H., Quinn, J. B. and Ghoshal, S. (Eds.), *The Strategy Process: Revised European Edition*. London: Prentice Hall.

Rumelt, R. P., Schendel, D. E. and Teece, D. J. (1994). Fundamental issues in strategy. In Rumelt, R. P., Schendel, D. E. and Teece, D. J. (Eds.),

Fundamental Issues in Strategy: A Research Agenda (pp. 9–48). Boston: Harvard Business School Press.

Santarelli, E. (1995). *Finance and Technological Change*. New York: ST Martin's Press, INC.

Saxenian, A. (1994). *Regional Advantage: Culture and Competition in Silicon Valley and Route 128*. Cambridge, Mass: Harvard University Press.

Saxenian, A. (1999). Inside-out: Regional networks and industrial adaptation in Silicon Valley and Route 128. *Cityscape: A Journal of Policy Development and Research, 2*(2), 41–60.

Saxenian, A. and Hsu, J. Y. (2001). The silicon valley-hsinchu connection: Technical communities and industrial upgrading. *Industrial and Corporate Change, 10*(4), 893–920.

Schaller, R. R. (2004). Technological Innovation in the Semiconductor Industry: A Case Study of the International Technology Roadmap for Semiconductors (ITRS). PhD Thesis, George Mason University, Fairfax, Virginia.

Schmitz, H. (1995). Collective efficiency: Growth path for small-scale industry. *Journal of Development Studies, 31*(4), 529.

Schneider, R. B. and Maxfield, S. (1997). Business, the state, and economic performance in developing countries. In Maxfield, S. and Schneider, R. B. (Eds.), *Business and the State in Developing Countries* (pp. 3–35). Ithaca and London: Cornell University Press.

Schumpeter, J. A. (1934). *The Theory of Economic Development*. Cambridge: Harvard University Press.

Schumpeter, J. A. (1942). *Capitalism, Socialism and Democracy*. New York: Harper & Row.

Scott, A. J. (1998). *Regions and the World Economy*. Oxford: Oxford University Press.

Shandong Statistical Bureau (SDSB) (2005). *Shandong Jingji Pucha Nianjian 2004 (Shandong Economic Census 2004)*. Beijing: China Statistics Press, Digital Version.

Segal, A. (2003). *Digital Dragon: High-Technology Enterprises in China*. Ithaca and London: Cornell University Press.

Segal, A. and Thun, E. (2001). Thinking globally, acting locally: Local governments, industrial sectors and development in China. *Politics and Society, 29*(4), 557–588.

Seth, A. and Thomas, H. (1994). Theories of the firm: Implications for strategy research. *Journal of Management Studies, 31*(2), 165–191.

Shaanxi Statistical Bureau (SAAXSB). (2005). *Shaanxi Jingji Pucha Nianjian 2004 (Shaanxi Economic Census 2004)*. Beijing: China Statistics Press, Digital Version.

Shanghai Integrated Circuit Indusry Association (SICA) (2006). Shanghai shi jicheng dianlu xiehui erjie erci huiyuan dahui wenjian (Documents of the second session of the second SICA meeting).

Shanghai Municipal Informatization Commission (SMIC) and Shanghai Integrated Circuit Industry Association (SICA) (2008). 2008 Nian Shanghai Jicheng Dianlu Chanye Fazhan Yanjiu Baogao (Report on the Development of Integrated Circuit Industry in Shanghai in 2008). Shanghai: Shanghai Educational Publishing House.

Shanghai Statistical Bureau (SSB) (1991). *Shanghai Tongji Nianjian 1990* (*Shanghai Statistical Yearbook 1990*). Beijing: China Statistics Press.

Shanghai Statistical Bureau (SSB) (1992). *Shanghai Tongji Nianjian 1991* (*Shanghai Statistical Yearbook 1991*). Beijing: China Statistics Press.

Shanghai Statistical Bureau (SSB) (1993). *Shanghai Tongji Nianjian 1992* (*Shanghai Statistical Yearbook 1992*). Beijing: China Statistics Press.

Shanghai Statistical Bureau (SSB) (1994). *Shanghai Tongji Nianjian 1993* (*Shanghai Statistical Yearbook 1993*). Beijing: China Statistics Press.

Shanghai Statistical Bureau (SSB) (1995). *Shanghai Tongji Nianjian 1994* (*Shanghai Statistical Yearbook 1994*). Beijing: China Statistics Press.

Shanghai Statistical Bureau (SSB) (1996). *Shanghai Tongji Nianjian 1995* (*Shanghai Statistical Yearbook 1995*). Beijing: China Statistics Press.

Shanghai Statistical Bureau (SSB) (1997). *Shanghai Tongji Nianjian 1996* (*Shanghai Statistical Yearbook 1996*). Beijing: China Statistics Press.

Shanghai Statistical Bureau (SSB) (1998). *Shanghai Tongji Nianjian 1997* (*Shanghai Statistical Yearbook 1997*). Beijing: China Statistics Press.

Shanghai Statistical Bureau (SSB) (1999). *Shanghai Tongji Nianjian 1998* (*Shanghai Statistical Yearbook 1998*). Beijing: China Statistics Press.

Shanghai Statistical Bureau (SSB) (2000). *Shanghai Tongji Nianjian 1999* (*Shanghai Statistical Yearbook 1999*). Beijing: China Statistics Press.

Shanghai Statistical Bureau (SSB) (2001). *Shanghai Tongji Nianjian 2000* (*Shanghai Statistical Yearbook 2000*). Beijing: China Statistics Press.

Shanghai Statistical Bureau (SSB) (2002). *Shanghai Tongji Nianjian 2001* (*Shanghai Statistical Yearbook 2001*). Beijing: China Statistics Press.

Shanghai Statistical Bureau (SSB) (2003). *Shanghai Tongji Nianjian 2002* (*Shanghai Statistical Yearbook 2002*). Beijing: China Statistics Press.

Shanghai Statistical Bureau (SSB) (2004). *Shanghai Tongji Nianjian 2003* (*Shanghai Statistical Yearbook 2003*). Beijing: China Statistics Press.

Shanghai Statistical Bureau (SSB) (2005a). *Shanghai Jingji Pucha Nianjian 2004* (*Shanghai Economic Census 2004*). Beijing: China Statistics Press.

Shanghai Statistical Bureau (SSB) (2005b). *Shanghai Tongji Nianjian 2004* (*Shanghai Statistical Yearbook 2004*). Beijing: China Statistics Press.

Shanghai Statistical Bureau (SSB) (2006). *Shanghai Tongji Nianjian 2005* (*Shanghai Statistical Yearbook 2005*). Beijing: China Statistics Press.

Shanghai Statistical Bureau (SSB) (2007). *Shanghai Tongji Nianjian 2006* (*Shanghai Statistical Yearbook 2006*). Beijing: China Statistics Press.

Shanghai Statistical Bureau (SSB) (2008). *Shanghai Tongji Nianjian 2007* (*Shanghai Statistical Yearbook 2007*). Beijing: China Statistics Press.

Shanxi Statistical Bureau (SAXSB) (2005). *Shanxi Jingji Pucha Nianjian 2004* (*Shanxi Economic Census 2004*). Beijing: China Statistics Press, Digital Version.

Shefer, D. and Frenkel, A. (1998). Local milieu and innovations: Some empirical results. *The Annals of Regional Science*, *32*(1), 185–200.

Shenzhen Municipal Committee (2004). Guanyu Wanshan Quyu Chuangxin Tixi Tuidong Gaoxin Jishu Chanye Chixu Kuaisu Fazhande Jueding (Decision about Improving Regional Innovation System and Promoting High-tech Industry).

Shenzhen Municipal Government (2001). Guanyu Guli Ruanjian Chanye Fazhande Ruogan Zhengcede Tongzhi (Document of Policies about Encouraging the Development of Software Industry).

Shenzhen Statistical Bureau (SZSB) (2005a). *Shenzhen Jingji Pucha Nianjian 2004 (Shenzhen Economic Census 2004)*. Beijing: China Statistics Press.

Shenzhen Statistical Bureau (SZSB) (2005b). *Shenzhen Tongji Nianjian 2004 (Shenzhen Statistical Yearbook 2004)*. Beijing: China Statistics Press.

Shenzhen Statistical Bureau (SZSB) (2006). *Shenzhen Tongji Nianjian 2005 (Shenzhen Statistical Yearbook 2005)*. Beijing: China Statistics Press.

Shenzhen Statistical Bureau (SZSB) (2007). *Shenzhen Tongji Nianjian 2006 (Shenzhen Statistical Yearbook 2006)*. Beijing: China Statistics Press.

Shenzhen Statistical Bureau (SZSB) (2008). *Shenzhen Tongji Nianjian 2007 (Shenzhen Statistical Yearbook 2007)*. Beijing: China Statistics Press.

Sheppard, E. (2002). The spaces and times of globalization: Place, scale, networks and positionality. *Economic Geography, 78*(3), 307–330.

Shi, Y. Z. (1998). *Chinese Firms and Technology in the Reform Era*. London and New York: Routledge.

Sigurdson, J. (2005). *Technological Superpower China*. Cheltenham: Edward Elgar.

Simmie, J. (2002). Knowledge spillovers and reasons for the concentration of innovative SMEs. *Urban Studies, 39*(5/6), 885–902.

Simmie, J. (2003). Innovation and urban regions as national and international nodes for the transfer and sharing of knowledge. *Regional Studies, 37*(6/7), 607–620.

Simmie, J. (2004). Innovation and clustering in the globalised international economy. *Urban Studies, 41*(5/6), 1095–1112.

Simmie, J. and Sennett, J. (1999). Innovative clusters: Global or local linkages? *National Institute Economic Review, 170*, 87–99.

Simon, D. F. and Goldman, M. (Eds.). (1989). *Science and Technology in Post-Mao China*. Cambridge: Harvard University Press.

Simon, D. F. and Rehn, D. (1988). *Technological Innovation in China: The Case of the Shanghai Semiconductor Industry*. Cambridge: Ballinger Publishing Company.

Sit, F. S. V. (1998). Geography and natural resources. In Hook, B. (Ed.), *Shanghai and the Yangtze Delta: A City Reborn* (pp. 74–118). Hong Kong: Oxford University Press.

Spreadtrum. (2008). 2008 Annual Report of Spreadtrum.

State Council. (1991). Circular of the State Council Concerning the Approval of the National Development Zones for New and High Technology Industries and the Relevant Policies and Provisions.

State Council. (1999). Guanyu Jiaqiang Jishu Chuagnxin Fazhan Gaokeji Shixian Chanyehua De Jueding (Decision about Enhancing Technology Innovation, Promoting High Technology and Realizing Industrialization).

Sternberg, R. and Arndt, O. (2001). The firm or the region: What determines the innovation behavior of European firms? *Economic Geography, 77*(4), 364–382.

Storper, M. (1995). The resurgence of regional economies, ten years later: The region as a nexus of untraded interdependencies. *European Urban and Regional Studies, 2*(3), 191–221.

Storper, M. (1997). *The Regional World: Territorial Development in a Global Economy.* New York: Guilford Press.

Storper, M. (1999). The resurgence of regional economies, ten years later: The region as a nexus of untraded interdependencies. In Bryson, J., Henry, N., Keeble, D. and Martin, R. (Eds.), *The Economic Geography Reader: Producing and Consuming Global Capitalism.* Chichester: John Wiley & Sons, Ltd.

Sturgeon, T. J. (2003). What really goes on in Silicon Valley? Spatial clustering and dispersal in modular production networks. *Journal of Economic Geography, 3*(2), 199–225.

Su, C. and Littlefield, J. E. (2001). Entering Guanxi: A business ethical dilemma in mainland China? *Journal of Business Ethics, 33*(3), 199–210.

Sun, Y. (2002a). China's national innovation system in transition. *Eurasian Geography and Economics, 43*(6), 476–492.

Sun, Y. (2002b). Sources of innovation in China's manufacturing sector: Imported or developed in-house? *Environment and Planning A, 34*, 1059–1072.

Sung, Y.-w. (1996). Dragon head of China's economy? In Yeung, Y. M. and Sung, Y. W. (Eds.), *Shanghai: Transformation and Modernization Under China's Open Policy* (pp. 171–198). Hong Kong: The Chinese University Press.

Sunley, P. (2008). Relational economic geography: A partial understanding or a new paradigm? *Economic Geography, 84*(1), 1–26.

Susskind, C. and Zybkow, M. (1978). The ecology of innovation. In Kelly, P. and Kranzberg, M. (Eds.), *Technological Innovation: A Critical Review of Current Knowledge.* California: San Francisco Press, Inc.

Suttmeier, R. P. and Yao, X. (2004). China's Post-WTO Technology Policy: Standards, Software and the Changing Nature of Techno-Nationalism. Available at: http://www.nbr.org/publications/specialreport/pdf/SR7.pdf, accessed on 20 August 2007.

Swyngedouw, E. (1997a). Excluding the other: The production of scale and scaled politics. In Lee, R. and Wills, J. (Eds.), *Geographies of Economics* (pp. 167–176). London: Arnold.

Swyngedouw, E. (1997b). Neither global or local: Globalization and the politics of scale. In Cox, K. R. (Ed.), *Spaces of Globalization: Reasserting the Power of the Local* (pp. 137–166). New York: The Guilford Press.

Swyngedouw, E. (2000). The Marxian alternative: Historical-geographical materialism and the political economy of capitalism. In Sheppard, E. and Barnes, T. J. (Eds.), *A Companion to Economic Geography* (pp. 41–59). Oxford: Blackwell Publishing.

Tödtling, F. (1994). The uneven landscape of innovation poles: Local embeddedness and global networks. In Amin, A. and Thrift, N. (Eds.), *Globalization, Institutions, and Regional Development in Europe*. New York: Oxford University Press.

Tödtling, F., Lehner, P. and Trippl, M. (2006). Innovation in knowledge intensive industries: The nature and geography of knowledge links. *European Planning Studies*, *14*(8), 1035–1058.

Tappeiner, G., Hauser, C. and Walde, J. (2008). Regional knowledge spillovers: Fact or artifact? *Research Policy*, *37*(5), 861–874.

Taylor, M. (2005). *Cluster: The Mesmerising Mantra*. Paper presented at the Regional Studies Association Conference.

Taylor, M. and Asheim, B. (2001). The concept of the firm in economic geography. *Economic Geography*, *77*(4), 315–328.

Teece, D. J. (1986). Profiting from technological innovation: Implications for integration, collaboration, licensing and public policy. *Research Policy*, *15*, 285–305.

Tianjin Statistical Bureau (TJSB). (2005). *Tianjin Jingji Pucha Nianjian 2004 (Tianjin Economic Census 2004)*. Beijing: China Statistics Press.

Torre, A. and Rallet, A. (2005). Proximity and localization. *Regional Studies*, *39*(1), 47–59.

Tsang, W. K. E. (1998). Can Guanxi be a source of sustained competitive advantage for doing business in China? *Academy of Management*, *12*(2), 64–73.

Van Waarden, F. (2005). A prototypical institution: Law, regulation and innovation. In Casper, S. and van Waarden, F. (Eds.), *Innovation and Institutions: A Multidisciplinary Review of the Study of Innovation Systems* (pp. 269–262). Cheltenham: Edward Elgar.

Vaona, A. and Pianta, M. (2008). Firm size and innovation in European manufacturing. *Small Business Economics*, *30*(3), 283–299.

Vogel, E. F. (1989). *One Step Ahead in China: Guangdong under Reform*. Cambridge: Harvard University Press.

Walcott, S. M. (2002). Chinese industrial and science parks: Bridging the gap. *Professional Geographer*, *54*(3), 349–364.

Wang, C. C. and Lin, G. C. S. (2008). The growth and spatial distribution of China's ICT industry: New geography of clustering and innovation. *Issues & Studies*, *44*(2), 145–192.

Wang, C. C., Lin, G. C. S. and Li, G. C. (2010). Industrial clustering and technological innovation in China: New evidence from the ICT industry in Shenzhen. *Environment and Planning A*, *42*, 1987–2010.

Wang, J. *et al.* (2001). *Chuangxin De Kongjian: Qiye Jiqun Yu Quyu Fazhan (Innovative Space: Industrial Clusters and Regional Development)*. Beijing: Peking University Press.

Wang, J. and Wang, J. (1998). An analysis of new-tech agglomeration in Beijing: A new industrial district in the making? *Environment and Planning A*, *30*(4), 681–701.

Wang, J. and Tong, X. (2005). Industrial clusters in China: Embedded or disembedded? In Alvstam, C. G. and Schamp E. W. (Eds.), *Linking Industries across the World: Processes of Global Networking*. Aldershot: Ashgate.

Wang, J. H. and Lee, C. K. (2007). Global production networks and local institution building: The development of the information-technology industry in Suzhou, China. *Environment and Planning A, 39*(8), 1873–1888.

Wang, L. X. (2008). Zhangjiang jicheng dianlu chanye chixu zengzhang, jishu chuangxin yeji feiran (Sustainable growth and remarkable technological innovation in the IC industry of Zhangjiang, Shanghai). *Zhangjiang Xin Jingji (Zhangjiang New Economy)*, *2*, 22–25.

Wang, T., Liefner, I. and Zeng, G. (2006). Xifang jiqun he jiqun zhengce de yanjiu jiqi dui zhongguo de jiejian yiyi (Western cluster studies and cluster policies and their implications to China). *Renwen Dili (Human Geography), 21*(5), 74–79.

Watts, H. D., Wood, A. M. and Wardle, P. (2003). "Making friends or making Things?": Interfirm transactions in the Sheffield metal-working cluster. *Urban Studies, 40*(3), 615–630.

Weber, A. (1929). *Theory of the Location of Industries.* Chicago: University of Chicago Press.

Wei, B. P.-T. (1987). *Shanghai: Crucible of Modern China.* Hong Kong: Oxford University Press.

Wei, J. (2003). *Chanye Jiqun: Chuangxin Xitong Yu Jishu Xuexi (Industrial Clusters: Innovative System and Regional Development).* Beijing: Beijing Science Press.

Wei, S., Wang, J. and Zhao, Y. (2002). Chanye jiqun: Xinxing quyu jingji fazhan lilun (Industrial cluster: A new theory of regional economic development). *Jingji Jingwei (Economic Survey), 2*, 18–21.

Wei, Y. D., Leung, C. K. and Luo, J. (2006). Globalizing Shanghai: Foreign investment and urban restructuring. *Habitat International, 30*(2), 231–244.

Wei, Y. H. D. (2007). Regional development in China: Transitional institutions, embedded globalization and hybrid economies. *Eurasian Geography and Economics, 48*(1), 16–36.

Wei, Y. H. D., Lu, Y. Q. and Chen, W. (2009). Globalizing regional development in Sunan, China. *Regional Studies, 43*(3), 409–427.

Weiss, L. (1998). *The Myth of the Powerless State.* Ithaca and New York: Cornell University Press.

Wen, M. (2004). Relocation and agglomeration of Chinese industry. *Journal of Development Economics, 73*(1), 329–347.

Wernerfelt, B. (1997). A resource-based view of the firm. In Foss, N. J. (Ed.), *Resources, Firms and Strategies.* New York: Oxford University Press.

White III, L. T. (1989). *Shanghai Shanghaied? Uneven Taxes in Reform China.* Hong Kong: Centre of Asian Studies, University of Hong Kong.

Wolfe, D. A. and Gertler, M. S. (2004). Clusters from the inside and out: Local dynamics and global linkages. *Urban Studies, 41*(5/6), 1071–1093.

Wong, K. Y. and Chu, K. Y. D. (1985). Export processing zones and special economic zones as locomotives of export-led economic growth. In Wong, K. Y. and Chu, K. Y. D. (Eds.), *Modernization in China: The Case of the Shenzhen Special Economic Zone* (pp. 1–24). Hong Kong: Oxford University Press.

Wong, Y. H. (1998). The dynamics of Guanxi in China. *Singapore Management Review*, *20*(2), 25–42.

World Bank (2009). *World Development Report 2009: Reshaping Economic Geography.* Washington, D.C.: The World Bank.

Wright, W. R. (1997). *The Competitive Advantage of Knowledge-Based Resources in the Semiconductor Industry.* New York & London: Garland Publishing, Inc.

Wu, F. (2008). China's great transformation: Neoliberalization as establishing a market society. *Geoforum*, *39*(3), 1093–1096.

Wu, W. M. (1990). China's Shenzhen Special Economic Zone: A Social Benefit-Cost Analysis. MA Thesis, University of Hawaii, Hawaii.

Wu, W. P. (1999). *Pioneering Economic Reform in China's Special Economic Zones: The Promotion of Foreign Investment and Technology Transfer in Shenzhen.* Aldershot: Ashgate.

Xinjiang Statistical Bureau (XJSB) (2005). *Xinjiang Jingji Pucha Nianjian 2004 (Xinjiang Economic Census 2004).* Beijing: China Statistics Press, Digital Version.

Yee, L. W. F. (1992). Economic and Urban Changes in the Shenzhen Special Economic Zone, 1979–1986. PhD Thesis, The University of British Columbia, Vancouver.

Yeung, H. W. C. (2003). Practicing new economic geographies: A methodological examination. *Annals of the Association of American Geographers*, *93*(2), 442–462.

Yeung, H. W. C. (2005a). The firm as social network: An organisational perspective. *Growth and Change*, *36*(3), 307–328.

Yeung, H. W. C. (2005b). Rethinking relational economic geography. *Transactions of the Institute of British Geographers*, *30*(1), 37–51.

Yeung, H. W. C. and Lin, G. C. S. (2003). Theorizing economic geographies of Asia. *Economic Geography*, *79*(2), 107–128.

Yeung, Y. M. (1996). *Introduction.* In Yeung, Y. M. and Sung, Y. W. (Eds.), *Shanghai: Transformation and Modernization under China's Open Policy* (pp. 1–24). Hong Kong: The Chinese University Press.

Yeung, Y. M. and Sung, Y. W. (Eds.). (1996). *Shanghai: Transformation and Modernization under China's Open Policy.* Hong Kong: The Chinese University Press.

Yunnan Statistical Bureau (YNSB). (2005). *Yunnan Jingji Pucha Nianjian 2004 (Yunnan Economic Census 2004).* Beijing: China Statistics Press, Digital Version.

Young, S. and Lan, P. (1997). Technology transfer to China through foreign direct investment. *Regional Studies*, *31*(7), 669–679.

Yu, Z. Y. (2005). China's IC Industry: The Status Quo and Future. Internal Report.

Zeng, G. (1997). Woguo gaoxin jishu chanye kaifaqu de xianzhuang ji fazhan (Status and development of high-tech parks in China). *Diyu Yanjiu Yu Kaifa (Area Research and Development)*, *16*(1): 48–52.

Zeng, G., Li, Y. and Fan, J. (2006). Jinghu quyu chuangxin xitong bijiao yanjiu (Comparison of regional innovation system of high-tech enterprises cluster in Beijing and Shanghai). *Chengshi Guihua (City Planning Review)*, *30*(3), 32–38.

Zeng, G. and Wen, H. (2004). Shanghai Pudong xinxi chanye jiqun de jianshe (A study on the IT industrial cluster in Pudong area, Shanghai). *Dili Xuebao (Acta Geographica Sinica)*, *59*(Supplement), 59–66.

Zhang, C., Zeng Z., Mako, W. P. and Seward, J. (2009). *Promoting Enterprise-Led Innovation in China*. Washington D.C.: The World Bank.

Zhang, J. (2008). China's dynamic industrial sector: The internet industry. *Eurasian Geography and Economics*, *49*(5), 549–568.

Zhang, L. Y. (2003). Economic development in Shanghai and the role of the state. *Urban Studies*, *40*(8), 1549–1572.

ZhangJiang High-tech Park. (2007). Report on Industrial Development of Zhangjiang High-tech Park, 2006. Internal Document.

Zhao, J. Z. (2002a). 2001 nian Shanghai jicheng dianlu chanye gaikuang (General situation of IC industry of Shanghai in 2001). *Jicheng Dianlu Yingyong (Application of IC)*, *06*, 1–2.

Zhao, J. Z. (2002b). Pengbo fazhan de Shanghai jicheng dianlu chanye (Rising and flourishing IC industry in Shanghai). *Jicheng Dianlu Yingyong (Application of IC)*, *11*, 1–5.

Zhao, J. Z. (2003). IT chanye biaozhun dui Shanghai IC shejiye fazhan de zhongyaoxing (Importance of IT industrial standards in the development of Shanghai IC design industry). *Shanghai Biaozhunhua (Standardization of Shanghai)*, *10*, 20–24.

Zhao, J. Z. (2004). Shanghai IC sheji jiqi chanyehua (IC design and industrialization in Shanghai). *Bandaoti Jishu (Semiconductor Technology)*, *29*(9), 1–7.

Zhao, J. Z. (2005). Shanghai jicheng dianlu chanye fazhan xianzhuang jiqi qushi (The status quo and the trend of development of the IC industry in Shanghai). *Shanghai Xinxihua (Informalization of Shanghai)*, *8*, 48–52.

Zhao, S. X. B. and Zhang, L. (2007). Foreign direct investment and the formation of global city-regions in China. *Regional Studies*, *41*(7), 979–994.

Zhejiang Statistical Bureau (ZJSB) (2005). *Zhejiang Jingji Pucha Nianjian 2004 (Zhejiang Economic Census 2004)*. Beijing: China Statistics Press, Digital Version.

Zhou, S. M. (2007). Shenzhen Shi Jicheng Dianlu Sheji Chanye Niandu Fenxi Baogao (2007 nian ban) (Annual Report of IC Design Sector in Shenzhen, 2007 version). Shenzhen: Management Center of Shenzhen National IC Design Industrial Center.

Zhou, Y. (2005). The making of an innovative region from a centrally planned economy: Institutional evolution in Zhongguancun Science Park in Beijing. *Environment and Planning A*, *37*, 1113–1134.

Zhou, Y. (2006). State and commercial enterprises in China's technical standard strategies. *China Review*, *6*(1), 37–66.

Zhou, Y. (2008). *The Inside Story of China's High-tech Industry: Making Silicon Valley in Beijing*. Lanham: Rowman & Littlefield Pub.

Zhou, Y., Sun, Y., Wei, Y. H. D. and Lin, G. C. S. (2010). Decentering spatial fix: Patterns of territorialization and regional technological dynamism of ICT hubs in China. *Journal of Economic Geography*, *11*, 119–150.

Zhou, Y. and Tong, X. (2003). An innovative region in China: Interaction between multinational corporations and local firms in a high-tech cluster in Beijing. *Economic Geography*, *79*(2), 129–152.

Index

Absorptive capability, 35, 36
Agglomeration, 2, 12, 22, 23, 47, 106, 109, 111, 112, 119, 120, 166, 188, 189, 221, 224. See also concentration
Agglomeration economies, 23, 38, 40, 166, 216
Agile business model, 202
Asia-Pacific region, 160, 196

Beijing, city of, 4, 27, 28, 47, 106, 107, 111, 112, 113, 116, 133, 134, 136, 137, 140, 151, 152, 168, 174, 175, 176, 180, 183, 184, 200, 211
Beijing-Tianjin city-region, 106

Caohejing high-tech park, 125, 127, 154
Capital profitability, 5, 103, 109, 110, 111, 120, 163, 165, 194
Capability Maturity Model, 170
Chengdu, city of, 176
Changsha, city of, 176
China circle, 161
Chinese Academy of Sciences, 73, 88, 91, 92, 175
Codified knowledge, 34, 36, 41
Collective learning, 6, 7, 29, 30, 31, 32, 38, 40, 41, 49
Collectively-owned enterprises, 75
Co-location, 6, 31, 32, 166, 207, 210
Concentration, 12, 20, 27, 37, 39, 91, 106, 109, 111, 120, 154, 159, 163,

166, 167, 186, 193, 194, 208, 227. See also agglomeration
Core technology, 4, 35, 77, 104, 166, 170, 171, 188
Cultural revolution, 93
Culture turn, 29

Dalian, city of, 176
Datang Telecom, 98
Decentralization, 56
Deng, Xiaoping, 93, 96
Dongguan, city of, 107, 109, 113, 116, 175
Dragon head, 200

Eastern coastal region, 4, 97, 106, 112, 120, 221
Economic census, 1, 13, 87, 104, 106, 109, 111, 207
Economic reform, 1, 3, 75, 76, 78, 80, 93, 199, 202, 207, 220
Economy under transition, 10. See also transitional economy
Electronics and information revolution, 172
Embeddedness, 2, 22, 25, 31, 32, 225, 226
European Union, 2, 87
Export processing zones, 160

Fetishing of proximity, 36
Five year plan, 94, 96, 97, 131, 139, 140